LEADERS IN MAKING

LEADERS IN MAKING

U.B. SINGH

KALPAZ PUBLICATIONS
DELHI-110052

Leaders in Making

Rs. 690

ISBN: 81-7835-585-X

Published in 2007 in India by
Kalpaz Publications
C-30, Satyawati Nagar,
Delhi-110052
E-mail: kalpaz@hotmail.com

Lasser Typesetting by: Rudra Computer Graphics, Delhi
Printed at: Salasar Imaging System, Delhi

Contents

Preface

Studies on leadership have assumed two approaches - the elite approach, mainly concerned with the explanation of leadership in top positions (political elites) and, organizational leadership, mainly concerned with the qualities required of an ideal leader in charge of groups and organizations. The first deals with leadership as a phenomenon in all societies and has been the favorite subject of political philosophers. The second deals with leadership as being a set of attributes which are required for achieving organizational objectives and has been taken up by students of management and organization. The political scientists and researchers across the world over the years have studied various aspects of politicians, including their socio-economic background, education and age, occupation etc. along-with the evolution and role of political parties in shaping the political leadership.

In a developing country having parliamentary democracy like India, the role of political parties assumes great importance. Under the colonial rule there was little participation of the people in the country's government. As such political parties in India had not developed before independence. There was freedom movement in the country but that was very different from a modern political party.

India has been one of the few new states of the post-second World War period which were able to foster a strong democratic set up and liberal growth of political parties. Unfortunately, studies available on the social bases of the political process in India do not throw a continuous light on the structure and processes of political leadership in the country.

Norman D. Palmer (1955) is of opinion that leadership principle has been particularly strong in India, reinforced by the traditional aspects of Indian life and social organization. According to him, in addition to the conservative authoritarian values which are traditionally rooted in Indian society, modern leadership shows the influence of religious mystics. Paul H. Appleby (1953) believes that one of India's outstanding assets has been the extraordinary national leadership. John Mender (1963) notes two patterns of political leadership existing in India since independence. There is the basic democratic party political pattern borrowed from Britain to which the great majority of educated Indians are attached. Besides it intersecting it at many points there exists an older semi-religious pattern of personal authority. This latter kind of leadership pattern is found to have a stronger and more stable influence on the village masses in India. According to Kothari (1970) the electoral and democratic process has shifted the levers of power from the hands of the first generation leadership to those in charge of state and district organizations, caste federations and rural panchayats and cooperatives. The men at the top of such trends are pragmatic men, less inclined to the modernistic ideas but modernizers in their own way. Sirsikar (1995) pints out that some of them are popular leaders, others ruthless managers but they control the vote. Sleigh Harrison (1960) notes that a trend in the evolution of leadership in India is that a new class of leaders with deeper roots in local and regional society is emerging in the Indian political scene.

According to Alfred De Souza (1976) the democratization of education since Independence has conferred education to a large segment of the population which was hitherto socially deprived. At the same time the removal of untouchability and other caste barriers through legislation and programmes of economic uplift have enabled the depressed and backward castes to come out of their low position and to play a significant role in politics. The conferment of universal adult franchise compelled the forward castes to woo their voters and to accommodate them in the political elite group which was hitherto a preserve of the western educated upper castes. The introduction of new modes of institutions of political decision making has strengthened the divisive forces of caste, language and religion and brought about a change in the social composition of political elites as well as in the styles of leadership and decision making.

The last decade of the 20th century witnessed a major breakthrough in the political framework in the country. The efforts of decentralisation initiated by (late) Rajiv Gandhi in the 1980's culminated in the form of historic 73rd and 74th Amendments to the Constitution of India. These revolutionary endeavors aimed to bring the administration nearer to people; to ensure participation of people in managing local affairs, and to make the grass-root administration accountable to people. As a result, the politico - administrative framework of the country saw a new era characterized with democratic decentralization, administrative decentralization, fiscal devolution and people's participation in the local administration - urban as well as rural. A turning point came in the political history of the country when mandatory provisions were made for granting reservations to all sections of the society. The Scheduled Castes and Scheduled Tribes were given representation to the tune of their respective proportion in the total population. The women irrespective of their castes were granted a blanket reservation to the extent of one-third, including the women belonging to SC/ST categories. The Constitution left the reservation to other backward classes on the State Governments. Thus political leadership was imposed overnight, without any preparedness, on the people irrespective of their social, economic and educational status.

Although a decade or so is not sufficient period to assess the effectiveness of such a revolutionary step on the society embedded with long complex traditions and customs, it is however appropriate for assessing its impact on mind set of the people as well as the society. The experiences thus learnt may help in knowing the direction to which the imposed political leadership is moving. It is in this backdrop, the present endeavor was conceived.

The volume is structured in such a way that a real life experience can be presented. It is broadly divided into two parts. The first part consists of the papers highlighting the experiences of a few states in the country, whereas the second part is the findings of research study undertaken under the aegis of the ICSSR. First two papers present the theoretical framework of political leadership, while other contributions discuss case studies of respective states. The last part is an empirical study of role-conflict among elected woman representatives in Uttar Pradesh.

Dr. V. Bijukumar discusses the various contexts of emerging the political leadership. He feels that democratic regimes not only provide certain political rights to the people but also facilitate them to exercise those rights. India being a democratic country has been under colonial rule for a long time and has mixed experiences of both the eras. He traces the genesis of political leadership to the freedom movement. The national movement disseminated democratic conceptions and popularized the idea of representative institutions. The modernization process in the post-independent period tried to transform the norms and structures of traditional political system into a modern political system, which led to ensure effective public participation in public policy making. The active role of the state in development process gave an opportunity to the political leadership to expand its democratic base among the cross-section of the people. Thus developmental planning became an essential instrument for patronage politics.

The second generation political leadership, according to him, emerged in the mid 1960s, when a feeling of anti-Congressism generated in Indian politics. Consequently, there emerged a new political leadership at the regional level (state level). Compared to the first generation political leadership which stood for universalistic ideas, the second generation leadership advocated regional autonomy.

Dr. Bijukumar recognizes the emergence of third generation of leadership in the 1990s when the 73rd and 74th Amendments to the Constitution created a new awareness among the marginalized social groups and accelerated the process of passive revolution. Decentralisation has made certain changes in the access to local power structures. The grass-root local institutions (municipalities and panchayats) have become the easiest way to fulfill aspirations for political power. This new leadership represents the diverse social milieu and hence faces enormous challenges from the traditional socio-economic conditions and emerging trends in the era of globalization. Thus the new leadership may suffer from real empowerment in the trajectory of developmental shift from state to market.

Dr. K. S. Saxena confines his discussion to the emerging leadership in women in urban politics. He sees a paradox of Indian public life that cities are both profoundly influential and politically weak. The ruralisation of politics, according to him, has been marked by increasing attention to rural development policies by government and the mobilisation of rural leadership in parties. He finds the emergence of women leadership in urban as well as rural areas as a significant development as a consequence of 73rd and 74th Amendments to the Constitution of India. The emergence of woman leadership has been a signal to the effect that women have realised their hidden strength and will come out with more vigour and courage.

Dr. V. Gnaneshwar links municipal leadership to the principles of good urban governance. According to him, municipal political spectrum has two dimensions - representation and leadership. Representation aims to ensure that the local governments strive to achieve the developmental goals set and serve the local communities according to the accepted principles of good governance. And elected leadership is the ability to infuse complex community problems with governing principles, practical competencies and measurable and sustainable results. Based on these assumptions he highlights the complexion of the municipal council in southern states and also the impact of the 74th Constitution Amendment Act, the facets of political executives and gender balance in political representation. He concludes with comment that "the new generation elected representatives will develop such an understanding going beyond the pressing and immediate partisan interests and become people's representatives in a true sense".

Sri Jairaj Phatak dwels exhaustively the local government in Maharashtra. He discusses at length the genesis and development of rural as well as urban governments in this western state. He feels that one of the objects of local self government is to give opportunities for as many citizens as possible to participate in public affairs and have continuous interest in them. He finds many similarities between leadership at different levels in the federal structure. In fact in Maharashtra many of the local leaders graduate to state and national levels.

Dr. N. Ashok Kumar talks of women leadership and empowerment. He traces of status of women over the ages and feels that poverty, physical form and biological functions, fear of their man folk, poor capabilities to meet the challenges are the other reasons for their poor representation in public life. He emphasises on enrolling as many women as possible as voters and on imparting practical education and teaching them to think independently, as these steps are strong enough to assure political strength and capacity for sacrifice and place of honour in the society for women. Dr. Kumar exhorted the political parties for their failure to allow scope for women to come up in the political arena in a big way. He is confident that empowerment will enable women to meet the challenges, creativity in organising and managerial capabilities. The government also has to take supportive measures with a view to ensure women's access to economic power.

Dr. Srinibas Pathi discusses the women leadership in Panchayati Raj Institutions in Orissa. He feels that the role and position of women in society have far-reaching consequences for the nature and quality of life of both men and women. He says that participation of women in the decision making process is considered as one of the most significant steps in connection with empowerment of women. He emphasises on regular and intensive orientation for women representatives. He sees that women have occupied the political space and it is time for them to consolidate their role, position and performance.

Dr. Rajesh Kumar presents political empowerment of weaker sections in municipal bodies in Haryana. He reviews the situation of elected women in urban local bodies as a result of 74th CAA. He feels that their contributions to deliberations and decision making processes leave much to be desired because of their lack of proper education, experience and training. He is however optimistic that they will certainly improve their political position with the passage of time and the national leadership will emerge from these sections in due course as has been in the case in respect of advanced sections of the India society.

Dr. Pawan Kumar Banta discusses the participation and development in relation to Shimla Municipal Corporation. He traces the history of Shimla city government since British days and describes the role of elected group in the functioning of the corporation. He feels that elected people are putting their best in development of the city.

Dr. Jogendra K. Das describes the municipal government in Assam in general and Palasbari Municipal Board in particular. The last chapter presents a case study related to role conflict among elected woman representatives in urban local government in Uttar Pradesh. The study was sponsored by the Indian Council of Social Science Research.

The 73rd and 74th Amendments to the Constitution provide representation to the tune of not less than one-third of seats for women. As such a large number of women per force have come forward and joined the political mainstream at the grass root level governance. These women representatives have multidimensional roles to perform. As a house-wife and as daughter-in-law she is responsible for managing the home affairs and as people's representative, she has to perform for the fulfillment of people's aspirations and expectations. Therefore these women have to perform two sets of roles i.e., traditional or prescribed as a woman and an achieved or ascribed by acquiring political role and status. As such, a woman as a role occupant finds now lesser a time for family. Her role is now divided over two sets of roles for family as well as for society. This leads to a constant and continuous phenomenon of role conflict. A woman representative has therefore to make a balance between the two roles for a harmonious and peaceful life and effective role in decision making.

In this backdrop, the present study was conceived and undertaken for identifying the major areas of conflict in both the roles of women entering in urban governance. For the purpose, municipalities from all the geographical regions of Uttar Pradesh were selected. They included Municipal Corporations, Nagar Palika Parishads as well as Nagar Panchayats. The elected and nominated women representatives belonging to these urban government units were contacted and personally interviewed. These local units consisted of municipalities with female chairpersons as well as male chairpersons. For a holistic view officials of urban local bodies and family members of women representatives were also interviewed.

The report is divided into many parts. Prologue covers the status of women in Indian society and their role in political arena, including identification of conflict areas at urban levels. The research methodology adopted also forms part of this section. Next part is devoted to introducing the universe and discussing the socio-economic profile of the women representatives. Part III highlights the conceptual framework of role conflict and its various dimensions, followed by section IV which attempts an analysis of adjustment and conflicts in family life of women representatives.

Next part deals with adjustment and conflict in municipal/political role. Part VI is devoted to discussing status of women represenatives in wider society and section VII presents the responses of family members whereas next part brings out the responses of municipal officials. Epilogue summarizes the study. The major findings are discussed at length. Conflict areas have been identified and the measures to reduce or minimize the conflict have also been discussed.

I am extremely thankful to all my friends who took a pain and contributed a paper and enrich the volume. This is my foremost duty to express my gratitude to the Indian Council of Social Science Research for sponsoring the study on role conflict. The research team consisting of Dr. Alka Singh, Dr. K.K. Singh, Ms. Priya Sinha and Sri Govind Shukla did tremendous job of collection and analysis of data. My special thanks to Dr. Alka Singh for preparing the first draft of the report. My colleagues in the University specially Dr. A.K. Singh and Dr. R.K. Trivedi deserve thanks for their contribution at various stages.

While working on the project, I had to cut time meant for family and they bore with me. I am extremely thankful to my family especially my daughter Nivedita who suffered a lot during my engagement and for all sorts of cooperation in completing this endeavour.

I am thankful to Sri Amit Garg for his encouragement and for publishing the book in a record time.

Christmas, 2005
Lucknow.

U.B.SINGH

Contributors

Dr. V. BIJUKUMAR is Lecturer in Political Science, Mizoram University, Aizawl (now with NEHU, Shillongp)

Dr. K.S. SAXENA was Reader in Political Science and Director, Academic Staff College, Jodhpur University, based at Jaipur

Dr. V. GNANESHWAR is Professor of Public Administration, Regional Centre for Urban & Environmental Studies, Osmania University, Hyderabad

Sri JAIRAJ PHATAK, I.A.S., Secretary to Maharashtra Government in the Department of Basic Education, Mumbai

Dr. N. ASHOK KUMAR is Professor of Public Administration, Regional Centre for Urban & Environmental Studies, Osmania University, Hyderabad

Dr. SRINIBAS PATHI is Reader & Head, Department of Public Administration,Mizoram University, Aizawl

Dr. RAJESH KUMAR is Lecturer in Public Administration, Kurukshetra University, Kurukshetra

Dr. PAWAN KUMAR BANTA is urban consultant associated with Department of Public Administration, Shimla University, Shimla

Dr. JOGENDRA KUMAR DAS is Reader in Political Science Mirza Collage, Mirza

Dr. U.B. Singh formerly Reader & Head, Department of Public Administration, Mizoram (Central) University, Aizawl is presently Joint Director, Regional Centre for Urban and Environmental Studies, Lucknow University, Lucknow.

1

Contextualising Political Leadership in India

V. Bijukumar[1]

Democracy is generally perceived as a form of government in which everyone has a share in the governance of the country. In fact, democratic regimes not only provide certain political rights in contrast to authoritarian regimes but also facilitate the citizens to exercise these rights. Among political rights, the right to vote is the cornerstone of the democratic structure. However, the right to vote also implies candidate standing in the election process and representing the people in the state structure. Thus, leadership has a special importance in democratic regimes than any other forms of governments.

Political leadership constitutes an important theme in comparative politics. A number of studies have analyzed the nature of political leadership, especially in post colonial states. In India, such studies have aroused much interest in political literature.

Like other post-colonial states, the genesis of political leadership in India can be traced back to the nationalist movement.

In fact, the nationalist movement was an amalgam of various ideas and ideologies from around the world, which the western educated Indian intelligentsia. The incipient form of political leadership pleaded for the political, economic and social modernization of India. According to Desai (1948) the liberal leadership of Indian National Congress, which emerged during the nationalist movement, 'infused national consciousness among the various sections of the Indian people, disseminated democratic conceptions among them, and popularized the idea of representative institutions'.[2] However, the stumbling block to the process of modernization was the continuing British colonialism which impoverished the nation. Thus, ending the alien rule and achieving sovereignty, both political and economic, constituted the prime agenda of the political leadership in India. In fact, the ideology and philosophy of the modernization process was nationalism. Nationalist leaders like Dadabhai Navoroji, M.G. Ranade, et. al. were active proponents of economic nationalism. The liberal and secular values of the leadership was not confined to the political sphere but encompassed the social modes and ways of living.

Decolonization paved the way for the western educated elite leadership to gain the high political status in India. The leadership evolved a consensus to formulate a new development strategy in to combat the underdevelopment created by colonialism. This was the first step towards 'modernisation'. The main agent of modernization was the state. The state, vis-à-vis market, took the initiative to modernize the society, polity and economy. The leadership concentrated all efforts towards this goal. In the state-led modernization process, the market was assigned a subservient role. The rationale for state-led modernization was to fight against grave problems like illiteracy, ignorance and backwardness. The direction of this modernization was echoed in the Jawaharlal Nehru's famous 'tryst with destiny' speech. Nehru reminded that the task ahead included, 'the ending of poverty and ignorance and disease and inequality of opportunity'. While emphasizing the need for achieving high economic growth, he stressed the importance of eradicating deprivation and improving the capabilities and also the quality of life of ordinary people. In the social arena, modernization process sought to emancipate the people from traditional social bondages and values. The leadership tried to replace the old value system even though it was half-hearted way. In the field of economy, the modernization process aimed at a state-centred developmental strategy. The Public Sector was given prominent role over the private sector.

Politically, the modernization process tried to transform the norms and structures of traditional political system into a modern political system. It tried to build a 'civic political culture' for the successful working of the democratic process. Moreover, it tried to ensure effective public participation in public policy making However, the 'half-hearted' social modernization had a direct bearing on the effective political modernization. Traditional identities and values posed hurdles for the effective working of democratic institutions. When modern political institutions were forced to function within the traditional social structures, identities like caste, religion, etc. hindered the smooth working of modern political institutions. Instead of transforming the traditional structures of society in a more egalitarian direction, political democracy was superimposed from above. This sparked off tensions in the working of political institutions. This contributed to the revival of many ascriptive identities like caste, religion, language, etc.[3] Though the process of political modernization faced a lot of strain, the political leadership took the credit as the champions of political modernization in India.

The active role of the state in development process gave an opportunity to the political leadership to expand its democratic base among the cross-section of the people. The leadership attracted new social forces and recruited them into the party system through a state focused strategy. It depended on the developmental state for its mobilization, electoral domination and political management. The abundant resources under the state control and its allocation to various social groups helped the leadership to garner electoral support. When the state was the sole agency for development, the political leadership who exercised state power had control over the public resources.

Thus, developmental planning became an essential instrument for patronage politics[4]. The institution of development and planning and other development programmes, by extending active agencies for development of the society, provided new social and economic opportunities. The introduction of poverty alleviation programmes, the adoption of redistributive measures, the launching of employment generation schemes, the high expenditure on the poor, programmes intended to empower socially marginalized sections, rural development schemes, high allocation in social expenditure, distribution of essential commodities through fair price shops to the poor, etc. had helped the local leadership of the party to approach the common masses and to expand its support base at the local level.[5] The elaborate network of patronage created by the political leadership under the aegis of the developmental state, enabled it to bargain with various social strata in rural and urban areas for political support.[6] The wide ranging PSUs provided job opportunities and recruitment to socially marginalized sections. The provision of affirmative action in the PSUs stands testimony to the government's commitment to the deprived sections of the society and established its linkage with these groups.

The second-generation political leadership emerged in the mid-1960s, as a result of the emergence of a new regional capitalist class in various states. They thought that since the Congress Party was protecting the interest of the national big bourgeoisie, it was no longer accommodating their interests. The newly emerged regional capitalist class felt that the national big bourgeoisie influenced the national policy initiated by the Congress. The opportunities for private investment created by planned industrialization were monopolized by the big business groups. The newly emergent class often accused the Central government of discriminating against them. Such a feeling generated anti-Congressism in Indian politics. The new regional bourgeois began to support regional political forces for protecting their interest at the political level.[7] Consequently, there emerged a new political leadership at the regional level. In addition to this, in the aftermath of the Green Revolution in various parts of the country especially, in Punjab, Haryana and Karnataka, an affluent middle class peasantry also emerged. This economically advantaged class aspired for political power. The regional parties fulfilled their aspirations for political power. Compared to the first generation political leadership which stood for universalistic ideas, the second generation leadership advocated regional autonomy and were the champions of sub-nationalism.

The emergence of regional political leadership at the state level put the Congress party in trouble. The Party's mass base was eroded at the cost of the expansion of regional parties. The fourth general election of 1967 was an indicator of the shrinking political space of the Congress party. The popular vote for the party declined from 44.73 percent in 1962 to 40.73 percent in 1967. In the case of share of seats in the Lok Sabha, its majority declined from 361 to 283. The stature of the Congress as a national political party was challenged, though it controlled power at the Centre. The party lost its hegemony over the Indian political system and regional political parties came to power at the state levels. In eight states Congress governments were replaced by the non-Congress ones. Thus, at the political level, the 1967 general election marked the beginning of a transformation of the Indian political system from a dominant one-party system to a multi-party system.[8] In fact, the period after the setback of the Congress in the general election in 1967 to 1980 is a period of co-option and mediation.[9]

In order to counter the exponential growth of the regional parties and the challenges posed by the regional leadership, the Congress party leadership adopted certain radical populist polices.[10] The Congress party under Indira Gandhi tried to woo the alienated social groups like the rich peasantry by giving economic benefits like subsidies and loans. Efforts were made to co-opt the rich peasantry into the ruling coalition. The new programmes (*garibi hatao,* nationalization of commercial banks, abolition of privy purses, etc...) initiated by the Indira Gandhi government in the post election scene in 1967 strengthened the position of the Congress party in Indian politics and finally secured its astounding victory in the 1971 general elections.[11] This shows the realignment of alienated social forces back into the party due to the effect of radical populism. Though, the radical populism of Indira Gandhi helped the party to win the 1971 and 72 elections, such populism provided the ground for rapid centralization.[12]

The third generation leadership emerged in the 1990s, in the aftermath of the implementation of Panchayati Raj Act by various state governments. The Panchayat Raj Institutions (PRIs) acted not only as a means of development but also a political laboratory to experiment and curve out new leadership at the grass root level. They not only became a stratum of political decision makers in the Indian political system, but also emerged as alternative centres of political power.[13] The 73rd and 74th Constitutional Amendments created a new awareness among the socially marginalized social groups in the rural areas, especially SCs, STs and Women. It accelerated the process of 'passive revolution'[14] in the countrysides of India. The reservation of seats for SCs, STs transformed them from passive spectators from passive spectators to active participants in local democracy. The provision of one-third reservation to women in PRIs (in some states like Karnataka (43.6%) and West Bengal (35%)) made possible the entry of women in the local level governance. Younger and dynamic leadership emerged through the Panchayats from these sections. Panchayats enabled them to acquire leadership skills at the local level. The leadership in PRIs, acted as 'springboards for social mobility and movement to institutions at the higher levels'.[15]

Decentralization made certain changes in the access to rural power structures. The Panchayat Raj Institutions (PRIs) became the easiest away to fulfill aspirations for political power. It also became the training ground for new leadership in reaching highest echelons in the power structure. The PRIs also emerged as instruments of democratization process. According to Jha (1999), this 'opened up the hinterland for recruitment of leadership which was represented by the 'limited elite' in the beginning and turned into "expansive" elite in the course of time to include leaders from diverse social categories'.[16] The new leadership not only actively engaged in public policy and developmental programmes but enjoyed more 'visible' control over allocative decisions concerning developmental goods and services. The devolution and deployment of developmental resources at the grass root level made proximity between voters and their elected representatives.[17] Thus, the new leadership could create a network of 'new patronage' politics at the local level.

In contrast to the early generations of political leadership, the new leadership represented by diverse social milieu, faced enormous challenges from the traditional socio-economic conditions and the emerging trends in the era of globalization. Traditional socio-economic hierarchy, primarily based on caste system, ownership of land, patriarchal society based on gender inequality were the stumbling bloc to the effective functioning of new political leadership. Instead of being the real instrument for the empowerment of the local people, the panchayats can be seen as a 'potential source of unlimited patronage to service needs of the party machines'.[18] The new leadership, especially from the socially marginalized sections, were often forced to act according to the dictates of party machinery to which he or she belongs to. In such a situation, the aspirations of the newly politicized groups were undermined. Moreover, the nexus between local bureaucracy and local leadership acted as a stumbling bloc to the effective democratic participation of newly politicized social groups.[19]

The emergence of the new leadership happened in the context of the trajectory of developmental shiftfrom state to market. The economic reforms of 1991 were about, the reworking of the idea of the state and its capacity to work on behalf of those who stand outside India's expanding social and economic elites.[20] The retreat of the state was not only manifested in its role as a producer state, regulatory state, distributive state, but it also altered its role as an agency for the empowerment of the socially marginalized sections. The developmental programmes were tampered with for attaining the ambitious target of high economic growth. It was a quite critical moment, when there was an upsurge of the poor and the socially margainlised sections to acquire increased shares in the allocation of economic resources and political power. The dominant classes and castes showed much enthusiasm in diverting the public policies of the government for acquiring more resources from the government. The resource capacity of the state might be increasingly rotten, but it continued to occupy a central place in the imagination of the deprived sections of the society.[21] Moreover, the retreat of the state in general and the privatisation of public sector in particular can be seen in the context of the upper classes and castes for calling specific control over the state power in the face of the emerging hordes of the lower castes.[22]

Unlike the previous generations of political leadership which developed under the shadow of the state and expanded its mobilization, the new leadership found it difficult to sustain mass mobilization. The lack of developmental funds adversely affected the developmental activities especially the programmes aimed at the welfare of socially marginalized sections. In such a situation, the new leadership found it difficult to meet the demands of the local people. It often mocked the effective mobilization of local leadership among the socially marginalized sections. To sum up, the new leadership that emerged in the aftermath of the implementation of the Panchayati Raj suffered from real empowerment in the era of globalization. The process of 'globalisation', the retreat of the state from socio-economic transformation and the penetration of the market forces exist real challenge before the political leadership trying to expand its mass base.

References

1. Lecturer, Department of Political Science, Mizoram University, Aizaw l -12
2. Desai, A. R. (1948), *Social Background of Indian Nationalism*, Bombay: Popular Prakashan, p. 303.
3. Ray, Aswini K. (1989), "Towards the Concept of a Post-Colonial Democracy: A Schematic View", in Zoya Hasan, S. N. Jha and Rasheeddin Khan (eds.), *The State, Political Processes and Identity: Reflections on Modern India*, New Delhi: Sage Publications, p. 130.
4. Patronage politics here refers to the appointments or privileges that a political party/politician can give to loyal supporters for mustering their political support. The Congress party leadership in early decades developed a kind of patronage politics through the strength of the developmental state. By assigning job opportunities in the wide ranging public sector units and by extending public subsidies like fertilizers, seeds, power and irrigation to the farmers and food subsidies for the poor, it could garner

their political support. The mobilisation of the party at the local level was through extending the patronage politics. The bureaucrats and the public servants holding key positions in the public sector units offered their political and monetary support to the party.

5. see Kohli, Atul (1987), *The State and Poverty in India: The Politics of Reform*, Cambridge: Cambridge University Press.
6. Mitra, Subrata Kumar (1992), 'Democracy and Political Change in India', *The Journal of Commonwealth and Comparative Politics*, Vol. 30, No. 1, March, p. 16.
7. Baru, Sanjaya (2000), "Economic Policy and the Development of Capitalism in India: The Role of Regional Capitalists and Political Parties" in Francine R. Frankel, Zoya Hasan, Rajeev Bhargava and Balveer Arora (eds.), *Transforming India: Social and Political Dynamics of Democracy*, New Delhi: Oxford University Press, p. 223.
8. Kochanek, Stanley A. (1968), *The Congress Party of India: The Dynamics of One-Party Democracy*, Princeton: Princeton University Press, p. 427.
9. Nayyar, Deepak (1998), 'Economic Development and Political Democracy: Interaction of Economics and Politics in Independent India', *Economic and Political Weekly,* Vol. XXXIII, No. 49, 5 December, p. 3125.
10. see Bijukumar, V. (2004) "Economic Reforms, Populism and Party Politics in India", *The Indian Journal of Political Science*, Vol. LXV, No.2, April-June, 161-180.
11. Kochanek, Stanely (1974), *Business and Politics in India*, Berkeley: University of California Press, p. 41.
12. Alam, Javeed (1982), 'Congress party: Consensus politics to autocratic regimes', *Economic and Political Weekly*, Vol. XVII, Nos. 28-29, 10-17 July, p. 1144.
13. Mathur, P. C. (1999), "Political Dynamics of the Institutional Pendulum of Democratic Decentralization: An Overview" in S.N. Jha and P.C. Mathur (eds.), *Decentralization and Local Politics,* New Delhi: Sage Publications, p. 105.

14. Antonio Gramsci, the Italian Marxist of 20th century coined the term, 'passive revolution' to refer to the accession of new claimants to power who lacked the social strength to launch a full-scale assault on the old dominant classes.
15. Jha, S. N. (1999), "Introduction" in Jha and Mathur, *op.cit.,* p. 38.
16. *Ibid.*, p. 38.
17. Mathur, *op. cit.* p. 100.
18. Mitra, Subrata K. (2000), "Making local government work: local elites, panchayati raj and governance in India", in Atul Kohli (ed.), *The Sucessof India's Demcoracy*, Cambridge: Cambridge University, p. 110.
19. Lieten, G. K. (2003), *Power, Politics and Rural Development: Essays on India*, New Delhi: Manohar, p. 23.
20. Corbridge, Stuart and John Harriss (2000), *Reinventing India: Liberalisation, Hindu Nationalism and Popular Democracy*, Cambridge: Cambridge University Press, p. 169.
21. Corbridge and Harriss further elaborated this view while reinventing India in the context of liberalisation and Hindu nationalism in the 1990s. Both these trends, according to them, eroded the social base of the state and its commitment to the weaker sections of the society. According to them, the faith of the upper classes and castes on the role of the state in development might be lost, but it is not accurate to say that ordinary men and women have lost faith entirely in the idea of the state.
    see Corbridge and Harriss, *ibid.*
22. Bardhan, Pranab (2000), 'The Political Economy of Reform in India', in Zoya Hasan (ed.), *Politics and the State in India*, New Delhi: Sage Publications, p. 168.

2

Urban Politics: Emerging Leadership in Women

K.S. Saxena

Cities have traditionally been centers of civilization and power. The special significance of cities for politics in developing countries, stems from their strategic contribution to process of economic development and modernization and from their potential for political disruption. Urbanization is seldom an unmixed blessing; it offers grounds for both hope and despair. Two inter related controversies permeate the literature on urbanization. The first concerns the effects of urbanization on economic development and secondly it drains urban and national resources and diverts the investment needed for economic growth.

It is a paradox of Indian public life that cities are both profoundly influential and politically weak. Urban forces persuade modern Indian politics but cities as corporate actors are not, as a rule individually powerful. Much of the political energy contained in Indian cities is not expanded on their behalf as communities but instead absorbed in national competition or on behalf of more specific interests.

While urbanites swept up most of the high positions of power and status after independence, there has been a steady growth in rural claims for power and recognition. The ruralization of politics, or as Rosanthal puts it, the "deurbanisation of the Indian political system" has been marked by increasing attention to rural development policies by government and the mobilization of rural leadership in parties. The process had its roots in the Gandhian movement which made the rural areas the focus of the historic nationalism, but it came to fruition with community development programmes and the Panchayati Raj System. Universal suffrage, the fact that nearly fourth-fifth of the population is rural has promoted a shift in the balance of power from urban to rural sectors.

"Political arenas" can be thought of as constellations of political activity "Islands of Power" in the urban political system. Power and incentive comprise the energy of politics – entirely palpable to the participant, but elusive for the observer. Patterns of power and influence can only be detected indirectly. They must be inferred from a variety of possible manifestations – from who participates in the making of, or, has access to, authoritative decisions, from who gains or loses by virtue of decisions as well as "non-decisions" from who occupies official positions in institutions or organizations; and from the possession of private resources such as money, information, and skills, or control over jobs and publicity.

However, empirical studies of urban society and politics have produced a more conditional and accurate picture of social change in the modern city.

In this background, the emergence of women leadership in urban as well as rural areas is a significant development. 73rd and

74th Constitution Amendments have given 33% reservation for women in urban and rural local bodies. Politics and political awareness are the critical factors. The emergence of women leadership has been a signal to the effect that "women have realized their hidden strength and will come out with more courage and vigour". The following table of Lok Sabha polls, 1998 shows the awakening among women:

Table -1

LOK SABHA POLLS, 1998

State/U. I.	*Women voters*	*Poll Percentage*
Andhra Pradesh	15403950	62.62
Arunachal Pradesh	267514	57.85
Assam	4048789	59.29
Bihar	15313219	56.79
Goa	257228	58.79
Gujarat	770957	55.10
Haryana	3319032	65.07
Himachal Pradesh	956712	71.15
Jammu & Kashmir	610097	34.64
Karnataka	9956901	60.96
Kerala	7689725	70.71
Madhya Pradesh	12051518	55.94
Maharashtra	14389358	53.54
Manipur	374569	55.95
Meghalaya	430317	74.91
Mizoram	153513	69.23
Nagaland	189024	43.07
Orissa	5929349	53.18
Punjab	4197162	58.07
Rajasthan	7785829	55.27

(Contd.)

(Contd. Table-1)

State/U.T.	*Women voters*	*Poll Percentage*
Sikkim	70828	62.50
Tamil Nadu	12484797	55.19
Tripura	670453	80.47
Uttar Pradesh	23043276	50.19
West Bengal	17449454	77.99
U.T.		
Andaman & Nicobar Islands	63906	65.19
Dadra & Nagar Haveli	36225	79.50
Daman & Diu	26025	75.34
Delhi	1713270	48.52
Lakshadeep	15537	87.70
Pondicherry	207195	63.11

The above poll-percentage shows that the women electorates have been politically awakened and their participation in the general elections have been overwhelmed. In this context, it would be in the fitness of things to examine the representation of women candidates in the Lok Sabha since the first general elections of 1952.

Table – 2
Representation of Woman

Year	*Total Seats*	*Women Member*	*Percentage of Women Members to total seats*
1952	499	22	4.4
1957	500	27	5.4
1962	503	34	6.7
1967	523	31	5.9
1971	512	22	4.2

(Contd.)

(Contd. Table-2)

Year	Total Seats	Women Member	Percentage of Women Members to total seats
1977	544	19	3.4
1980	544	28	5.1
1989	517	27	5.2
1991	544	39	7.4
1996	544	35	6.4
1998	543	43	7.0

The above table indicates that the percentage of women members elected to Lok Sabha remained below 10 per cent. Though the performance of women candidates have not been very satisfactory during last half of the 20th century it reflects to the emergence of women leadership, as evident in Table No.3.

Table – 3
Performance of Women Candidates
(Lok Sabha Polls, 1998)

States/U. T.	No. of Seats	No. of woman candidates	No. of women elected
Andhra Pradesh	42	18	02
Arunachal Pradesh	02	-	-
Assam	14	03	01
Bihar	53	21	04
Goa	02	01	-
Gujarat	26	07	04
Haryana	10	06	01
Himachal Pradesh	03	-	-
Jammu & Kashmir	04	01	-

(Contd.)

(Contd. Table-3)

States/U.T.	*No. of Seats*	*No. of woman candidates*	*No. of women elected*
Karnataka	28	10	-
Kerala	20	10	01
Madhya Pradesh	40	28	04
Maharashtra	48	20	02
Manipur	02	01	01
Meghalaya	02	02	-
Mizoram	01	-	-
Nagaland	01	-	-
Orissa	21	10	02
Punjab	13	09	01
Rajasthan	25	20	03
Sikkim	01	-	-
Tamil Nadu	39	13	01
Tripura	02	01	-
Uttar Pradesh	85	56	09
West Bengal	42	21	05
Andman & Nicobar Islands	01	-	-
Chandigarh	01	02	-
Dadra & Nagar Haveli	01	-	-
Delhi	07	10	02
Lakshadeep	01	-	-
Pondicherry	01	-	-
Total	539	271	43

Though majority of the political parties support 33 per cent reservation for women in Lok Sabha even then women's reservation bill has not yet been passed by Lok Sabha. Which shows that in hearts of hearts political parties are not willing to give 33 per cent reservation to women. However, in-spite of heavy odds like traditional or orthodox customs and conventions, family, out-look of the society, conservative attitude of the male-dominated system, the things are rapidly being changed and women in good number are now coming forward to contest the elections right from the Panchayats, Municipalities, Assemblies to Lok Sabha. Women like Smt. Rabri Devi, Chief Minister of Bihar, Ms. Uma Bharti, former Chief Minister of Madhya Pradesh and Ms. Mayawati former Chief Minister of Uttar Pradesh have emerged as leaders from the non-elite classes. Ms. Jayalalitha, Chief Minister of Tamil Nadu, Ms. Vasundhara Raje, Chief Minister of Rajasthan and Ms. Sheila Dixit, Chief Minister of Delhi have already established themselves as an undisputed women leader of their party. Ms. (Dr.) Najma Heptulla, has been the Dy. Chairman of Rajya Sabha four time in a row.

The Assembly elections held in December 2003 in Rajasthan, Madhya Pradesh and Delhi have seen three women Chief Ministers – Smt. Vasundhara Raje, Ms. Uma Bharti (later on resigned) and Ms. Sheila Dixit of the States respectively in a row in independent India.

In case of Rajasthan, in particular, the emerging leadership in women was witnessed in the State Assembly elections held on December 01, 2003 when BJP Chief Ministerial candidate – Smt. Vasundhara Raje and the Dy. Chief Minister – Ms. Kamala Beniwal (Congress) were among the 114 women candidates contesting Assembly elections in Rajasthan.

For Rajasthan, it has been a long journey from the time that four women contested the first Assembly elections in 1952 in a feudal atmosphere that saw none of them successful. However, the first House saw two women members including Ms. Kamala Beniwal, who entered the Legislature in by-elections. In the elections of December 2003, the State BJP had fielded the maximum number of women candidates, numbering twentyone, followed closely by the Congress, which had nineteen candidates of the fairer sex. The BSP had seven, Indian National Lok Dal six, Samajwadi Party five, NCP and LJP three each. Besides, 42 women contested as independent.

To conclude, this shows the emergence of leadership in women, where a record number of women were in electoral battlefield. This is a good beginning in the democratic history of Independent India.

References

1. Donald B. Rosanthal; Deurbanization, Elite Displacement and Political Change in India.
2. D.C. Potter: Government in Rural India
3. K.S. Saxena, Women's Political Participation in India
4. Hindustan Times, dated 29-11-2003

3

Representative Dimension of Municipal Political Leadership-Emerging Scene in South India

V. Gnaneshwar

Ideally, municipal leadership should be attuned to the principles of good urban governance. Municipal political leaders in varying positions viz. mayors, chairpersons/presidents, vice-chairpersons/vice-presidents and councilors should be fore runners in realizing these principles in their respective local situations. Though there can be contextual variations, certain principles are widely recognized at the global level. Most discussed and recognized principles are[1]:

- *Sustainability* in all dimensions of local development.
- *Subsidiarity* of authority and resources to the closest appropriate level consistent with efficient and cost effective delivery of services.
- *Equity* of access to decision-making processes and the basic necessities of community life.
- *Efficiency* in the delivery of public services.

- *Transparency and Accountability* of decision-makers and all stakeholders.
- *Civic Engagement and Citizenship* with all men and women participating in and contributing to the common good, and
- *Security* of individual men and women and, their living environment.

The municipal political spectrum has two main dimensions: representation and leadership. By vote of the people and the legal mandate of the office, elected men and women are responsible for representing the rights and needs of all citizens within their local government jurisdiction.[2] Representation aims to ensure that the local governments strive to achieve the developmental goals set and serve the local communities according to the accepted principles of good governance. And elected leadership is the ability to infuse complex community problems with governing principles, practical competencies, and measurable and sustainable results. It is managing the paradoxes and predicaments through varied knowledge and personal competencies viz., communicating, facilitating, and using power, decision-making, policymaking, enabling, negotiating and institution building. Competency here means a judicious combination of knowledge, skills, understanding and attitudes.

We shall discuss the representative dimension of the municipal councils as also the councilors in the post-Constitution 74th Amendment Act, 1992 scenario in India in the following pages. The discussion is based on data obtained from four southern states, Andhra Pradesh, Karnataka, Kerala and Tamil Nadu as part of a Study on the Impact of the 74th CAA in Southern States by the Regional Centre for Urban and Environmental Studies, Hyderabad.

1. Complexion of the Municipal Councils in Southern States

As the democratic bodies, the municipal councils primarily consist of the elected members. This apart, municipal councils also comprise of ex-officio, nominated and co-opted members in the southern states. In Kerala, the municipal councils are constituted only with the elected members. In this sense, the municipal councils in Kerala could be considered more democratic institutions compared to the other states. Ex-officio members exist in Andhra Pradesh, Karnataka and Tamil Nadu. If nominated members are there in Karnataka, co-opted members exist in Andhra Pradesh. In Tamil Nadu, though the provision exists in the municipal Acts, discussions with the officials reveal that nominated members do not exist in practice. There are variations, however, in extending the voting rights to the nominated, ex-officio and co-opted members in different states. In Andhra Pradesh and Karnataka, the ex-officio members i.e., MLAs, MLCs and MPs have voting right while in Tamil Nadu, the ex-officio members can participate in the deliberations of the municipal council, but have no right to vote. In Andhra Pradesh, the co-opted members and in Karnataka, the nominated members have no right to vote.

2. Impact of the 74th Constitution Amendment Act (74th CAA)

The implementation of the provisions of the 74th CAA had undoubtedly impacted the operant political leadership in the ULBs in India. This has been more pronounced in respect of two vital areas of municipal democracy viz., regular conduct of elections and representation to the weaker/disadvantaged sections of the society and women through adoption of a more rationalized reservation policy uniformly across the states. Now, we shall examine these aspects in detail.

Municipal Elections-Ensuring Regularity

Municipal democracy suffered due to postponement of elections indefinitely for quite long periods and indiscriminate use of the dissolution and supersession provisions of the municipal Acts. In contrast, after the 74th CAA, all the four states have conducted elections twice to the ULBs based on the amended Acts. Table -1 gives details of the elections held so far to the ULBs and the elections due. The third elections were held in September2005 in Andhra Pradesh and Kerala. Though the state government postponed elections for about six moths, maximum period allowed in the 74th CAA, it had to conduct the elections in majority of the ULBs. However, elections to certain municipalities/ corporations were not held due to proposed restructuring of the municipal areas. In the municipalities surrounding Hyderabad, elections were postponed as the State Government proposes to constitute Greater Hyderabad by annexing these municipalities and select panchayats. In a broader sense, elections were more or less regular in the post-74th CAA period.

Table -1: Elections to Urban Local Bodies

State	*First Elections*	*Second Elections*	*Third Elections*
Andhra Pradesh	1995	2000	2005
Karnataka	1996	2001	2006(Due)
Kerala	1995	2000	2005
Tamil Nadu	1996	2001	2006(Due)

Balancing Representation Through Reservation

A true representative democracy entails that all the sections of the society are proportionately represented in the legislative bodies which are the main policy making instruments of modern democratic governments. Unfortunately, serious imbalances in the representation developed in the democratic countries across the world. Certain sections of the society including women could not find proper place in the country's legislative bodies due to various social and historical factors, leaving a critical mass of the populations outside the policy making ambit. In this situation, reservation as a policy ensures a sort of balance in the legislative bodies. It enables the previously un-represented sections of the society to participate in the decision making process thereby influencing the issues that are discussed and the policies being made.

Representation to the weaker sections is being ensured through the mechanism of reservation in India in the Parliament and State Legislatures. This is extended slowly to the local bodies over a period of time. Following this trend, the municipal Acts of all the four southern states provided for reservation of seats in the councils to the weaker sections like STs and SCs and women even before the 74th CAA. The procedure of reservation and the numerical strength varied from state to state based on the local demands and situations. The policy was to adopt a percentage formula. In Andhra Pradesh, the percentages of reservations for SCs, STs, BCs and women were 15, 6, 20 and 9 respectively. In Karnataka, for SCs, STs and women, the percentages of reservations were 15, 3 and 20 respectively. Kerala and Tamil Nadu provided for reservations for SCs and STs in proportion to their population in the municipal area. In Kerala, three seats were reserved for women in each urban local body and in Tamil Nadu, one-third strength of the council was reserved for women. There was no reservation for BCs in these two states.

The 74th CAA rationalized this practice in respect of the SCs, STs and women in all the ULBs and it was made discretionary in respect of the BCs. The provisions stipulate that:[3]

- the number of seats reserved should be in proportion to the SC and ST population in the municipality as the case may be;
- not less than 1/3rd of the total number of seats belonging to SCs and STs respectively should be reserved for women; and
- not less than 1/3rd seats in the council including the seats reserved for SCs and STs, should be reserved for women.

All the four states made provision for reservation of seats for SCs, STs and women in conformity with the CAA. The states of Andhra Pradesh and Karnataka have provided reservation for BCs too. Table-2 gives details of the number of elected members of municipalities from the general and reserved categories in the four states as per municipal elections held in 2000/2001.

In respect of the political chief executives, there was a provision for reservation of offices of mayors and chairpersons of corporations and municipalities respectively on the same lines as that of reservations to councilors even before 74th CAA in Andhra Pradesh. The percentage of reservations for STs, SCs, BCs and women are 6, 15, 9 and 20 respectively. There were two important provisions in the municipalities Acts relating to reservations. Firstly, the system of rotation of the reserved seats was introduced in 1987. Secondly, in a district, the total reservations under different categories should not exceed, as far as practicable, 50% of the total number of such offices. Though reservations were provided for different categories, there was no reservation for women under each of the ST, SC and BC categories. Therefore, in general women only got elected in the general category rather than the reserved categories.

Later, all the states have provided for reservation to the offices of the mayors and chairpersons for SCs, STs and women as per the mandatory provisions of the 74th CAA. The number of reserved offices in the state is in proportion to the total number of offices to be filled as the population of SCs and STs as the case may be. Exercising the discretionary provisions of the CAA, Andhra Pradesh and Karnataka have also made provision for reservation in favor of backward classes. In Andhra Pradesh and Karnataka, one-third of the total number of offices in the state are reserved in favor of backward classes. In Karnataka, 80% of the total offices

Table-2: Social Composition of the Elected Councilors of ULBs

(In Numbers)

Category	Andhra Pradesh			Karnataka			Kerala			Tamil Nadu		
	Corp	Mun	Total	Corp	Mun	Total	Corp	Mun	Total	Corp	Mun	Total
a) General												
G	141	1082	1223	149	1502	1651	190	967	1157	283	2593	2876
W	78	550	628	78	844	922	91	504	595	140	1225	1365
b) SC												
G	25	198	223	26	341	367	8	79	87	32	312	344
W	15	127	142	16	276	292	9	45	54	19	225	244
c) ST												
G	7	109	116	0	41	41	-	1	1		-	-
W	0	7	7	5	77	82	-	1	1		3	3
d) BC												
G	87	669	756	88	986	1074	-	-	-		-	-
W	46	383	429	48	598	646	-	-	-		-	-

(Contd.)

(Contd. Table 2.)

Category	*Andhra Pradesh*			*Karnataka*			*Kerala*			*Tamil Nadu*		
	Corp	*Mun*	*Total*	*Corp*	*Mun*	*Total*	*Corp*	*Mun*	*Total*	*Corp*	*Mun*	*Total*
Sub-total												
G	260	2058	2318	263	2870	3133	198	1,047	1,245	315	2905	3220
W	139	1067	1206	147	1795	1942	100	550	650	159	1453	1612
Grand Total	399	3125	3524	410	4665	5075	298	1,597	1,895	474	4358	4832

Corp =Corporations; Mun: Municipalities including nagar panchayats/town panchayats; G: General ; W: Women.

Source: C & DMA, Government of Andhra Pradesh, Urban Development Department, Government of Karnataka, Kerala State Election Commission, and Tamil Nadu State Election Commission

of mayors and chairpersons reserved for BCs are further reserved for BC-A category and the remaining 20% to BC-B category.

Impact of Reservations on Representation to Weaker Sections-The Case of Guntur Municipal Corporation, Andhra Pradesh

The social complexion of the municipal councils changed in certain respects due to adoption of the provisions of the 74th CAA. In the changed system, representation to certain categories increased while it decreased to others. Even the total reserved strength also changed in the process. The following example of Guntur Municipal Corporation from Andhra Pradesh clearly brings-out this comparative perspective.

The government fixed the strength of the municipal council at 50 on the basis of population of the city, which was 3.67 lakhs as per 1981 census.[4] A fifty-member municipal council was elected in 1987. Even after its up-gradation as Municipal Corporation in 1994, the strength of the council remained at 50. But, it was slightly increased to 52 in election in September, 2005.

Reservations were provided in 1987 in the municipal council for SCs, STs, BCs and women. After its up-gradation as a municipal corporation in 1994, the first election to the corporation was held in 1995 as per the incorporated provisions of the 74th CAA. Elections to the corporation were held thrice in the post-74CAA period. A comparative picture of the reservations provided in the municipal council before and after the 74th CAA clearly brings out the impact of the CAA on the composition of the councils, particularly in terms of providing representation to women and other disadvantaged sections (Table-3.)The women representation was 8 % with 4 seats before the 74th CAA (the statutory provision being 9%) which increased over fourfold to 17 that is, about 34 % of the total number of seats in the council in 1995 elections. The number increased to 18 in 2005 due to increase in the total strength of the council on account of revision of wards but the percentage remains same. Increased representation to women from the weaker sections was another vital feature.

As there was no reservation for women from the SC, ST and BC categories, no woman was elected to the council in 1987. The representation to women under SC and BC categories stands at 2 and 6 respectively during post-CAA period. There was no representation to women, however, under ST category even after 74th CAA as their population was very limited in the city. Evidently, greater representation to women in the corporation council has been the dominant feature of the post-74th CAA period.

Reservations to SCs, STs and BCs, including women in these categories, has also a clear impact as is evident from the number of councilors elected under these categories before and after the 74th CAA. In some cases, the representation has come down while in others representation has increased. For example, the representation for SCs was 16% with 8 councilors in 1987 while it was only 8% with only four councilors including women councilors after the 74th CAA in 1995 and 2000 elections. The number increased slightly to five in 2005 due to revision of wards and increased strength of the council with 10% representation. This was mainly because in l987, there was l5% reservation, whereas in 1995 and 2000, the reservation was related to their population in the city. During the pre-CAA period, as per the provisions of the municipalities Act, 6% of the seats were reserved for STs. This enabled three members to get elected as councilors under this category. In 1995, 2000 and 2005 when representation to STs was provided in proportion to their population in the municipal area, only one person was elected. Thus, there is a reduced representation for STs also in the municipal council in the post-

Table-3: Social Composition of the Guntur Municipal Council

Reservation Category	*Election Year*							
	1987		*1995*		*2000*		*2005*	
	Number	*%*	*Number*	*%*	*Number*	*%*	*Number*	*%*
General	25	50	20	40	19	38	19	36
General (Women)	4	08	9	18	9	18	10	20
S.C.(General)	8	16	2	04	2	04	3	6
S.C.(Women)	-	-	2	04	2	04	2	4
S.T. (General)	3	06	1	02	1	02	1	2
S.T.(Women)	-	-	0	-	0	-	0	-
B.C.(General)	10	20	10	20	11	22	11	21
B.C.(Women)	-	-	6	12	6	12	6	11
Total Women	4	08	17	34	17	34	18	34
Total	50	100	50	100	50	100	52	100

Source: Guntur Municipal Corporation.

CAA period. Representation to BCs, which was only 10 with 20% reservation before CAA, increased to 16 in 1995 and again to 17 in 2000/2005 with the percentage representation ranging between 32% and 34%. Their representation has increased substantially in the post CAA period.

3. The Facet of Political Executives

In Andhra Pradesh, Tamil Nadu and Kerala, political executives of the municipalities are designated as chairpersons and in Karnataka they are designated as presidents. In corporations, they are called mayors uniformly in all the four states. Recognizing the significance of political executives, the 74th CAA provided for reservation of offices of the mayors/chairpersons for SCs, STs and women. However, the manner of election of mayors and chairpersons and reservation of offices of the mayors and chairpersons in the corporations and municipalities for backward class citizens was left to the discretion of the state governments on the lines of the councilors.

Political Executive Election Politics

Historically, the elected members of the corporation or the municipal council elected the mayors or chairpersons. In some states, they are being elected directly by the eligible voters of the civic community. The 74th CAA has left it to the discretion of the state governments to determine the manner of election of mayors and chairpersons of ULBs. In all four states, the pattern existing before passing the conformity legislation continued even after 1994. The practice, however, varies from state to state. In Andhra Pradesh and Tamil Nadu, they are directly elected by all the eligible votes in the city and in Karnataka and Kerala they are indirectly elected by the elected members of the council.

The Case of Andhra Pradesh

Comparative advantages and problems associated with the direct and indirect election of political executives has been a subject of debate. Often there are discussions and debates to change the practice, particularly before elections to ULBs. For instance, the mode of election of the chairpersons is changed from direct to indirect election just before the on-going municipal elections of September 2005 in Andhra Pradesh.[5] There has been wide criticism for such a change just before the municipal elections. The opposition parties attributed this to political reasons. It is alleged that the ruling Congress Party at the state level wanted to win maximum mayor/chairperson posts, even by horse-trading. Added to this, the Government had also given voting powers to the ex-officio members namely, MPs and MLAs in the election of mayor/chairperson which only strengthens these allegations. This measure is widely and strongly criticized on the ground that it goes against the local democracy and the spirit of 74th CAA. The State Government, at the other end, feels that indirect elections will ensure more stable functioning of the municipal councils. It is put-forth that direct election will create problems to the functioning of the municipal councils in case the majority of the councilors belong to the party other than that of the mayor/chairperson. Many a time, it is argued, this situation led to stalemate in the councils stalling the proceedings affecting its functioning in the past. Irrespective of these arguments and counter arguments, the political parties continue to play a very significant role in maintaining the stability or otherwise of the municipal councils rather than the personal charisma and qualities of the aspirants.

The multiparty environment and hung legislative bodies are virtually wrecking the governments at the central and state levels often leading to opportunistic politics and fragile governance. The problems arising out of indirect method of election of the mayors/ chairpersons are bound to complicate the political environment in the municipal councils too. In a way, the events witnessed in the recently concluded municipal elections (September, 2005) in Andhra Pradesh clearly brought-out the complications involved in the indirect election of the mayor/chairperson virtually testifying these arguments and apprehensions. In the elections, there was hung situation in as many as 23 municipalities and two corporations namely, Karimnagar and Nellore. Majority of the hung municipalities are found to be in the Telangana Region as voters did not give a clear verdict in as many as 17 of the 32 municipalities that is over 50%.[6] The Telangana Rashtriya Samithi (TRS) which is spearheading the separate Telangana State movement did not have an alliance with the Congress Party as was done in the last Assembly elections. This is considered to be one of the main reasons for this hung situation as each party fought on its own resulting in the split of votes. In the corporations, the Party-wise position is presented in table-4. It is evident that no party could get a clear majority that is, 26 seats to get the mayoral position. The Telugu Desam Party got slightly more seats in both the corporations. But interestingly, the Congress could get elected its candidate as mayor in both the corporations. Evidently, independents, who are mostly rebel candidates from the recognized parties, played a very significant role in the election of the mayor.

Ultimately, the ruling Congress Party could get as many as 85 municipalities out of the 98 municipalities. The TDP, the opposition party could get only 7 chairperson posts. The party-wise status as per the recently concluded municipal elections in AP is presented in the table-5. The information relating to the vice-chairpersons is incomplete as elections were postponed in some municipalities. In the corporations, the Congress could get all the 10 mayoral posts. Though the ruling Congress Party could get majority seats in the Vijayawada Corporation, the mayor post was given to CPI due to pre-poll alliance between the parties.

Interference of Ministers/MPs/MLAs

Another dimension of the problem relates to the interference of the MLAs and MPs in council elections. There has been heavy lobbying to get the coveted posts of the mayors and chairpersons

Table-4

Political Complexion of Parties in Hung Municipal Corporations in AP.

Corporation	*Total Strength*	*Congress (INC)*	*Telugu Desam*	*BJP*	*CPM*	*TRS*	*MIM*	*Inde-pendents*
Nellore	50	19	20	2	4	-	-	5
Karimnagar	50	13	15	2	-	1	9	10

TRS- Telangana Rashrtiya Samithi, MIM – A Muslim minority party in AP.

Table-5
Party-wise Status of the Municipal Councils in AP

ULB	*Total*	*INC*	*TDP*	*BJP*	*BSP*	*TRS*	*CPI*	*CPM*	*MIM*	*Independents*
Municipalities										
Chairpersons	98	85	7	-	-	2	-	1	-	3
Vice-Chairpersons	89*	63	6	2	1	6	3	1	1	6
Corporations										
Mayors	11	10	-	-	-	-	1	-	-	-
Deputy Mayor	11	9	-	-	-	-	-	1	1	-

Source: Gathered from the news papers, The Hindu and Vaarta, Hyderabad.

* 9 municipalities no data

in favor of their relatives by the ex-officio members. For instance, the mayoral election in Guntur Corporation was postponed twice due to internal conflicts within the Congress Party which got majority seats in the council. There has been a tough fight between a state minister and a local MP to get the mayoral post for their respective relatives. It is unfortunate to note that a local MLA and the MP came to blows publicly in respect of the election of the Tenali Municipal Chairperson resulting in the postponement of the election.[7] And in Kadapa and Nizamabad Corporations, close relatives of the state ministers/chief minister got elected as mayors. In other civic bodies too there was hectic lobbying to get these posts for their relatives

Crazy Tie-ups or Opportunistic Politics?

Apart from the party politics and MLA/MP interference, the election of the political executives was full of surprises and unpredictable events. In certain cases, the councilors defied the party whip and supported the rival party candidates in spite of the danger of loosing their councillorship. There were also local level unexpected alliances between the rival parties like Telugu Desam, Congress, Telangana Rashtriya Samithi and Bharatiya Janata Party. In Bhainsa Municipality, three of the TDP councilors quit the party and floated an outfit called the Telangana TDP overnight and got elected one of its members as chairperson with the support of the TRS, a rival party of the TDP at the state level, BSP and some independents. The local TRS MLA and the MP also supported this move. In Medak Municipality, six TRS councilors voted for the TDP candidate for chairperson in defiance of the Party Whip. Further, Mr. Narendra, the TRS leader and the Central Minister voted for a Congress candidate to become the chairperson while utilizing his critical ex-officio vote.[8] It was reported that the internal dissident problems in Congress led to gifting of the chairperson post to TDP in Gudur Municpality. Further, in Guntakal Municipality, the BJP councilors supported the Congress candidate for the chairperson while the Communist Party supported the BJP in the vice-chairperson election.[9] In Pithapuram and Dharmavaram Municipalities also the BJP helped the Congress win the chairperson elections. As the TDP had no election tie-up, the BJP councilors chose the local convenience to support the Congress.

These events only prove that the political parties in India behave most unpredictably, sometimes even defying the Party Whips. The local media termed these happenings as bizarre events and unholy or crazy tie-ups. These events depict the opportunistic and parochial political picture at the municipal level and are potential enough to become a major threat for stable functioning of the municipal councils in future. One consolation amidst all these affairs is that the political chiefs once elected cannot be removed by no-confidence motion till three years as per the newly amended municipal Acts.[10] But, the informal understanding similar to Guntur and Vijayawada Corporations is always there to share the power.

Fixed Term – No Bar for Sharing Power

An interesting feature of the 74th CAA is that though it provides for a mandatory five-year tenure for the elected councils, it does not make any mention about the tenure of mayors and chairpersons. The Governments of Andhra Pradesh, Kerala and Tamil Nadu have provided for a five year tenure for mayors of corporations as well as chairpersons of municipalities and nagar panchayats. In Karnataka, however, for the mayors and chairpersons a different tenure-one-year for mayors and 30-months (two-and-a-half years) for the presidents was provided. In case of tenure of the offices of mayors and chairpersons, pre-74th CAA practice continued without any changes in all the four states.

In all four states, provision has been made for the rotation of offices of mayors and chairpersons as per the 74th CAA. In Andhra

Pradesh, Karnataka and Kerala, the period of rotation is only one term, whereas in Tamil Nadu, the period of rotation is two terms. In case of any casual vacancy either due to resignation or incapacitation, death or for any other reasons, the vacancy is filled in the same manner as the person who was holding office was elected. The person, however, will hold office for only the remainder period of the person who was elected for the office in whose place a new person was elected. However, the casual vacancies of mayor and chairpersons should be filled within six months after the vacancy occurs. There is no need to fill the casual vacancy, however, if the elections are due within six months.

In Karnataka, because of the shorter tenure and rotation policy, reservations of the political executives change every year in case of mayors and every 30 months in case of the presidents of municipalities. It was observed that in certain cases, two persons are sharing even the 30 months period of the president enjoying a term of 15 months each by mutual understanding. The mechanism is, the incumbent resigns midway after a year paving way for election of a new president as per the Act. This was evident in respect of Guntur and Vijayawada Corporations in AP too. The mayor post was shared during the five year term. In Guntur Corporation, the sharing is between the Congress Party candidates only. There was a tug of war for the post between two aspirants- one, the son of a state minister and the other relative of a local MP. The tussle was resolved ultimately by 50:50 solution wherein each group will get the mayoral post for half of the term that is, two and half years. In Vijayawada, the sharing is still interesting. Vijayawada Corporation will see three mayors during its five-year term. In the first year that is, 2005, the CPI candidate was elected as the mayor. During the subsequent three years from 2006 to 2009, Congress candidate will be elected as the mayor. And again in the final year of 2010, the CPI candidate will occupy the mayor post as per the understanding between the political parties.[11]

Sharing of political executive posts based on local situational political understanding appears to be common irrespective of the statutory fixation of the term akin to the state and central governments.

Personal Background of the Political Executives- the Case of AP

The municipal governments, in general, are seen in a very low esteem in India in spite of the fact that they perform significant role in wellbeing and development of the communities at the grass-root level. The common impression has been that they do not attract educated and young into its stream of governance. But, in recent years, there has been a change. One comes across talented and educated youth taking part in the municipal political process. This is demonstrated in elections across the states in the post-74th CAA period. For instance, in the recent 2005 municipal elections, preliminary information collected about background of the mayors and chairpersons reveal this trend. In respect of the mayors, out of 9 mayors where information could be collected, 5 are either graduates or post-graduates (table-6). From age perspective, Ms K.Saroja, first mayor of the Kakinada Corporation, is considered the youngest mayor in the state with just 24 years, a record of a sort. The Mayor of the Guntur Municipal Corporation, Mr Nagaraj aged 25 also can be considered very young Out of the 8 where information is available, 3 are below 45 years. But, most of the mayors are inexperienced with no earlier municipal experience. In respect of the chairpersons, of the 92 municipalities where information could be collected, more than 50% are well-educated with 16 post-graduates and as may as 34 graduates. Of these, five are observed to be from medical profession and four from law. Interestingly, only two have no formal education. From the point of age, it is observed that 13 are below 30 years and as many as 47 are in the age group of 30-45. It means more than 50% are below 45 years age. It is observed that

Table-6

Background of the Newly Elected Political Executives in AP (In numbers)

Category	*Education*						*Age Group in Years*				*Past Experience*			*Total*
	No Education	School	Inter	Graduate	Post Graduate	No Data	Below 30	30-45	Over 45	No Data	Yes	No	No Data	
Mayors	1	1	2	2	3	2	2	3	5	1	1	8	2	11
Chairper-sons	2	18	22	34	16	6	13	47	30	8	23	69	6	98

Source: Vaarta daily 1st October, 2005, a local Telugu news paper and Commissioner and Director of Municipal Administration, Govt. Of AP

about 23 elected chairpersons have served the municipal councils in one capacity or other. Incidentally, most of these experienced chairpersons are from the Telangana Region.

4. Gender Balance in Political Representation-Toward 50-50

The right to political representation is considered a human right today. But, the global situation reveals that women are grossly underrepresented in government and other policy-making bodies. The situation appears to be similar in the developed as well as the underdeveloped or developing countries. It was brought-out that women formed mere 10 percent of the members of the legislative bodies in 1995.[12] Ten years down the line, the global average of women's Parliamentary representation is still 15.8% and in India it is mere 8.3% as per the UNFPA report 2005[13]. It is clearly brought-out that the countries with relatively high women representation in Parliament, viz., Sweden (45%), Norway (38%) Finland (37%) and Denmark (36%), figure high in human development indices too[14]. While conscious of this disturbing situation, the UN General Assembly in a Special Session in June, 2000 committed the governments all over the world to set and encourage the use of explicit short and long-term time bound targets or measurable goals, including women's equal access to and full participation on a basis of equality with men in all areas and at all levels of public life, especially in decision and policy-making positions, in political parties and political activities, in all government ministries and at key policy-making institutions as well as in local development bodies and authorities.[15] Simultaneously, a global campaign of the Women's Environment and Development Organization (WEDO) was launched during the Beijing + 5 Review which called for all governments to work for a provisional minimum target of 30% representation of women in cabinet ministries and legislatures as well as local authorities by 2003 and equal representation by 2005.[16] The 50:50 campaign was launched in different parts of the world and the Asia Pacific Campaign was launched on March 20, 2001 in Manila, Philippines.

The constitutional and legislative quotas, known as reservations in India, are one form of set-righting the gender imbalances. It is heartening to note that the Government of India provided such a quota, that is, reservation of one-third of the seats for women as back as 1992 through the 73rd and 74th Constitution Amendment Acts uniformly across the country as far as the local governments are concerned. As stated earlier, the quota system existed even in the late 1980's in some states like Andhra Pradesh. Some other countries have also followed this quota system. For instance, 25% of seats at the local level and 20% of seats at the national are reserved for women in Tanzania legally. At the political level, one-third of the African National Congress (ANC) Party lists must be women. Such a political quota system is followed in several Scandinavian and European countries.[17]

Political empowerment of women, thus, has been a recurring theme of discussion at international and national levels. Several policies and programs are being formulated across the globe to improve the status of women, mainstreaming them into public affairs, and addressing their specific developmental issues. In India, the constitution provides for equal rights and privileges in political, economic and social spheres. Politically, their representation in the elected bodies is being pursued at central, state and local levels. The central and state level representation though yet to be realized, the 74th CAA ensured participation of women in urban local governance through the provision of reservation of 1/3 of total seats for women in the municipal councils. It is estimated that there are over 23,000 elected women representatives in ULBs in India at present of which, 670 are in the capacity of chairpersons. In the four southern states, the total strength of councilors, including mayors and chairpersons is 15,872 and the strength of women councilors is 5,589, constituting about 35 percent. This is a positive impact of the 74th CAA.

In certain cases, the women representation was more than the reserved strength. For instance, in the 2005 municipal elections in Andhra Pradesh, women chairpersons were more than the actually reserved strength at the state level as shown in the table-7. Further, 49 women chairpersons were elected whereas the actual reserved strength was 38 out of the 98 municipalities where election was held in the state. .[18] Incidentally, it is exactly 50:50 as

Table-7

Gender Impact of Reservation on Political Executives in AP.

ULB	*Women-Reserved Strength*	*Women Actual Winners*	*Men*	*Total*	*% of Women Political Executives*
Chair persons	38	49	49	98	50
Vice-Chair Persons	-	11	79	90	12.2
Mayors	4	4	7	11	36.3
Deputy Mayors	-	-	10	11 (one no data)	100

Source: Office of the Commissioner and Director Municipal Administration, Govt. of AP, and information gathered from daily news paper-Vaarta and The Hindu.

aimed by the UN by 2005. In six municipalities viz., Srikakulam, Vizianagaram, Tanuku, Kadiri and Sangareddy and Sadasivapet, women candidates won chairperson posts from the unreserved category. Another interesting fact has been that women belonging to weaker sections won from the general category of seats within the reserved categories in Nuzivdu (BC-G), Ponnur (SC-G), Chittor (SC-G), Sattupally (ST-G) and Bongir (SC-G) Municipalities. Further, two Muslim women were also elected as the chairpersons from Khammam and Kadiri Municipalities. Women representation exceeded the fixed statutory share in all the reserved categories which could be considered a very positive and encouraging trend in the municipal governance. There is no reservation of posts of Deputy Mayor/Vice-Chairpersons. The situation, therefore, explains the impact of reservation.

Two generations of women representatives have already occupied the seats in the local councils in all the four states and the third generation too in Andhra Pradesh and Kerala where elections are held in September, 2005. No doubt, reservations provided scope for political empowerment of women at the local government level. Yet, there is much to be done. There are problems concerning the proxy women representatives, rotation, party influences, etc. Research evidence, though meager, shows that women representatives are yet to make their voice felt and play their representative role with confidence. For instance, women had inherited the reserved constituency previously held by their relatives due to reservation policy and it is brought-out by some studies that more than 50% of the successful women candidates are relatives of the political activists in the Kolkata, Ludhiana, Mumbai, Ahmedabad and Hyderabad municipal corporations. [19]

Women's role is better recognized and being utilized in the poverty schemes like SJSRY in the urban sector. In Kerala, the implementation of Kudunbarsree programme, with its network of institutions at the neighbourhood and city levels has contributed to strengthening urban local government institutions. They have contributed enormously through their active and effective participation in the meetings of the ward committees and sabhas, which have a responsibility to prepare the local development plans which are integrated at the district level. This practice should also be encouraged in the other development projects at the local level. It is important to promote effective participation of women in urban local governance by creating a congenial atmosphere where women can express their problems and issues freely; encouraging and building the capacities of grass-root women organizations and the women elected representatives to make understand their role, improve leadership capabilities and to develop confidence.

Different strategies must be adopted to mainstream women and achieve the gender balance in the governance process. Some of these could be:

- Improving gender consciousness among the elected representatives by making men and women equal partners and also by gender sensitization of men.
- Preparing the potential women representatives through training in skills like running and managing election campaigns and enhancing their political knowledge and awareness levels.
- Networking of women working in different sectors.
- Focused capacity building initiatives.

5. Role of MPs and MLAs - the ex-officio members

The representative role of members of legislatures and parliament is unquestionable. Extending this role, the municipal Acts in several states have provided for their representation in the ULBs. There are, however, wide variations in the states both in terms of their representation as also their right to vote. In most cases, the states followed pre-74th CAA practice in terms of representation of MLAs and MPs in the post-CAA period also with marginal changes. In the four southern states, three patterns have emerged. In Andhra Pradesh and Karnataka the legislators and parliamentarians are members of the ULBs, which form part of their constituency with a right to participate and vote. In Tamil Nadu, MLAs and MPs can participate in the discussions but without a right to vote. In Kerala, they have no role in the ULBs. Thus, there are variations in the pattern of representation to the members of legislature and parliament in the local bodies.

Representation to the legislators and parliamentarians in the ULBs has been a point of debate for quite a long time. The Constitution Review Commission, which examined this aspect in detail, felt that "the provision for the representation of MPs and MLAs in panchayats and municipalities appear to go against the spirit of the constitution and its overall scheme of elected bodies at various levels".[20] It further states that *prima facie*,[21] the provisions underArticle 243R are against the grain and spirit of Articles 101 and 190 of the Constitution irrespective of the fact whether prohibition of dual membership is a basic feature of the Constitution or not. It expressly recommends that in keeping with the spirit and substance of the 73rd and 74th Amendments envisaging panchayats and municipalities as institutions of self-government, the provision for representation of MPs, MLAs and MLCs in Articles 243C and 243R should be deleted. It recommended that if such representation is considered necessary, it should be without voting rights and as invitees. The Commission also felt that dual membership in a municipality on one hand and state legislative or parliament on the other should be specifically prohibited. This recommendation needs to be critically examined.

But, the mood of the central and state governments, undoubtedly favors their membership in the municipal councils and they are destined to play significant role in functioning of the municipalities especially, their councils. The recent stance of the Government of Andhra Pradesh demonstrates this trend. In Andhra

Pradesh, the election of the chairpersons and the mayors is changed from direct to the indirect system and the MLAs and MPs are provided with voting right to participate in the election of the chairpersons/mayor in their respective municipality/corporation. Many argued that this measure goes against the spirit of local self-governance so strongly advocated through the 73rd and 74th Constitution Amendments. The bizarre events that were witnessed during the election of the mayors and the chairpersons in Andhra Pradesh as narrated earlier only prove the stance taken by the Constitution Review Commission. It also led to certain legal problems. Under the A.P .Municipalities Act, the MPs/MLAs who are ex-officio members in the municipal councils should give their preference of Municipality for which they desired to utilize their voting right to the commissioner concerned in writing. They are, however, free to participate in the discussions in other municipalities under their constituency but without voting right. In the recent elections, some MLAs/MPs changed their preference municipality just to enable their party candidates to win the chairperson post. As they have not given in writing, they defended that they are eligible to vote although they are exercising their voting right routinely in the council and also taken oath in other municipality. For instance, a local MP who has been exercising his ex-officio voting rights in Hidupur Municipality till the election changed his preference to Dharmavaram Municipality and exercised his critical ex-officio vote to enable a Congress candidate to win the chairperson election. The opposition candidate belonging to the TDP Party approached the High Court seeking disqualification of his vote. But, the High Court ruled that the action of the MP right and upheld the election of the chairperson in the absence of written evidence testifying the ex-officio membership of the MP in the Hindupur Municipality. The administrative lapse on the part of the commissioner to get the MP preference in writing led to such a situation. This only shows the opportunistic attitude of the MPs/MLAs.

The MPs and MLAs have an important role to play in promoting urban development and improving urban governance. They, being representatives in the Parliament and State Legislatures respectively, should provide macro level policy guidance and support to the local bodies. Ideally, they should play an advisory role than playing politics at critical moments. Their participation, with or without membership and with or without right to vote becomes meaningful only when they:

- take development above partisan politics and contribute to political development;
- see local problems in a broader perspective and represent them at higher level representative bodies in which they are members;
- coordinate and help in formulating and implementing the development schemes and programs;
- help the local bodies in mobilizing the financial resources from the central and state governments, financial institutions, etc.; and
- utilize their local area development funds for infrastructure development in the ULBs.

6. Conclusions

The complexion of the municipal councils, which was in existence before 1994 more or less, continues. In Andhra Pradesh and Karnataka, the MLAs and MPs are ex-officio members with a right to vote while in Tamil Nadu, they have membership without voting right. Kerala is the only state where they do not have a membership of ULBs. Regularity of elections and more wider and enhanced representation to the disadvantaged sections of the urban community are the two pronounced impacts one witnesses on the urban scene in the post-74th CAA period in India. This has been true in respect of ULBs in all the four southern states too. A significant feature is that some of the ULBs had the elected councils for the first time after a prolonged suspension of their elected councils, as is the case with Coimbatore Corporation in Tamil Nadu. The supersessions and dissolutions of ULBs can be said to be non-existent in the four states during the last 10 years and in a couple of cases where ULBs were dissolved as in Tamil Nadu, elections were held within the stipulated time providing for democratically elected councils.

One of the very significant roles of the elected bodies is providing representation to all the sections of the society. Their representative role was limited mostly to the elite and advantaged sections of the society till recently in India. To overcome this problem, the policy of reservation has been introduced in India. Initially, the most disadvantaged sections like SCs and STs were provided reservations in various legislative bodies including the municipal councils in India. As a result, provision for reservation to SCs and STs existed even before the passage of the 74th CAA in 1992 in the southern states. The percentage and methodology however varied. Reservation for BCs, which is a discretionary provision under 74th CAA, was provided in Andhra Pradesh and Karnataka. Provisions relating to reservation to women have been incorporated in all the four states. The reservation scheme stipulated in the 74th CAA was incorporated in case of the political executives as well as the councilors. The constitutional provisions of making reservations to women and other disadvantaged sections have considerable impact on the composition of the councils. In some cases, the representation was provided for the first time to the categories like women under STs and SCs and in other cases, there has been a significant increase in the percentage of representation to these groups. A significant and visible impact of 74th CAA can be said to be the political empowerment of women as also STs and SCs. Often, criticisms are voiced against the proxy role being played by the husbands of the women councilors in the states like Andhra Pradesh and Karnataka. This brings us to the next important issue of capacity building concerning the municipal councils.

An important question that is being raised by the political executives of corporations and municipalities in all the states is their powers. The demand for more powers appears to be a burning issue among all the elected representatives in all the four states. Another question relates to their training and capacity building. Large numbers of councilors are getting elected for the first time as a result of 74th CAA and the needs of training orientation and capacity building are enormous. Reservations merely provide opportunities and scope for involvement but cannot ensure participation. The function of representation can become effective and purposeful only when the elected representatives understand their representative roles properly and develop their leadership skills to play these roles effectively. They should understand that[21]:

- Representation is the measure of how well the local government serves all of its citizens in accordance with widely accepted principles of good governance.
- Representation involves the development and enforcement of policies, allocation of public goods and services, assisting local men and women in their interactions with their local government, and keeping in touch with all citizens on a continuing basis.
- Conflicting demands, pluralistic pressures, and problems challenge effective representation when no one is in charge of solving them.
- Representation and good governance share common values: participation, respect for the law, equity and inclusiveness, transparency and accountability, effectiveness and efficiency, and subsidiarity.
- Representation is enhanced through a rich network of partnerships, which is different from a network of rich partnerships.

It is hoped, the new generation elected representatives will develop such an understanding going beyond the pressing and immediate partisan interests and become peoples' representatives in a true sense.

References

1. UN- HABITAT, *Global Campaign on Urban Governance.*
2. Quick Guide(Volume 1), The Local Elected Leadership Series Key Competencies for Improving Local Governance ,United Nations Human Settlements Programme, 2005.
3. Sections 243 T, The Constitution 74th Amendment Act, 1992.
4. Andhra Pradesh Municipal Corporations Act, 1994, Section 5(1) and G.O.Ms.No.605, Housing, Municipal Administration and Urban Development, Government of Andhra Pradesh, dated 29.10.1986. After 1988, there was no delimitation of constituencies. As a result, the strength of council remained 50 fixed based on 1981 census even during 1995 and 2000 elections.
5. Andhra Pradesh Ordinance No. 17 of 2005, Government of Andhra Pradesh, dated August 8, 2005.
6. Varta, a Telugu daily in AP, dated 27th September, 2005.
7. The Times of India, October 1, 2005, Hyderabad.
8. Ibid.
9. Vaarta (Telugu News Paper), October 1, 2005, Hyderabad.
10. AP Ordinance 17 of 2005, op cit.
11. The Hindu, 8th October, 2005, Hyderabad.
12. Report on Asia Pacific Workshop on Gender Balance in Political Representation, March 21-22,2001, Manila, Philippines, www.cld.org/Manila Conference.htm.
13. Times of India editorial, October 22, 2005, Hyderabad.
14. Ibid.
15. Asia Pacific Report, op.cit.
16. Ibid.

17. Ibid.
18. The Hindu, October 1, 2005, Hyderabad.
19. Shipra Maitra, The Empowered Women-Implications for Urban Governance, Nagarlok, Vol.XXXIV, No.4, October-December, 2002, p19.
20. Constitution Review Commission, p.1058.
21. UN- HABITAT, Op.cit.

4

Local Leadership as a Representative National Leadership

Jairaj Phatak

Local Government in Maharashtra

Maharashtra, arguably the leading state of the Indian Union, has a long history in elected governments at the local level, both of the urban and the rural areas. Elected councilors constitute the municipal councils in smaller towns and the municipal corporations for cities with a population of more than three lakhs. Now, there are twenty two municipal corporations and more than two hundred municipal councils. The councilors in a municipal corporation are also called corporators. Similarly, elected councilors form the village panchayts for village or group of villages. For about hundred villages, there is a block panchayat samiti with elected councilors and at the district level i.e. for about 1000 villages or ten blocks there is a zilla parishad (district council) with elected councilors. Now, there are thrity-three Zilla Parishads. The Mumbai City District and the Mumbai Suburban District, both being hundred percent urban, do not have zilla parishads. The elected head of the zilla parishad is called the president, who is assisted in his duties by a vice-president and four subject committee chairmen. At the block level, the elected head is called the chairman, panchayat samiti and at the village level, the sarpanch is the elected head. The Mayor is the elected head and the presiding authority in a municipal coporation and the president of the municipal council is the elected head and the presiding authority in the municipal council.

In the urban areas, the Mumbai Municipal Corporation that was set up under the Act of 1888 has served as a role model for the local governments in Maharashtra and Gujarat. The Municipal Corporation of Greater Mubai became the trendsetter for a sound municipal system in Maharashtra. Maharashtra today has twenty two municipal corporations and more than two hundred municipal councils. The Municipal Commissioners, for the purpose of administrative control, report to the Secretary in the Urban Development Department. The Commissioner, Municipal Corporation of Greater Mumbai (MCGM), who is usually of the rank of Additional Chief Secretary/Principal Secretary reports directly to the chief secretary of the state government. The nodal department for the MCGM, too, is the Urban Development Department. The chief officer of the municipal councils report to the district collector and through him to the Director of Municipal Administration, a field officer of the urban development department with the rank of a commissioner. In view of the importance of cities in Maharashtra, the portfolio of urban development department is usually with the chief minister himself.

In the rural areas, apart from the traditional village panchayats that have existed in India since historic times, the state set up a strong panchayati raj system in the year 1962. A three-tier model of panchayati raj, that has now been recommended for the country vide the seventy-third admendment to the Indian Constitution has successfully worked in the state for more than forty years. The chief executive officer of the zilla parishad (district council) is a senior-scale officer, of the same rank but usually junior to the district collector. The block development officer (B.D.O.) is a class I officer of the Maharashtra Development Service and is of the same rank as the tahsildar. The gramsevak, who is also the secretary of the village panchayat is the administrative support to the village local body.

It is not unsurprising that Maharashtra has devolved a number of administrative functions and has bestowed adequate resources on the local bodies. Vieira had carried out an interesting study of forty-five countries during the sixties. His study shows that the degree of devolution (measured by the ratio of local government revenues and expenditures to total government spending and receipts over a ten year period) in both western and developing countries is significantly correlated with five factors. These five factors are the following.

1. The age of the nation; older nations devolve more
2. The size of the GNP
3. The level of development of news media
4. The level of industrialization
5. The number of local governments

Maharashtra is ahead of most states in India on four of these above five factors. It has the highest state domestic product, well developed industries and very enlightened media. Thus, it is logical that local governments should get adequate administrative and financial powers in this state.

Elections take place regularly for all levels of local bodies and elected representatives are associated with all decision-

Table-1

Authorities in Various Levels of Government

Level of Government	*Legislature*	*Executive*	*Legislative Secretariat*	*Audit*	*Appointments*	*Income*
1. Centre	Parliament	Council of Ministers	Lok Sabha/Rajya Sabha Sectt.	C and AG	UPSC	Excise, Customs Income Tax
2. State	Legislature	Council of Ministers	Legislature Sectt.	C and AG	State PSC	Sales Tax, M.V. Tax
3. Municipal Corporation	Corporation	Commissioner	Municipal Secretary	Own audit	Selection Committee	Property Tax, Octroi
4. Municipal Council	Council	President	Chief Officer	AC/LFA	Selection Boards	Property Tax, Grants
5. Zilla Parishad	Parishad (Council)	Chief Executive Officer	Under Dy. CEO	AG/LFA	Selection Boards	Grants, Z.P. Cess
6. Block Panchayat Samiti	Samiti	Block Development Officer	B.D.O.	AG/LFA	-	Part of cess
7. Village Panchayat	Panchayat	Sarpanch /Gram Sevak	Gram Sevek	AG/LFA	-	Grants, tax on lands and building

making. Although the chief executive in all the local bodies, except the municipal councils, is a career bureaucrat, the non-officials have considerable say in the decision-making. Many ministers and M.L.As in Maharashtra have come up after experience at the local level. Shri S.B. Chavan, who went on to become a snior union minister and was chief minister more than once started his career as President of Nanded Municipal Council. Shri Vilasrao Deshmukh was first Sarpanch of his village Babhalgaon and then Deputy Chairman of the panchayat samiti, Latur before becoming an M.L.A. and later on Chief Minister. Shri Manohar Joshi, former Chief Minister and now Speaker of the Lok Sabha was Mayor of the Mumbai Municipal Corporation. So was Shri Chhagan Bhujbal, former Deputy CM, Shri Narayan Rane, former CM was Chairman of the BEST Committee of the Mumbai Municipal Corporation, which runs a bus transport of more than 3500 buses and also distributes electricity to the city of Mumbai. Thus, the leaders at the national and state level usually have personal experience of local government and hold it in esteem and respect.

The Table 1 illustrates the local government structure in Maharashtra.

The elected corporators are thus trained in the art of governance by taking decisions at the local level.

Urban Local Government

Local government in urban India, owes its origin to the British initiatives and not to the ancient village republics or panchayats. The Government of India suitably acknowledges this. The Memorandum of Development and Working of Representative Institutions says: 'Local government in India, in the sense of representative organization, responsible to a body of electors, enjoying wide powers of administration and taxation and functioning both as a training in responsibility and a vital link in the chain of organism that make up the government of the country is a British creation. The ancient village communities were constituted on a narrow basis of hereditary privilege or caste, closely restricted in the scope of their duties collection of revenue and protection of life and property were their main functions and were neither conscious instruments of political education nor important parts of the administrative system.'

After India became independent in 1947, local government was made a state subject. However, vide Article 12, the Constitution of India has recognized that local government institutions are an integral part of the national government. The subject of local government is listed under the 'state list' i.e. entry 5 of List II of the Seventh Schedule to the Indian Constitution. They are created by the state governments who are to provide them with adequate finances. They possess the powers and functions that are passed on to them by the state legislatures under the state enactments.

The 'corporation' is comparable to the parliament or the state assembly and meets at least once a month. The Mayor, whose protocol rank as numero uno in the corporation is undoubted, presides over the corporation. However, the Mayor individually has no administrative control over the commissioner or the subordinate staff. Although he presides over the meetings of the corporation, the commissioner or his officers are expected to give replies to the questions in the house. Again, the commissioner is to introduce the agenda items in the corporation meeting and also to defend the policies and measures taken by the corporation when they are criticized or questioned by the corporators. The Mayor's position in the house is that of the Speaker of the legislative assembly while the Commissioner plays the role of the Chief Minister answering questions and defending the policies of the executive. Since the Mayor is also the nominal head of the corporation, it might be appropriate to say that the

Mayor's position in the city government is that of the Governor and the Speaker combined.

The Standing Committee of the Corporation meets every week and the Commissioner cannot enter into contracts involving certain amounts or higher without the approval of the Standing Committee. Thus the commissioner cannot push through his proposals through the corporation or the standing committee unless he enjoys a respect and a majority support in both the bodies. For smooth governance, he has to keep good working relationship with both the Mayor and the Chairman of the Standing Committee. Some people defend this "Commissioner" model of city governance by saying that it is designed to offer effective administrative leadership. The Commissioner, who is the chief executive officer of the Corporation, is drawn from the highest echelons of the public service in the State viz. the I.A.S. and he is expected to provide administrative leadership. However, the origin of such an arrangement may also be searched in the history of the Bombay Municipal Corporation Act, 1888. This was a time when the Commissioner was British member of the I.C.S. while the corporators were democratically elected Indians. Thus, it could be said the government chose to rely more on the Commissioner than on the elected Mayor or the corporators. It was administratively not possible for the British government to post I.C.S. officers as chief executives of smaller municipal bodies. Thus, in the smaller bodies the government vested the Chairman/ President with executive powers and gave the controlling powers to the Collector and District Magistrate, who was a member of the I.C.S.

In the municipal councils, thus, the elected President is the chief executive. He is not a gubernatorial functionary like the city Mayor. He is the head of the deliberative and executive wing and wields authority over the executive wing.

The Rural-Urban Relationship Committee, appointed by the Government of India in 1963 recommended that Municipal Corporations be set up for cities with population of 5 lakhs or more or annual revenue of Rs.1 crore or more. A financial limit in an inflationary economy is of an ephemeral nature. However, in Maharashtra a population of about 300,000 has been generally based as the parameter for setting up of municipal corporations.

The Corporation Acts

The Corporation Acts, wherever the municipal corporations exist, are separate legislations from the municipal councils Acts. Chronologically, some of the important enactments have been:

1. The Bombay Municipal Corporation Act, 1888
2. Madras City Municipal Corporation Act, 1919
3. Bombay Provincial Municipal Act, 1949
4. Bangalore Municipal Corporation Act, 1949 (Karnataka M.C. Act, 1976)
5. The City of Nagpur Municipal Corporation Act, 1950
6. The Calcutta Municipal Corporation Act, 1951
7. Delhi Municipal Corporation Act, 1957
8. The U.P. Nagar Mahapalika Abhiniyam, 1959 (U.P. Nagar Nigam Adhiniyam, 1959)

The broad frame of these Acts is similar. The relationship between the deliberative wing (corporators) and the executive wing (the commissioner and officers) has been a subject of controversy over the last few decades. However, to argue that the Mayor or the chairman of standing committee is a ceremonial office is far from truth. In fact, every major work taken up in a local area is after an approval of the corporation/works committee. It rarely happens that Mayor or other important party functionary wants to take up an activity and it is not taken up. The Commissioner, a non-local career civil servant, is generally not interested in particular individual works unless there is some complaint or nuisance because of them. Again, the Commissioner cannot give work order for any work except with a prior approval of the standing committee. Thus, the Mayor and the Chairman of standing committee enjoy considerable clout as long as they enjoy the majority support within the corporation.

Authorities

The original Mumbai Act as well as Nagpur and the Bombay Provincial Acts mentioned three authorities vested with the powers of implementation of the Acts. The authorities are the corporation, the standing committee and the commissioner. Interestingly, the Mayor was not included in the list of authorities since he was not expected to discharge any powers independently.

The Calcutta Municipal Corporation Act, 1980, on the contrary, lists the corporation, the Mayor-in-council and the Mayor as the three authorities. The Mayor-in-council has been made collectively responsible to the corporation while the commissioner has not been listed as an authority. The Calcutta Act, thus, tries to emulate the state government model with the Mayor-in-council replacing the council of ministers and the Mayor replacing the Chief Minister. Interestingly, the Constitution of India, which lays down the staturoty basis for the central and state government, does not mention the posts of Cabinet Secretary or the State Chief Secretary as authorities. The Calcutta Act does not mention the Municipal Commissioner as an authority and places the Municipal Commissioner as the chief administrative officer of the corporation, who more like the Chief Secretary of a state, wields considerable influence but little statutory powers of his own.

The Maharashtra Municipalities Act, 1965 lists five authorities that are charged with carrying out the provisions of the Act. These are the council, the president, the standing committee, the subjects committee, if any, and the chief officer.

The Corporation/Council

The Corporation meeting, in which all the councilors are present, usually takes place once in a month. The Mayor presides over this meeting. The questions are, however, answered by the Municipal Commissioner or his officers who also table and defend various proposals for consideration of the corporation. All major policy decisions pertaining to the corporation, approval of the budget and administrative approval to major works are within the purview of the Corporation. Under the Maharashtra Acts, the Corporation meeting is to be held before the 20th day of each month. The corporation meeting should not be adjourned on frivolous grounds. The Supreme Court has observed. This power must be exercised bonafide and not for a collateral purpose. The power must be exercised for a proper purpose. If the Mayor is unable to show this, then the postponement of the meeting must be held to be bad.

Similar procedure prevails for the conduct of business in the municipal councils. However, the Municipal President is not a gubernatorial functionary like the city mayor. He is the chief executive in the real sense. In Maharashtra, he even writes the Annual Confidential Report of the chief officer. He is thus both the Chief Minister and the Speaker combined for the town administration.

An important difference between the corporation and council is regarding the power to remove individual councilors for misconduct. Under the Maharashtra Municipalities Act, 1965, councilors misbehaving or misusing their position for wrongful gains can be removed by the government either on the recommendation of the council or suo motu. In the case of municipal corporation, however, such proposals for removal can be considered only on the recommendation of the Corporation supported by not less than two-thirds of the total number of Councillors and it is very difficult, if not impossible, to get such a recommendation.

The procedure for the motions to be taken up in the meeting is usually laid down in the Acts. Under Rule 24(1) of the Mahrashtra Municipalities Rules:

- 'On a motion or amendment being moved and seconded, the presiding authority shall read it or cause it to be read to the meeting.
- It shall then be considered before the meeting for discussion.
- The mover may then speak in support of the kmotion or amendment, and the seconder may either follow or reserve his speech for a latter stage of debate thereon.
- Other Councillors may, save as otherwise provided, speak on the motion in the order in which they are called upon by the presiding authority.'

Most other Acts have similar position about the discussion in the Corporation/council meeting. The role of the Commissioner/ Chief Officer is crucial in the meetings since he alone can tell clearly what is legal and what is proper. A good Municipal Commissioner is also sure of the facts. If the Commissioner/Chief Officer is well versed with his work he can also tell the councilors whether a particular course of action is advisable or otherwise.

The meeting is generally open to the public unless the Presiding Authority directs to the contrary. This is in keeping with the practice to keep meetings of the legislature open to public.

Following the practice in the legislature, the system in Mumbai Municipal Corporation is not to call the police in case of a disturbance and disruption of proceedings in the corporation meeting. Marshals have been appointed for keeping order. However, in Pimpri-Chinchwad and Navi Mumbai Municipal Corporations there are instances of calling the police inside the house to separate the warring corporators and to restore order.

The Committees

Most corporations have a single 'standing committee' elected on the basis of proportional representation. All the matters of entering into contract pass through this committee. The term of office of this committee is usually one year. *The commissioner cannot enter into a contract for execution of work unless the Standing Committee approves it.* The standing committee can approve or reject the proposal of the commissioner but cannot change it. In case of the standing committee having doubts about the proposal, the Commissioner's personal presence helps as to what extent he is ready to modify his proposals. The Mumbai practice is to allow the Press in the meetings of the standing committee although the Pune practice is to the contrary. The Pune practice is based on the fact that the standing committee is more like the cabinet or the council of ministers in the central/state government. Members of the press are not allowed in the meetings of the cabinet. However, there is no harm in making the procedures transparent and there is nothing objectionable in the Mumbai practice of allowing press reporters to sit through the meetings of standing committee. In fact, presence of the press helps in orderly conduct of the meetings.

The Bombay High Court has clarified the powers of the Standing Committee as follows:

6. Primarily the power to enter into a contract is the power of the Commissioner, and, on this power, there is a restriction.

In case the contract involves expenditure exceeding one lakh rupees, the Commissioner has to seek the previous approval of the Standing Commissioner.

7. What the Standing Committee is expected to do is specified in the proviso. The Committee is expected to consider and dispose of the proposal made by the Commissioner. There is no power in the Committee to substitute its own proposal made by the Commissioner."

Following the Bombay pattern, legal provisions exist in the Municipal Acts of western India that the municipal corporations may set up a transport undertaking. The affairs of the transport undertaking are looked after by a statutory transport committee, which functions as the standing committee for the purpose. Bomaby City and U.P. Mahapalikas (now Nagar Nigams) have separated Improvement Committees (presently Development Authority) while Patna has a separate water board. The Delhi Municipal Corporation has six statutory committees as under;

1. Standing Committee
2. Delhi Electric Supply Undertaking
3. Delhi Transport Undertaking
4. Delhi Water Supply and Sewage Disposal Committee
5. Rural Area Committee
6. Education Committee

The Bombay Primary Education Act provides for the setting up a School Board in each municipal town. The School Board acts as the committee for primary school education in western India.

In addition to the statutory committees created by the Act, the corporations in western India set up subjects committees. The important subjects committees are the Works Committee, the Health Committee, the Social Welfare Committee and the Slum

Improvement Committee. The corporation delegates authority for sanctioning/administratively approving works below a certain limit by these subjects committees. The system of governance by committees is a British legacy based on the age-old tradition in local government. The Commissioner requires approval of the corporation or of the concerned committee for the course of action suggested by him. Thus, the proactive role is with the Commissioner while the reactive role is with the Corporation of its committees. Of course, in reality the committees also make useful suggestions that the Commissioner can examine and thereafter bring a suitably worded appropriate resolution for the consideration of the body. The commissioner, however, cannot prohibit a committee from passing a resolution. If a committee passes an inappropriate resolution, the commissioner may refrain from acting on it or alternatively forward the resolution to the government for its cancellation Whether the resolution is just to be ignored or it is to be forwarded to the government for cancellation would depend upon the seriousness of the resolution. In a Navi Mumbai case, the Corporation passed a resolution that building permission should not be given to a developer because CIDCO, the new town development authority had disposed of the concerned plot without consulting the corporation although earlier it was reserved for a hospital. The Commissioner thought it prudent to forward the resolution to the government for appropriate action/guidance since there were many political overtones in the resolution and in a way, the corporators had a genuine grievance since the law required that corporation be consulted before changing a reservation. However, there are instances of Commissioners plainly ignoring resolutions to buy luxury cars or mobile phones for the non-officials.

The High Court has further held that under the Maharashtra Municipalities Act, 1965, the General Body can nullify or modify decision of standing committee because standing committee is subordinate to general body in view of Section 73(2) of the Act.

There are, however, important differences between the Standing Committee and the Council of Ministers at the state level. First, unlike the Chief Minister, the Chairman of the Standing Committee, on his own, does not have much authority. Secondly, the members of the standing committee do not belong to the same political partly. They do not owe their office to the Chairman, standing committee. Thus, they do not accept the authority of the Chairman in the same way in which the ministers accept the authority of the Chief Minister. In fact, the opposition members may appeal to the fairness of the commissioner against some resolutions passed by brute majority by the ruling partly.

Ward Committees

When a city government becomes too big, it is necessary to constitute lower tiers that can handle the day to day problems of the people. Just like the block panchayat samities are area committees of the Zilla Parishad (District Council) in India, the ward committees are expected to be the area committees of a large municipal corporation. Robson recognized this need quite some time back.

'One of the objects of local self-government is to give opportunities for as many citizens as possible to participate in public affairs and have continuous interest in them. But in big cities like Calcutta and Bombay and even in ordinary towns a single municipal council does not create all the opportunities required for the purpose. It is, therefore, desirable and necessary that statutory ward committees are constituted to look after the affairs of each ward on the basis of powers delegated to them by the Council. The Committee may consist of all the councilors elected from the ward and certain other residents of it co-opted for the purpose. The committee may be entrusted with the work of supervising the municipal institutions in the ward – schools, dispensaries, maternity homes etc. – bringing to the notice of the Council the way in which its sanitary and other staff does its work in the locality and the needs of a special character which the residents of the ward may have. This will be something like the introduction of two-tier government in the urban areas. It is sure to foster greater interest among the people in municipal affairs and will be an antidote to the indifference usually shown by citizens in such affairs.'

Even before the Seventy-fourth Amendment to the Constitution of India, cities like Mumbai, Delhi, Kolkota, Chennai and Hyderabad had moved in this direction and had taken steps to decentralize their administration by creating a lower level of local government. The lower tiers in Kolkota and Chennai were created through a statute while in Mumbai and Hyderabad they were created through administrative actions. The decentralization in Delhi Municipal Corporation has, on the other hand, a historical origin. The Municipal Corporation was formed in 1957 as a result of the amalgamation of nine municipalities that were earlier operating in the area. After the setting up of the Corporation, these municipal offices were retained as zonal offices for the limited function of attending to day-today public complaints about civic amenities and recovering civic dues.

Now, the ward committees have been introduced in all Municipal Corporations through the Seventy-Fourth Amendment to the Constitution. For the ward committees to be really effective, it is necessary that a reasonable budget, powers to approve smaller works and to approve the work orders, and sufficient staff must be made available to them. This decentralization should actually help the Corporations to concentrate on problems of larger significance for the city. The Maharashtra Municipal Councils Act also allows for constitution of these ward committees for councils with a population of more than three lakhs.

The Mayor

The position of the Mayor has been a subject of debate. As compared to the position of the Chief Minister at the state government level or that of a municipal President at the municipal council level, the Mayor has virtually no executive powers. The Mayor of Patna had narrated an amusing and certainly apocryphal story in the All India Mayors' Council meeting at Delhi in 1989 about the weakened position of the political executive when a municipal council is upgraded as a municipal corporation. The story runs as under:

'The Persian King Nadir Shah had not seen an elephant till he invaded India in the year 1739. When the Persian forces marched towards India, he asked some people enroute, "How big is an elephant? Is it bigger than a horse? He was told, "Yes, Your Majesty, much bigger than a horse". He again asked, "Is it larger than a camel?" A reply was given that an elephant is much larger than a camel. Nadir Shah's curiosity knew no bounds. After he entered India, an elephant was brought and shown to him. He mounted the elephant and asked for the reins. He was given a polite reply, "Your Majesty, you don't have to hold reins. The mahout sitting in your front would control the reins." Nadir Shah immediately dismounted the elephant and said, "I don't want to mount an animal that I cannot control. I would rather mount a horse which follows my instructions'. The then Mayor of Patna had explained that when a Municipal President is upgraded as a City Mayor, his feelings are akin to those of Nadir Shah mounting an elephant.

Following the Calcutta Municipal Corporation Act, which tried to invest the Mayor with the powers akin to the chief minister of the city government, some states have taken initiatives to constitute a Mayor-in-Council and to vest it with executive powers. The nomenclature "Mayor-in-Council" seems to owe its origin to the 'Governor General-in-Council' before independence. The British Government had constituted a council to assist the Governor General and Viceroy of India in the discharge of his executive responsibilities and members of the council were assigned different departments for that the Governor General combined the offices of the President and the Prime Minister. Moreover, being directly appointed by the Crown, he did not have to worry about maintaining a majority in the Cabinet or the council.

Following the Calcutta model, there was a major initiative in Maharashtra, particularly by the then Chief Minister, Shri Manohar Joshi, for introduction of a similar pattern in Maharashtra. The pattern was introduced in the Mumbai and Nagpur Municipal Corporations. However, the pattern generated a great deal of controversy. It was alleged that the Mayor-in-Council in Mumbai took many decisions in complete disregard to the rules. The government, therefore, scrapped the Mayor-in-Council. However, they invested the Mayor with some executive powers so that the Mayor does not remain only a ceremonial functionary.

The present position of the Mayor, as it exists in most places is ceremonial; someone who leads by influence by virtue of his majority support among the corporators and his personal equation with the Commissioner rather than by statutory powers. However, it cannot be said that he is a weakling. He enjoys the powers similar to the Guardian Minister or the MLAs in district administration. No file goes to him for final decision. However, when a subject requires the approval of the corporation the files do go to him. A seasoned Commissioner knows that a Mayor with a majority support can block his proposals in the corporation meetings and gives him due respect while taking important decisions affecting the city. The chairman of the standing committee, similarly, needs to be given due respect and importance since failure to do so can lead to avoidable trouble in the meetings of the standing committee.

An author, however, observes about the position of the Mayor as under, "According to the Act, the Mayor's position is weak as compared to the municipal commissioner. His position is not only comparable to the chief minister but is also not comparable to the Governor as the Mayor does not have any emergency powers. His position is perhaps comparable to the speaker of the state assembly." It is true that the role of the Mayor in a corporation meeting is that of the speaker. He only presides over the meetings. He cannot reply to the questions since he does not see the background files. He cannot defend the proposals for consideration of the corporation for a similar reason. An effective municipal commissioner, however, has to keep the mayor on his side in the same way a ruling party in the state assembly has to keep the speaker on their side. Although the Mayor does not have emergency powers like the State Governor, he indisputably enjoys the highest protocol rank in the city. For consultation, the commissioner must go to the Mayor, like the Chief Minister calls on the Governor. The Mayor's position thus is that of the Governor and the Speaker combined.

The Municipal Commissioner

The strong position of the municipal commissioner in the corporation as the head of the executive has been discussed by several authors. Anil Bhatt writes, 'The role of the municipal commissioner is visualized as a guardian of the state government vis-à-vis the elected corporators who (it is suspected) may be swayed by the narrow personal or political considerations. The Act has made the commissioner's position so strong that the underlying distrust of the representative body becomes apparent'. S.R. Maheshwari writes, 'To sum up, the commissioner form local government in India partakes of the character of a presidential type of government with the significant difference that the 'president' owes his appointment to the state government and is a regular, generalist civil servant'.

Maheshwari is right in comparing the position of the commissioner to that of the U.S. President. The executive powers are with the commissioner but he can be blocked by the standing committee or the corporation's general body. This is quite similar to the Senate or the House of Representatives blocking a President's new initiatives. In this connection, one remembers the fate of President Clinton's health bill that could not get past the Republican controlled Congress. The commissioner's ability to persuade the standing committee/corporation to his point of view is a sine qua non of his successful tenure. Even about the U.S. President, it has been said that the real test of a president's greatness in the While House is 'his ability to lead the Congress'. The same thing can be said about the municipal commissioner. His ability to lead the discussion in the corporation/standing committee determines his success as a commissioner.

Since the executive powers are vested in the commissioner and not in the Mayor, most Acts provide for a no-confidence motion against the Commissioner but not against the Mayor. The state government is to withdraw the Commissioner if required by a resolution adopted by the council by a simple majority in Patna, clear majority in Kolkota, 3/5th in Delhi, 2/3rd in Bangalore, Kerala and Hyderabad, 3/4th in Chennai and M.P. and 5/6th in others. The court has held that the word 'removal' can only mean the transfer of a Municipal Commissioner from one place to another and by removing the Municipal Commissioner and withdrawing him from the post, the same can neither amount to dismissal nor removal nor reduction in rank. The court observed in the same case, "When there is an incompatibility between the Corporation and the Commissioner, the Legislature has provided a way out in the shape of the aforesaid third set of circumstances in section 36(3). A Municipal Commissioner, when such a resolution is passed against him by the elected body, cannot be thrust upon the elected body indefinitely when the statute only requires to remove him from the office of the Municipal Commissioner and deal with him in such manner as the State Government may think proper. We are of the opinion on a construction of the said Section 36(3) and the facts and circumstances of the present case that it is a mandate issued by the statute that the State Government should act on such a resolution forthwith; when it is called upon to do so by virtue of the said resolution. The Municipal Commissioner, can hold the office so long as he enjoys the confidence of the councilors in keeping with the statute." The court further observed, "It is mandatory on the part of the State Government to remove the Municipal Commissioner forthwith in view of Section 36(3) of the Bombay Provincial Municipal Corporation Act, 1949, if at the meeting of the Corporation not less than 5/8th of the total number of the councilors vote in favour of a resolution requiring his removal".

The crucial role of the commissioner as the kingpin of city governments has been summarized aptly by S.K. Gupta. He observes: 'It is hardly fair to take the worse type of councilors and to compare them with the best type of commissioners'.

In any case, so long as the councilors are prevented from interfering in administration, they cannot do much harm except by putting off decisions which call for expeditious disposal. But the harm an inefficient commissioner can do is infinitely worse. He is the pivot round which the administration moves or should move. While the corporation fix the rate, he assesses the valuation and collects the tax. He sanctions the plans of all new buildings so long as they are supposed to be within rules and refers to the building committee only those cases in which minor infringements are to be overlooked. The decision whether a building is insecure or not and whether a demolition order should issue is his exclusive jurisdiction. While the corporation has the obligation to provide water, lay down sewers and maintain roads, it is the commissioner who has to be applied to in order to get water or sewer connection; he can force sewer on a recalcitrant householder who wants to avoid the costs, and he alone is entitled to take action against infringements. In providing and maintaining these services the vast corporation machinery has to be moved, plans and designs made, specifications prepared, tenders called and accepted and work executed. It is the duty of the commissioner to see that the machine moves smoothly, quickly, unerringly, that officers do their duty to the ratepayers and the citizens promptly without having to be spurred on by illegal gratification, and that the councilors get all possible assistance by being supplied with information, data and suggestions to evolve their policies and come to their decision.

His presence and persuasive arguments at committee meetings can go a great way in prompt disposal of even apparently controversial matters. The assumption behind vesting the commissioner with supreme executive powers is that he will do all these things. It presupposes that he will be endowed with abilities of a high order and inspired by the highest ideal of public service. As a critic once expressed, it is a gamble in an individual. If the gamble succeeds, the result will be good and the harmonious combination of an enlightened council and a dynamic commissioner will be able to work wonders. If it fails, the entire administration may be thrown out of gear. An important contract involving several crores and affecting the lifeline of the city may not even be signed within a year of acceptance of the tender, not to speak of the work being started and the commissioner may yet be completely unaware of the progress of the case and unconcerned about it. Committees may wrangle and members talk at cross-purposes without the commissioner guiding the discussion unobtrusively to the relevant points and a fruitful end. Assessments may show ridiculous variations in the same area without any supervising authority trying to secure reasonable uniformity. Building plans in full conformity with rules may be kept pending for over six months or a year without being sanctioned or frivolous objections taken because the party has not appeared on the scene to grease the palms, while plans in flagrant violation of these rules are passed in no time for reasons which are best left unsaid. Old tube wells may be drawn out and resunk elsewhere and passed off as new without anybody being wiser. Officers may come late and go early and spend unconscionable long hours at lunch without being pulled up. Office hours may be wasted in gossip while files accumulate. In fact, all the malaise in the administration due to delay and inefficiency will appear if the commissioner is inefficient. What will happen if he is also venal, it is dreadful to imagine.

For keeping an excellent liaison with the elected corporators, it is essential that the commissioner should personally attend not only the corporation meeting but also the meetings of the standing committee. It is even desirable if he can attend a few meetings of important subjects committees for health, works, education and transport by rotation so that he is fully aware of the real problems in the city. It has been rightly observed, 'Commissioner's participation in the deliberations of the council seeks to serve two purposes: first, he may guide the councilors in their discussions and, secondly, he is enabled to remain in constant touch with public opinion as voiced by people's representatives. It must be admitted at the same time that the commissioner has in this role to act as the spokesman of the administration and even to defend it – often with the help of other councilors – in the council. This indeed, is a difficult role, taking him unwittingly into the political arena.'

Many corporations in western India run their own municipal transport undertaking under the provisions of the Acts. The General manager/Transport Manager of these utility undertakings exercise the same powers as the Municipal Commissioner in so far as the activities of the transport undertaking are concerned. Thus, the budget of the transport undertaking is passed by the Transport Committee of the Corporation. Administrative approval is granted by the Transport Committee for individual works. Tenders are issued and accepted by the Transport Manager. However, the Transport Manager cannot give the work order unless the contract is approved by the Transport Committee.

For day to day working of the corporation, the Commissioner can delegate powers vested in him to his deputies. The High Court has held that delegation of powers by the Municipal Commissioner to the Town Development Officer was legal and proper. In an Ahmedabad case, it was decided that the action of a Deputy Municipal Commissioner to sign a vakalatnama was legal. However, an irregularity would creep in if the appointing authority is the Commissioner and the dismissing authority is the Deputy Commissioner. The Supreme Court has held that an illegality crept in when the Deputy Commissioner took the final decision.

The President of the Municipal Council

Unlike the City Mayor, the municipal President is the chief executive of the municipal council. He wields executive powers, approves decisions on files, presides over the council meeting as well as the standing committee meeting and even writes the Annual Confidential Report on the performance of the Chief Officer. A large number of our leaders of the freedom struggle had got their first exposure to governance as presidents of municipalities. Pandit Jawaharlal Nehru was Chairman of the Allahabad Municipal Council, Sardar Patel was the Chairman of the Sanitary Committee of the Ahmedabad Municipal Corporation while Netaji Subhash Chandra Bose was an elected commissioner in the Calcutta Municipal Corporation. In Maharashtra, S.B. Chavan was President of the Nanded Municipal Council.

There is no provision of a 'No Confidence' motion against the City Mayor because he usually has tenure of only one year and he does not wield executive powers. However, usually a 'No Confidence' motion is provided by law against the Municipal

President. Similarly, a President can be removed from his post for misconduct etc. President can resign his office with a resignation letter to the Collector. It has been held that Additional Collector is also competent to receive this letter.

The Municipal President, at his smaller level, is thus far more powerful than the City Mayor is. The specific sections under which the Municipal President inherits these powers vary from Act to Act. The relevant sections of the Maharashtra Municipalities Act, 1965 are used below:

1. Section 58 of the Act prescribes certain definite executive functions for the president.
2. The Chief Officer of the Municipal Council is supposed to work under the control, direction and supervision of the President (vide section 71 of the Mahrashtra Municipalities Act, 1965).
3. The President is the Chairman of the Standing Committee, which is vested with considerable executive power in Municipal Councils. The President also has the right to take part in the meetings of subject committees.

About the 'No Confidence Motion' the Supreme Court has observed that there is no imperative requirement in the case of a motion of 'No Confidence' that it should be passed on some particular ground. The Supreme Court observed, "It is pertinent to observe in this connection that there is a difference between a motion of no confidence and a censure motion. While it is necessary in case of a censure motion to set out the ground or charge on which it is based, a motion of no confidence needs not set out a motion or charge. A vote of censure presupposes that the persons censured have been guilty of some impropriety or lapse by act or omission and it is because of that lapse or impropriety or lapse while moving a motion of censure. No such consideration arises when a motion of no confidence is moved. Although a ground may be mentioned when passing a motion of no confidence, the existence of a ground is not a prerequisite of a motion of no confidence. There is no legal base to the passing of a motion of no confidence against an authority in the absence of any charge of impropriety or lapse on the part of that authority. The essential connotation of a no confidence motion is that the party against whom such motion is passed has ceased to enjoy the confidence of the requisite majority of members."

Rural Local Government

A number of authorities on the subject of democratic decentralization view the concept of district government as a logical finale to the process of devolution on a Panchayat Raj Model. It is, however, necessary to point out that the role of Zilla Parishads in Maharashtra, even when they are fully developed, would remain confined to the rural area only. At present, 42 percent of the population of Maharashtra resides in urban areas. In fact, in three districts viz. Nagapur, Pune and Thane, the proportion of urban population is already around 50%. Thus the Zilla Parishads do not represent the districts as a whole and we can look at them more as counterparts of Municipal Corporations for the rural areas rather than counterparts of the State Government at the district level. They work more as service agencies for the rural areas. However, there does not seem to be any objection, *per se*, to the use of the word 'district government' for the Zilla Parishads since the term municipal government has been often used for the municipal administration.

On an analysis of the reports of the various committees on P.R. Is., there appear to be three broad models of the Zilla Parishads:

Model – I : District Governance – The end of Collector Raj advocated by some authors

Model – II : The Karnataka Model – Separation of entire development functions from regulatory functions

Model – III : Naik Committee Model – Separation of Local sector from State sector.

The first model is actually, a step ahead of the Karnataka model of democratic decentralization. An author observes, "In the Karnataka Model the lathi will not be in the hands of Zilla Parishad and Mandal Panchayat. Therefore, it is unlikely to serve as a radical change agency. It is likely to come under pressure from vested interests who will try to destabilize it. In other words, the Karnataka model is as inherently unstable as the earlier versions, because it has been unable to get out of the "development only" syndrome". Thus the author advocates that even law and order and police should be under the Zilla Parishads, which is his concept of district government.

The Karnataka model visualized the separation of the developmental functions from the regulatory functions. The Chief Secretary of the Zilla Parishad (counterpart of the C.E.O.) was visualized to be senior of the Collector so as to give primacy to the development functions. This model has been recommended by the G.V.K. Rao Committee of the Government of India. However, this model did not survive the test of time. The M.A.L.s rebelled against the local bodies which were perceived stronger than the district units of state governments. In layman's terms no father can afford to give a pocket money to his children that would be greater than the balance left with the father.

The Naik Committee model which is prevalent in Maharashtra for the last fifty years, on the other hand, does not visualize a separation between regulatory and developmental functions. The separation is between the local sector and the state sector. The Chief Executive Officer of Zilla Parishad who is in charge of the local sector schemes is generally junior to the Collector who supervises the state sector schemes in addition to his regulatory duties.

While analyzing the concept of decentralization it would be worthwhile to refer to the book "Devolution: The End of Britain", by Tom Dalyell. Bringing government closer to the people, is one of those easy panaceas which sounds attractive with an elaborate execuse for shying away from difficult and unpopular decisions. The read problems are economic – the low investment, poor industrial relations, growing unemployment, low productivity, poor quality etc. which cannot be solved by devolution.

A senior officer of the Government of Maharashtra was once arguing with me about the advantage of democratic decentralization in Maharashtra. He observed that the green revolution in agriculture was catalysed by the Panchayat Raj institutions in Maharshtra. On this I replied that there was no green revolution worth the name in Mahrashtra. The real green revolution has been in Punjab, Haryana and Western U.P., where there are no Zilla Parishads. Thus the growth of agricultural production has taken place in areas where there are no P.R. institutions. While it is true that structural constraints do affect the agricultural growth in Mahrashtra, the only point I am making that we should not falsely take credit when it is not due.

Participation can result in unimaginable delays. It does dilute responsibility and diffuse accountability. Participation cannot be an end in itself. The theme of participation for the sake of participation would sound the death-knell of good administration.

Participative managements demand administrative skills of a high order. Jayaprakash Narayan had wisely warned that by more devolution of power from above, the organs of Panchayati Raj would not come automatically to acquire the necessary competence to wield power entrusted to them. The competence for self-government and self-management has to be developed by a process of education and experience. When such competence is created, power would not have to be given from above, but it would be taken from below even unwilling hands.

It is felt that we have not yet been able to create necessary enlightened opinion for a full-scale district government suggested by Shri N.K. Mukherjea. A large number of our Gram Sabha meetings get adjourned for want of quorum and petty squabbles affect our village politics. In this connection, the observations of Dr. Ambedkar in the Indian Legislative Assembly debates are very pertinent: "The love of the intellectual Indians for the village community is of course infinite, if not pathetic... I hold that these village republics have been the ruination of India... What is a village, but a sink of localism, a den of ignorance, narrow-mindedness and communalism? I am glad that the draft Constitution has discarded the village and adopted the individual as a unit". While we may not agree with Dr. Ambedkar, we must be careful to avoid the pitfalls which he has pointed out long ago.

The district government visualized by the first model, would also not fit in the federal structure visualized by the Constitution of India. The Seventy-third and Seventy-fourth Amendments to the Constitution precisely lay down the subjects to be entrusted to the local bodies.

The Karnataka Model visualizing a total separation between the executive and developmental functions also appears to be unrealistic. The regulatory powers do make the task of development easier when the vested interests are likely to resist the change. Actions such as forcible possession in a land acquisition proceeding or removal of encroachment do require exercise of regulatory powers. Development does not consist in mere spending of funds, but it also visualizes redistribution of assets which may be resisted by the vested interests.

The Naik Committee model visualizing a separation between the local sector and state sector, appears to be much more realistic and successful. However, it needs to be implemented in its spirit. When a Secretary to Government asked me as to whether the departments of social foresty and horticulture should be entrusted to the Zilla Parishads, I told him that they should have always been under the Zilla Parishads since their creation in 1981. All new departments and new activities which are mainly for rural areas and are of a local nature should be entrusted to Zilla Parishads. Recently the Government of Mahrashtra has transferred to Zilla Parishads many schemes that belong to the local sector as per the Seventy-third Amendment of the Constitution.

The Zilla Parishad because of its exclusively rural orientation and limited subjects delegated to it, cannot take over the overall co-ordination and planning. Thus the question of higher status to the C.E.O. does not exist. In this connection it may be mentioned that when the posts of senior scale Municipal Commissioners were created for Solapur and Kolhapur Municipal Coporations, the Municipal Commissioners were senior to the local Collectors but then this pattern was soon changed and the officers senior to the local Municipal Commissioners were posted as Collectors. The Collector has to undertake a number of co-ordination activities on behalf of Government and ideally he should be senior to the officer in charge of local body.

I would now come to organizational problems faced by the Zilla Parishads in Mahrashtra. The P.B. Patil Committee (Evaluation Committee, 1986) has suggested in this connection that officers of the State Government should not be posted under the Zilla Parishads. The Zilla Parishad should recruit most of its staff and a separate Local Government Service may be created. It is pertinent to note that the Committee praises the I.A.S. on one hand and criticizes the State Government officers on the other. This only shows the confused state of mind of the committee. The strength of I.A.S. comes from the fact that an I.A.S. officer has an opportunity to work at different tiers in Union Government, the State Government and the local bodies and this varied experience strengthens the administrative efficiency of an I.A. S. officer. Similarly, the Zilla Parishad would actually stand to gain if they can have officers who have worked under the State Government in different capacities.

In this connection the experience of the Municipal bodies is worthwhile to note. A former Municipal Commissioner of Delhi Municipal Corporation has observed that the efficiency of the municipal staff is only 60% of that of Government employees. Municipal administrations are notorious for faulty assessments on one hand and wasteful expenditure on the other. No sector of Government suffers more from poor management and chaotic conditions of staff control and supervision. The failure of the municipal administration has often been attributed to the absence of a well organizing personnel system, and all the commissions and committees appointed since Independence have recommended creation of state or provincial cadres for municipal bodies. This experience of the municipal bodies should be taken for guidance while advocating for Zilla Parishads, their own staff to run the Zilla Parishads.

The Karnataka model provides that the annual confidential reports of the Chief Secretary of Zilla Parishads would be written by the 'Adhyaksha' (the President). A number of other committees have also made similar recommendations. In this connection Weber's observations on bureaucracy are very relevant:

"Bureaucracy concentrates power in the hands of those who are in charge of bureaucratic machinery and such a concentration of power is against the very premises of democracy....However, without a civil service class, democracy would be plagued by a spoils system, public waste and lack of technical efficiency. *Thus democracy has to promote what reason demands and what democratic sentiments hate".*

The Chief Executive of local bodies has to take many decisions which democratic sentiments hate but which reason demands. Thus, it would be improper to entrust his annual confidential report in the hands of the political chief viz. the President. In Maharashtra municipalities the confidential report of the Chief Officer is written by the President of the municipality. This has led to Chief Officers being weak and unduly flexible in their decisions. The municipalities in Maharshtra, thereby, suffer from lack of administrative leadership.

One of the most common areas of confrontation between the political executive and the permanent executive has been recruitment of the employees. Time and again, Corporators/ Councillors try to pressurize the administration so as to get their relatives, friends and supporters appointed to jobs under local bodies. This has led to a considerable deterioration in the quality of staff in local bodies. In this connection, I must say that even the State Government has been given protection under the Constitution of India by setting-up of the State Public Service Commission. A similar protection to the administration in local bodies of State Government is necessary. The Supreme Court has observed in a Haryana case that 87% marks of recruitment tests should be on a written examination and only 13% should be reserved for the interview, which is broadly the distribution of marks kept by the U.P.S.C. for recruitment to the I.A.S. and higher civil services. It is necessary that the State Governments give similar directives to the local bodies under their control. I am happy to mention here that the State Rural Development Department has already issued guidelines to the Zilla Parishads that their recruitments should be based on written tests, which carry 80% of marks. The word 'State' in Article 12 of the Constitution of India, includes local bodies and it is necessary that all recruitments to jobs under local bodies are governed by the same objective standards.

Another area of constant friction between officers and the political executives of Zilla Parishads in Maharashtra has been the transfers of staff. The elected office-bearers have often shown undue interest in transfers of employees. Here too I am glad to mention that the Rural Development Department has issued detailed guidelines governing transfers and they have been of great use for handling this delicate and difficult function.

The role of the Subjects Committees in the local bodies should be to decide policy. They should not be given any powers which pertain to distribution of spoils. The Zilla Parishads in Vidarbha, for example, have been empowered to distribute surplus timber logs (phatas) made available from the Forest Department. The Committees distribute these logs with quota of 10 logs for each Z.P. Councillor and 5 logs for each P.S. Councillor. All these logs go to the political supporters of the councilors. It is necessary that some objective standards such as poverty should govern the distribution of these logs. However, such discretionary allotments of favours is seen at all levels of government and there is nothing unique about the rural local bodies in this regard

The provision of no-confidence motion against the Chief Executive has been a subject of debate time and again. It has been argued that the local bodies have tried to get rid of their Chief Executive Officer by passing no-confidence motion whenever the Chief Executive Officer came in the way of vested interest.

However, it is my submission that the provision of no-confidence motion is like a safety valve. The provision exists in almost all enactments of Municipal Corporations too. The State Government is to withdraw the Municipal Commissioner, if required by a resolution adopted by the Council, by a simple majority in Patna, clear majority in Kolkata, 3/5 in Delhi, 2/3 in Bangalore, Kerala and Hyderabad, 3/4 in Chennai and M.P.and 5/8 in others. The Maharashtra Zilla Parishads also provide for a no-confidence motion against the Chief Executive Officer, which if passed by a 2/3 majority leads to the transfer of the Chief Executive Officer. Although there is a point of view that this provision needs to be deleted, I personally favour the retention of this provision. In any case, there are powerful ministers in states who can get senior scale I.A.S. officers transferred if their interests are hurt. It is felt that the chances that a single senior minister will get annoyed with an officer are more than the chance that 2/3 of the Councillors would come together to pass a no-confidence motion against the officer. It has been my experience that so many councilors would not come together against an honest and upright officer, unless the body has a history of notoriously bad administration which has seen a symbiotic role between the Chief Executive and the corporators for their personal interests. The provision of no-confidence ensures that the officer would be loyal to the body and to the public at large. If this provision is deleted, it may give a handy tool to the Ruling Party in the state to post unwanted or inefficient officers to local bodies under the control of opposition parties and it may become impossible for the body to get the officer changed.

It has been argued that the creation of District Planning and Development Councils (DPDC) has led to an erosion of powers of the Zilla Parishads. While it is true that actually only 30% of plan funds are spent through the Zilla Parishad, the Zilla Parishads also spend a large amount of non-plan funds. The salary of the primary school teachers, for example, constitutes almost 50 per cent of the expenditure of Zilla Parishads and this item, although it is a non-plan item, contributes to the development of the District in a great way. In this connection it may not be out of place to add that the items which are within the jurisdiction of the Zilla Parishads such as location of a P.H.C. are never interfered with by the D.P.D.C. and thus the contention that the D.P.D.Cs. have eroded the powerws of Zilla Parishads is not wholly true.

On the whole, it is felt that there is no need of a substantial structural change in the panchayati raj institutions in Maharshtra. However, there is a need to give them all the functions which belong to them in law and spirit and which were entrusted to them in 1962.

Elections

1. The Constitution Amendments (73rd and 74th) came into effect in 1992 by which Part-IXA was introduced into the Constitution. Part IX deals with the elections to the Panchayats and Part IX-A deals with the elections to the Municipalities. As per the provisions of Article-245-K, the State Election Commission was established in every state. So also, under the provisions of Articles 243-K and 243-ZA, the superintendence, direction and control of the preparation of electoral rolls and conduct of elections to the Panchayats and Municipalities is vested in the State Election Commission.

2. In Maharashtra State there are 33 Zilla Parishads, 349 Panchayat Samitis, about 27,000 Village Panchayats, 22 Municipal Corporations, 224 Municipal Councils and 2 Nagar Panchayats. As per the provisions of the Constitution, every local body unless sooner disoolved under any law for the time being in force shall continue for 5 years from the date appointed for its first meeting and no longer. So also, an election to constitute a local body shall

have to be completed before the expiry of its duration. It will be clear that an election will have to be held and completed before the expiry of duration of every local body.

3. An election to local body comprises of 3 stages viz. (i) delimitation or ward formation, (ii) preparation of electoral rolls, (iii) actual conduct of election.

(1) *Delimitation or ward formation:* As per the provisions of law, the number of seats are fixed for every local body and the area of a local body is to be divided, taking into consideration, the number of seats admissible for the body. The State Government has recently made provisions for multi-member ward elections. So each ward will elect not less than 3 and not more than 5 members. This provision is not applicable to the Greater Mumbai Municipal Corporation. The delimitation is done according to the latest census figures, the census blocks and the location or layout maps etc. After the draft ward formation is ready, it is published for calling suggestions and objections from the residents of the local body. After considering the suggestions and objections, the ward formation is finalized.

(2) *Preparation of electoral rolls:* Assembly rolls are the basis on which the electoral rolls for a local body are prepared. As per the provisions of the relevant laws, the assembly electoral rolls existing on the date notified by the State Election Commissioner are to be divided into corresponding wards. This is just a cut and paste operation. After dividing ward-wise voters' lists, those are printed and authenticated by the authorized officer. For election to the Brihan-Mumbai Municipal Corporation, people have complained that they did not find their names in the electoral rolls. I want to make it clear that if the name of any person is not included in the

assembly roll or it is deleted from the assembly roll, it will not appear in the municipal voters list. It is important that names of persons should be included in the assembly roll on the date notified by the State Election Commission.

Many people normally do not care to see if their names are in the assembly roll or not. Some choose to vote only for local elections. If a voter votes for every election, he will come to know of addition/deletion/correction of his or his family names in the voters' list.

(3) *Actual conduct of election:* This stage includes the stages from nomination of the candidates, scrutiny, withdrawal, allotment of symbols and the actual poll and counting. These stages are fixed as per the provisions of the relevant law of the local body. This stage is important. Actual elections take place in this stage. Allotment of symbols, ballot papers printing etc. has to be completed in this stage.

4. Multi-member system elections: It is believed that due to multi member elections, the persons of good stature and recognition are elected and the number of independent candidates is decreased. So also earlier when single member system was in operation, if the ward was reserved for some other category, then the person from category for which the ward was reserved earlier had no chance to contest the election from the same ward, but since introduction of the multi-member system, each ward has to elect not less than 3 or more than 5 councillors. Persons from different categories including the open category may contest election from the same ward. Each voter will have a right to vote equal to the number of members to be elected from the ward.

The State Election Commission has prescribed that each voter will be given 3 or 4 ballot papers depending upon the number of candidates to be elected from the ward. Each ballot paper has been given a specific colour, so that voters can differentiate between candidates. This system has worked very well and about 200 Municipal Councils have elected their President directly in the recent polls.

5. Direct Election of the President: Earlier the President of Municipal Council was elected from amongst the councilors. Now, the Municipal Act has been amended and direct election has been provided. By this system, residents of the Municipal Councils can vote for the person of their choice for the post of President. This system has also worked well and about 200 Municipal Councils have elected their President directly in the recent polls.

6. Issues on which the political parties contested the elections: As far as elections to the local bodies are concerned, the local issues get prime importance. Most of the parties promise to improve the life of people living in the slums, to improve the roads, public health facilities, environment protection, education to all, play grounds, improvement in the water supply and potable water and sanitation and solid waste management etc. The promises made by all political parties are more or less on the same line.

7. Problem of impersonation during the poll: The State Election Commission issued an order that the voters have to produce some evidence while coming for voting. If they don't have an identity card issued by the Election Commission of India, they have to produce one of the following documents:

- Passports,
- Driving Licenses,
- Income Tax Identity (PAN) Cards,

- Service Identity Cards to its Employees by State/Central Government, Public Sector undertakings, Local Bodies or other Private Industrial Houses,
- Bank/Kisan/Post Office Pass-Books,
- Ration Cards issued prior to 1st September, 2001,
- SC/ST/OBC/VJ/NT/SBLC certificate issued by Competent Authority,
- Student Identity Cards,
- Property Documents such as Pattas, Registered Deeds, etc.,
- Arms Licences,
- Conductor Licences issued by Transport Authority,
- Pension Documents such as Ex-Servicemen's Pension Book/Pension Payment Order
- Ex-Servicemen's Widow/Dependent Certificates,
- Railway Identity cards for Railway pass issued prior to 1st September, 2001,
- Certificate of Physical Handicap,
- Freedom Fighter Identity Cards,
- Any other similar document establishing the identity of the elector to the satisfaction of Presiding Officer.

It will be seen that the State Election Commission has given elaborate list of evidence for a voter's identity. Earlier, no evidence was necessary for a voter to produce while voting. The only check was that the polling agents present in the booth could raise objections if certain voters were no credible. However, in a city like Mumbai, it is difficult for a polling agent to know each and every person that comes for voting. It is possible in the rural areas but not in the cities like Mumbai and other metropolitan cities. To a large extent, bogus voting was reduced by this order of the State Election Commission.

8. What is a Code of Conduct? The model Code of Conduct for guidance of political parties and candidates is a unique

document, evolved with the consensus of political parties and is a singular contribution by them to the cause of democracy that the political system in the country. It has no statutory backing and many of its provisions are not legally enforceable; for public opinion is the moral sanction for its enforcement. Armed with such moral sanction, the Election Commission ensures its observance by political parties including the ruling parties in the corporations and panchayats and candidates in the discharge of the Election Commission's constitutional duties of superintendence, direction and control of elections to the Local Self Government Bodies. The fact that political parties have themselves consented to abide by the principles embodied in the model Code of Conduct also binds them to respect and observe it in letter and spirit. Various conferences were held under the aegis of the Election Commission of India with the various political parties in the past and the last such conference was held in 2001.

Elections are in a way festivals of democracy celebrated during the political campaign. Originally, minimum campaign period for any election from parliamentary/assembly/council constituencies was 30 days. It was reduced to 20 days in 1966 and since August 1966 it was reduced to 14 days. In our cases also the State Election Commission has curtailed the period of operation of Code of Conduct as compared to our earlier stipulations.

The State Election Commission, this time, has curtailed the period of Code of Conduct. Earlier in the elections, to the local bodies, Code of Conduct was made applicable from the date of publication of draft delimitation order calling objections and suggestions from the residents of the local body. As a result, the Code of Conduct remained in operation for about 3 months. It was complained that due to the application of this Code of Conduct, the development work came to halt. This time, the Code of Conduct is being made applicable from the issue of nomination papers till the date of polling. However, from the date of declaration of election programme no policy decision can be taken without the prior approval of the Commission. The period of Code of Conduct for these elections is about 30 to 40 days.

9. Elections Reforms carried out by the State Election Commission: The State Election Commission carried out certain reforms as far as the elections to the local bodies are concerned. Those are stated below:

i) To prevent impersonation or bogus voting, the State Election Commission prescribed certain documents which will have to be produced by the voters while going for voting. This has certainly reduced the amount of bogus voting.

ii) Information of the candidates regarding criminal background: Since the submission of the affidavit regarding criminal background has been made compulsory, the voters have knowledge as to where all candidates stand and they can choose right candidates as per their choice, based on the information given in affidavits.

iii) The period of Code of Conduct: Previously, the Code of Conduct was in applicable for almost three months due to which the development work in the local bodies came to stand still, which was criticized by the residents of local bodies. The State Election Commission responded and the Code of Conduct has been now reduced to almost a month or so.

iv) Prohibiting the candidates from submitting bogus caste certificates: In local bodies, the seats are reserved for S.Cs., S.Ts. and Backward Class of Citizens. The State Election

Commission made it compulsory to present the original caste certificate at the time of scrutiny of nominations and certificates are verified by the Scrutiny Committee after the candidates are elected. If the certificate is found to be bogus, then the candidates are disqualified from their post, so also the candidates are liable for imprisonment and fine.

Expenditure ceilings for various elections in the Maharashtra State as per the orders issued by the State Election Commission from time to time

1. In case of an election as a Councillor to the Brihan Mumbai Municipal Corporation (Single Member Ward) Rs. 75,000.
2. In case of an election as a Councillor to all other Municipal Corporations (Multi Member Ward) Rs. 1,00,000.
3. In case of an election of a Councillor to the Municipal Council/ Nagar Panchayat (Multi Member Ward) Rs. 45,000.
4. In case of an election as a President to Municipal Councils/ Nagar Panchayat (Direct Election of President) Rs. 4,00,000- "A" Class Municipal.
5. In case of an election as a Councillor to the Zilla Parishads Rs. 45,000.
6. In case of an election of a Member of Panchayat Samiti Rs. 30,000.
7. In case of member of a Village Panchayat Rs. 7,500.

Committee System

In the national and state governments, the chief executive is the council of ministers with the prime minister or the chief minister at its head. In the municipal corporation, on the other hand, the chief executive is the municipal commissioner. Even in the Zilla Parishad, the Chief Executive Officer shares many characteristics of the chief executive. This is why there is a provision of no confidence motion against the chief executive officer, too. There is no such provision of no confidence motion against the chief secretary of the state. This is because the chief secretary is not the chief executive. The chief executive is the chief minister against whom there is a provision of a no confidence motion.

Again, unlike in the state government or the national government, where the minister is in charge of his department while it is the duty of the secretary to ensure that the rules of business are followed, the chief executive in the zilla parishad is the chief executive officer. The zilla parishad members wield little individual power and most of the powers are vested in the committees. This dilutes the power of an individual office bearer.

The Report of the Evaluation Committee on Panchayati Raj, 1971 observed as under:

"In this connection we would like to record here that quite a few of our respondents and persons whose oral evidence we have recorded had suggested to us that the Committee having become ineffective should be abolished and replaced by a system known as the "Cabinet System" or the old Local Board System. The desirability of introducing the Cabinet system was also considered by the Naik Committee and that Committee had expressed its preference for the Committee system. To quote the "Naik Committee: "As the District Council will be too large to meet frequently and to attend to day-to-day business, it will be necessary to provide some machinery for the latter purpose. This can be done either by providing a committee system which is the general pattern followed by local self-governing institutions all over the world or by adopting a cabinet system which is in vogue at the State and National levels".

Each system has its own advantages and drawbacks. It has been suggested that if the cabinet system is introduced into local administration it will lead to greater speed and efficiency in the dispatch of business. It will also provide scope to young leadership to show initiative and to exercise specified powers so that in course of time it is trained to assume higher positions of responsibility. It will further eliminate the necessity of calling meetings of the committees for deciding even minor issues and make available to the council full time services of capable popular leaders. On other other hand, it is argued that under the committee system decisions are the result of the application of collective wisdom and they are arrived at after giving an opportunity to all members to participate in the discussions. The Committee as a whole thus shares the responsibility for all decisions and is in a position to exercise proper supervision over their execution. If a Committee is elected by means of a single transferable vote all important sections of opinion in the council would find some representation on it.

Thus, the parties in opposition get an opportunity to participate in decision making and to make constructive suggestions. As the functions of the district body involve selection of development schemes, their locations, etc. which intimately affect the welfare of the local population, it will necessarily follow that decisions in respect of such schemes should be arrived at with as much unanimity as possible. This can be more easily achieved in a committee system. Since each of these systems has certain advantages which are not available in the other, we feel that a method should be evolved to combine the advantages of both. We, therefore, recommend that the District Council should function through committees but at the same time the President and the Chairman of the committees be made full time functionaries responsible for implementation of the decisions of the council and its committees'. We are in agreement with the Naik Committee's view brought out above and would suggest that the present committee system, which is in fact functioning well and which has, as pointed out above, a number of built-in-arrangements to take care of all possible sources of trouble, should continue".

Incidentally an effort was made in the Mumbai City to have a cabinet kind of government by introduction of the Mayor-in-Council form. However, the system was not successful and was given up after some time. The committee system has worked very well over the past many years and has stood the test of time.

Reservation

The wards in the local bodies are reserved by rotation for the scheduled castes and scheduled tribes candidates. Thus, the corporation or the zilla parishad represents the society that it represents. In Mahrashtra, the Other Backward Classes (OBCs) and other communities are also represented on the local bodies in proportion of their general reservation.

An interesting feature of local bodies in Maharashtra is that there is a 30 per cent lady councilors/corporators in the local body. I have worked as chief executive of the local bodies both before and after this reservation was introduced. The behavior of the male corporators certainly sobers after ladies are present in the house. The Mayor's position and other positions are also reserved for different categories by rotation. This has made the local bodies truly representational.

Similarities with the national and the state government system

Having worked at almost all the levels of government, I can say that there are no basic differences between the type of elected leadership at the local and national levels. By experience the national leadership is of course more mature. The national leadership also has the advantage of a high caliber advice while taking more important national level decisions. The differences between the national and local level elected leadership is similar to the differences between senior level bureaucrats and local level bureaucrats. Although the level and their pay-scales are different; basically both swear by the same Constitution of India and similar civil services rules are applicable to them. For the leadership, too, a similar situation prevails. An M.P. represents a wider areas, a zilla parishad councillor or an urban corporator represents a smaller area but their accountability to the voters and their concern for making a mark during their tenure are similar. In fact, in Maharashtra many of the local leaders graduate to state and national level.

5

Women Leadership and Empowerment in Urban India

N. Ashok Kumar

Indian Woman

In the days gone by, that is before the arrival of the Aryans (1500 B.C.), Indian family was more matrilineal in which the family holds control over male and female. The Aryans brought with them the patrilineal form of family system. Historical evidences reveal the fact that, woman enjoyed upper status over the man in all spheres of life, particularly in the field of education during the Vedic period. It may be recalled that much of our Vedic hymns were composed by women only during the Aryan period. It is also true that Islam as a religion was born in the arms of a woman, Khadija. She was the first person to accept Islam too. However from the dawn of Post-Vedic period women's status started declining and male's hegemony over women in all the decision making processes blossomed. Woman was being subjected to subordination to man. Values and customs that were in practice in our social system affected the freedom of women. Women belonging to upper caste groups were the worst sufferers. Women belonging to lower caste groups were not affected because of purely economic reason. Therefore, gender discrimination problem was more conspicuous in the upper caste groups.

Pro-Man Environment

Access to education for women was abundant during the Vedic period and such facility was denied for women by the society in post-Vedic period. The need for education for women was realized during the Colonial rule. Lord William Bentinck introduced the English education for women when he was Governor General of British India in 1828. Gender discrimination in social, economic, political and cultural fronts of human life was conspicuous in this country even during the Arab, Turk, Moghuls and British rule periods. Women are therefore the most distressed section of our community and they bear the burden of exploitation. Humanists of yester years like Vivekananda and Mahatma Gandhi denounced exploitation, subjugation and oppression of women on the ground of gender division. They have given a call to women asking them to rise above the situation prevailing at that time and march forward. While voicing his opinion on status of women in the society, particularly their role in politics, Gandhiji said that, "*woman in our scriptures is called ardhangini. But, instead of girl spreads gloom, whereas the birth of a boy is considered to be a festive occasion.*" He further said that, "*so long as this evil custom is not done away with root and branch, women can make no progress whatsoever. Man and woman will attain equality only when the birth of a girl is celebrated with as much joy as in the case of boy.*"

A country which boasts the Constituent Assembly after assuming power for the governance of the country accepted the National Flag from the hands of a woman, Mrs. Hansa Mehta, and the country which proudly says that it is committed to extend opportunities to women on an equal basis with men is not able to implementing a policy of reservation of seats for women in the elected bodies on the basis of men and women population ratio. Except a few cases like Sarojini Naidu, the first popular Governor of the United Provinces, very rarely Indian women have opportunity to be at the helm of the affairs. This is not peculiar to India alone. Any where in the world, the same phenomena one can witness. It has become a universal custom of man protecting his privilege in the decision making process overlooking the equation between a happy wife and a happy home. Male chauvinism is therefore dominates all fronts of human life like education, employment, administration, politics, business, technical, information technology, space, etc. This could be gleaned through the historical and the recent past events.

During the Colonial rule many kinds of reforms were introduced in this country in favour of women, '*Sati*' was the most significant reform. Enforcement of Widow Remarriage Act, raising the marriage age in respect of girls and education for women were the other major reforms that were undertaken by the British rulers. Right of admission into the schools for girls was introduced and it was a boon for girls. These reforms not only ensured security and freedom of sharing thoughts in women but also brought in a great deal of change in diversity based relationship between man and woman.

Women fare far worse than men and inevitably bear the brunt of their life. This is because most of the women do not have education. Poverty, physical form and biological functions, fear of their men folk, poor capabilities to meet the challenges, etc. are the other reasons for their poor representation in the public life. The other significant reason for the backwardness of women in this country is poor commitment on the part of our leaders about women. National leaders who vowed for the development of women hood before the attainment of Independence completely turnabout setting aside their commitment about bridging the gap between development and women. Added to this our own social customs and values is the other factor for sex discrimination. It may be recalled that, during the freedom struggle movement, when Gandhiji asked women to take part in Satyagraha movement and got courted arrest in 1930, about 17000 of around 30000 who courted arrest were women volunteers only. Women's participation in freedom movement was an entry point in their struggle for equality and justice in the society. Similar instances of women's participation in different types of national struggles including the economic, political, military, etc. are not seldom. All these events inculcated awareness in women about their rights and duties as citizens of this country and helped them in a long way for their personality development.

New Awakening

Various women's rights activities and national women's organizations initiated people's movements more often raising their fore fingers pointing at the rude nature of men against women and the failure of the national leadership in fulfilling the ideology enunciated by Mahatma. They echoed about women's right of sharing power with men on an equal basis and women's changing role in nation's developmental process. Before and after the attainment of Independence, economic and political critiques have been debating the relationship between women and the national progress. It may be recalled that, during the freedom movement when the Indian National Congress constituted the National Planning Committee in 1938 for preparation of a blue print for the nation's development, it formed 29 subcommittees. One of which was on women's role in planned economy. But unfortunately no serious initiative was taken in this regard in the first, second and third Five-Year Plans.

Feminists argue that, social, economic and political gains that are being made by the country are not reaching the most vulnerable sections of the society who includes women and children resulting in pushing the equity and social justice to the corner. Socialists opined that, emancipation of women will be possible only if women involve freely in economic front since this will ensure development of women's personality. So long as women are declined opportunities to improve their position in the society so long the country will never progress. Social equity and justice for women can be achieved if only the needs of women are realized and empowered them socially and economically. Cumulative result of opinions and reactions of various groups of people brought a paradigm shift in the policy makers and political leaders thinking process. This was reflected in their job of drafting the Sixth Five Year Plan. They lay stress and emphasis on women's participation in the nation's development process.

It is now realized that the more women participate sharing their views, needs the more they could be integrated into the nation's economic developmental process. To this effect, government initiated steps by adopting the concept of empowerment to ensure women too would enjoy the rights on par with men. To this effect, government initiated a slew of measures and of which awareness building schemes for women about their strength, role, areas feasible for their involvement and their rights was the major initiative. Quite a number of national and international voluntary and quasi-governmental agencies have been involving over the past years in organizing various kinds of capacity building workshops like income generation activities, leadership building, personality development, etc.

Strategies

Political and economic empowerment of women is gaining its importance. If empowerment is dissemination of knowledge among women it is certainly a need of the hour. This would be possible only it communication methods that we have today are exploited rationally. Acquisition of knowledge through education will enrich women with the power of reasoning, authority, will and action. When knowledge matures it becomes wisdom and through wisdom one would get the power of questioning and rational reasoning. This we refer to as new awakening. Any effort to create new awakening will enable women to climb out of the black hole of ignorance.

Empowerment of women politically could be realized by two ways; enrolling as many women as possible as voters and secondly, imparting practical education and teaching them to think independently. These two steps are strong enough to assure political strength and capacity for sacrifice and place of honor in the society for women. As Abdul Kalam spelt out that "learning gives creativity, creativity leads to thinking, thinking provides knowledge, knowledge makes you great" women could nurture a dream in this backdrop. To make this more realistic the government has to reconstruct the existing laws, policies, traditions. Added to this people's attitude about gender also have to be changed.

In political front, not only women's representation in the elected offices is far below men but also their representation does not match to their size of population. It is in this backdrop, the Government of India initiated action through amendment of the Constitution for the 73rd and 74th time and incorporated a provision for reservation of one-third of total seats for women in urban and rural local bodies. This Act (74th CAA) has quietly become a force to reckon with. The immediate impact of this action of the government is difficult to analyze at this moment. True, numerically the strength of the women members in the municipal councils might have been increased but in reality their performance in the councils is more male dictated and male manipulated form. It is observed that most of the women members do not have the required skills to counteract their opponents, or in putting forward their ideas in the council meetings. However, the government failed to get the bill for reservation of one-third of seats in the Parliament and the State Legislative Assemblies passed in the Parliament. It is interesting to note that, majority of the members of the Parliament who opposed the bill were males only. This reflects male chauvinism. One might ask if women determined to face the elections to Parliament or to the State Legislative Assembly or even to the local bodies there is little need for amending the Constitution. They should come out even there is resistance from men. This capacity they should built first. It is possible only through exposure and here comes the importance of information technology and other electronic media. The only doubt is about pushing through this idea. Since the majority of the members of the Parliament constitute males only, there is no guarantee that the policies drawn up through their eyes will concern about the needs and rights of women.

Historical review of actions of women's organizations/groups at different period of time lead us to concede women do have capacities to wear the mantle of leadership. Women's participation in Freedom Movement, anti liquor movement in Andhra Pradesh a few years ago and in the liberation of Hyderabad movement are the exemplary instances to quote here in this context. Sarladevi, Kamaladevi and Suseeladevi who participated in the movement for liberation of Hyderabad region from the tyrannical regime of the Nizam were women only. An attempt to quote Yolanda King's observations in this context is appropriate. She says "if there were a woman at the helm of affairs her Government's policy would be different" and she continued to say that, "if there were more women in positions of leadership, things would not only be different, they would be better". Her observation as a womanist draws us to conclude that if both men and women participate in social, economic and political spheres of the nation on an equal basis, again in her own words "certainly things are better, as more and more people realize that we must work together or we will perish together as fools".

Tomorrow is not too far away. Demand for economic, social and political justice for women is increasing. Gender discrimination cannot be wiped out overnight since there is a very strong lobby behind the whole campaign to keep this issue alive. On the other hand, participation capacity in decision-making process is dismally low. It is in this backdrop, the Government of India sponsored multifarious schemes investing money in the area of women and development.

Constitution of National Commission for Women is one more step taken by the government underpinning the cleansing role of women to play in economic, political and cultural fronts of the nation. The Commission too stressed the importance of imparting new skills and knowledge for women particularly to build leadership qualities among them. As directed by the Commission, the Government of India sponsored a Center for Gender Training, Planning and Research. This was established at Mussoorie in collaboration with the DFID. This apart, the Government of India has introduced various welfare programs underpinning its commitment to create pro-woman atmosphere in the country. Similarly state governments like Andhra Pradesh on their part have been sharing their mite of comforts by providing opportunities to women to improve their position. For instance, implementation of DWACRA, DWACUA, self help and thrift groups. Women's involvement in these programs is very conscious. By involving in these programs they got benefited financially and in the acquisition of managerial/leadership skills.

Leadership in human world is male bastion. In this kind of situation women should surmount gender bias to storm males' dominance in the community. This involves indomitable courage. At times men have to give a serious thought about this aspect. Our country has enough resources and these could be exploited by both men and women on an equal basis. Barrier free access to resources and information is an entry point for women's empowerment in all fields of human life. And this will be a gateway for them to enter into the decision making process from outside the decision making process.

Over the past few years there witnessed mushrooming of women's forums like ALIDWA across the globe striving for the betterment of women hood. Having considered raging wars against the practice of subordination of women to men is as good disinfectant as the Sunshine disinfectant. These forums led many a kind of women's movements drawing the attention of the international agencies including the United Nations. Their major objective was to bring women above poverty level and from here to politics, in simple, from hunger to politics. Evolving a gender friendly society is the ultimate motive of these forums.

Role of Political Parties

The ruling regional party and the main opposition national party in Andhra Pradesh have been spearheading mass campaigns with a view to enroll many women members into their respective parties. Both the parties have a separate cell for women. These cells are responsible to conduct seminars, meetings, demonstrations, slogan raising and enlightening women on social, economic, political and cultural issues and enrolling as many women as possible. The remarkable development in Andhra Pradesh is that state government is committed to strengthen women's force. This could be very well substantiated with the benefits which women particularly the poor women in rural and urban areas accruing by their active involvement in DWACRA and DWACUA schemes. This apart, the state government introduced Mahila Janmabhoomi program a people's participation program exclusively for women on the similar lines of the Janmabhoomi Program (People's Participation Program). These programs are successful in enriching the skills, particularly leadership qualities and self confidence in women folm particularly the low income women groups who were with never a say in the house and were with shy of expression and hesitant to venture out on their own. It is a turning point for women from that passé. It is said that these programs made waves not only in the country but abroad too. It is evidently seen that, members of the DWACRA/DWACUA have turned to be more confident, enthusiastic with a lot of hope in their journey on the road of their economic development. Most of the members of the DWACRA/DWACUA have neither educational qualifications nor any exposure to the worldly things. But they were successful because they were blessed with worldly wisdom. A few success stories are mentioned in the following paragraphs.

Like political parties, voluntary organizations, both national and international, like the Lion's and Rotary Clubs have created its branches exclusively for women where all the members are women only. These branches are rendering yeomen service for the betterment of women by conducting various types of capacity building programs and economic and cultural developmental programs.

In the DWACRA Bazaar where the women members sell different types of ware, handicrafts, handlooms, herbal products and eatables. Interaction with a few members of the DWACRA group and the managers of the bazaar reveal that the sales average is Rs. 50 lakhs a day. With more confidence they say that even the passers by along this bazaar become shoppers. They agree the fact that, once they were assisted by their men in all aspects but now they have their own money and they manage their enterprises by themselves in terms of responsibility in work, income and decision making. Many of these DWACRA women members had the opportunities of participating in exhibitions both at the national and international levels with their works. One woman member said that she is a mother of three in 20s and has visited

Malaysia as part of this DWACRA group, managed a big stall on her own and topped sales. Another woman said that she makes toys and other utility items and is an illiterate. For her it was a dream sending her kids to school but now her position is entirely changed and it was all due to DWACRA, she continued. Another woman said that, earlier before joining the DWACRA making ends meet was tough for her. Now she said that her family is happy and "her youngest daughter is studying at BITS, Pilani". Another member proudly said satisfaction writ all over her face that, though she is an illiterate but the garments which she manufactures like handloom sarees, dress material and salwar suits are very popular. She said proudly that she made a record stock sale worth Rs. 8 lakhs in the exhibition held at Sri Lanka.

Similar types of stories and narrations are many. This was possible because of the amount of exposure and experience they underwent in the field of self employment through state sponsored awareness programs like the Mahila Janmabhoomi, Clean and Green, etc. Various government departments got involved in giving training to women in the manufacturing of goods like Commissionerate of Women Empowerment and Self Employment, NIFT, etc. Some times these women form into groups, mutually aided cooperative societies and work at common facility centers created by the state government. Cases of whopping turnover of one crore and even more by those women who work from the common facility centers and home. This is really a remarkable achievement. Thanks to the government of Andhra Pradesh which has put in efforts in promoting self employment and decision making power in women by extending its cooperation and support for successful functioning of the DWACRA program in the state. To day there are sixty one lakh women in 4.5 lakhs groups earning income from Rupees one thousand to three thousand a month.

One could infer from the way women are responding to the new initiatives which the governments both at the national and state levels have been taking for the betterment of women, they need motivation and awareness about opportunities that are available in the country. The national and state women commissions should take note of this and put in their efforts with commitment to propagate the initiatives that are being taken by the government. This could be done easily by taking the advantage of the latest information and communication technology that is on hand to day with us.

Empowerment of women will be practicable if they are strong in their thinking process, ability to meet the challenges, creativity, organizing and managerial capabilities. This will be possible through learning process. The departments concerned like women and child welfare as part of their regular activities could undertake as many training and workshops on various aspects like community development, management of infrastructure, communication and leadership building, economic activities, participation in decision making process, etc. There are number of training and research organizations in the country which are known for its work in the field of human resource development. The task of exposing women, particularly poor women to the changing development scenario in the world can be entrusted to these organizations and other non-government agencies. As on to day the centrally sponsored SJSRY scheme is being implemented in almost all municipal towns in the country. Number of women members from women's organizations, self help/thrift groups, municipal councils, and other voluntary organizations are being participated in this program and gaining knowledge in economic and political fields. Having gained practical experiences through these programs there are humpty instances of women becoming leaders both at the community, occupational, decision-making and income generation activity levels. Enrichment of women's knowledge and skills is therefore key element of women's empowerment, economically and politically.

The government can take other supportive measures with a view to ensure women's access to economic power. This may be through provision of access to credit, training and extension programs in agriculture and allied sectors to those women involved in agriculture and similarly in the fields of information technology and food processing and even in textiles to those women who are working in these fields. These measures will improve their job performance and can meet the competition from men.

Conclusion

The basic philosophy of liberalism refers to mainly the rights of individuals to life, liberty and property. In Indian context, this philosophy is being understood in a more critical way and this is the reason there exists tension about discrimination on grounds of gender. Despite the fact that, women's organizations both national and international like the All India Women's Conference have been demanding their share of participation in the nation's economic and political development, women were being condemned to remain in the timeless universe of domesticity.

References

1. The Hindu, 14 October, 2003.
2. Nubile Clara, The Danger of Gender, Sarup and Sons, New Delhi, 2003.
3. Gandhi, Night, "In the Shadow of Inequality", The Hindu, 19 October 2003.
4. Chaudhuri, Maitrayee, Gender in the Making of the Indian nation – State in Rege, Sharmila (ed) Sociology of Gender, Sage Publications, New Delhi, 2003.

6

Women Leaders in Panchayati Raj: A Study of Orissa

Srinibas Pathi

An estimated sixty to one hundred million girls and women are banished from the world each year as victims of foeticide, infanticide, malnutrition, neglect and other types of rights violations. This is mainly attributed to practices that favour male over female children. Also women and girls are discriminated against and are denied access to basic health care and education. Girls account for nearly sixty per cent of more than 113 million school aged but educationally deprived children. In India, more than six lakh women meet their fatal end every year during childbirth or due to pregnancy related complications. Most of such women do not have the power to decide when and how often they should bear children. They are denied their reproductive rights, equality as well as timely health care, proper nutrition, health-related information and counseling facilities. Again there are unequal employment opportunities available to women which are also conditioned by social stigmas and family-related issues. There are issues like crime against women, violence and deprived childhood which act as handicaps for women in gaining access to development opportunities.

It may be mentioned that differences between men and women are conditioned by societal norms as well as biological factors. In every society, gender roles are prescribed by custom, convention, social norms and other economic, political and cultural factors. Biology determines a wide set of characteristics, attributes, features and capabilities that exist in men and women as distinct entities. However, social factors largely determine gender roles. They are conditioned by the whims of the decision-makers in each society which can be modified and renegotiated over a period of time. The role and position of women in society have far-reaching consequences for the nature and quality of life of both men and women in the society. They have a definite impact on the over-all prosperity, well-being and development of the society. Studies have shown that those states in India which strive to ensure that women have equal rights and just positions in the society account for higher rates of economic development, literacy, education and lower rates of infant mortality rate and maternal mortality rate.

But the fact remains that while women in India in recent years have gained ground in the spheres of literacy, education and access to primary health care, they still have a long way to cover in sharing social, cultural, economic and political empowerment and opportunities at par with men.

Empowerment of women and improvement in the quality of life being the corner stone of women's emancipation, it is pertinent to discuss the issue at this juncture. Empowerment stands for acquiring the power to think, to act freely, to exercise choice, to raise voice and to be able to take a decision. This is equally true for both men and women. Coming to the notion of women empowerment, it may be added that women should enjoy certain amount of autonomy for fulfilling their potential as full and equal members of the society. They should be able to enjoy basic human rights, dignity and respect. They should have the right to pursue development paths that reflect their needs and aspirations. Such a situation is in the interest of both men and women due to its wider socio-economic implications that come as natural corollary to gender equality and equity.

Participation of women in the decision-making process of our democratic polity is considered as one of the most significant steps in connection with empowerment of women. The 73rd and 74th Amendments to the Constitution of India along with a large number of state Acts provide for the participation of women in the rural and urban local self-government institutions through reservation of one-third of seats in the Panchayati Raj Institutions and urban local bodies in India. Now that we have experienced a political scenario in which women at the grassroots level have joined the political decision-making process, it is time to take stock of the situation and also to evaluate the same in the context of our democratic decentralized administration as well as empowerment of women.

The present study was conducted in Satyabadi Block of Puri district in Orissa. Satyabadi is situated forty kms. south east of Bhubaneswar, the capital city of Orissa on the national highway no. 203. It is famous for its coconut plantation and allied industrial activities. The literacy level of the place is well above the state average. The place is also known for its contribution to education, culture and social reform movements in the state. During the national struggle for freedom, it was in the forefront of nationalist activities. And to cap it all, it was the seat of the Satyabadi Vana Vidyalaya (first open school of India that Inspired Kaviguru Ravindranath Tagore to go for Shantiniketan which later on became the now-famous Viswa Bharati). Pandit Gopabandhu Das, the great nationalist leader, freedom fighter, writer and social reformer of the pre-Independence era who along with four other equally illustrious friends formed the 'Pancha Sakhaa" made Satyabadi their headquarters.

So far as the political scenario in Satyabadi is concerned, it may be pointed out that there are twenty-two Gram Panchayats out of which eight are reserved for women where they hold the position of Sarpanch. And among the women, six belong to the other Backward Classes, one to the Scheduled Castes and one to the Scheduled Tribe. There are 297 ward members in the Gram Panchayats out of which 191 are male members and 106 are female members. But one significant aspect that needs a special mention here is that while 104 women ward members have been elected from the reserved seats, two women have been elected from general or unreserved wards by defeating male contestants.

During our study, we contacted a number of elected women representatives in Satyabadi with the help of a questionnaire. And thirty-three of them responded to the same. Out of them there were three Sarpanchs (Heads) of the Gram Panchayats and thirty were ward members. So far as the age-group is concerned, four of them belonged to 21-25 years. While 13 of them were in the age group of 26-35; 12 belonged to the age group of 36-50 years; and rest four of them were above 51 years of age. Coming to the educational qualifications of the elected women representatives, we found that all of them were literate. While eight of them have school education; 17 of them have passed the high school certificate examination; three of them have Intermediate qualification; another three are graduates; and, rest two are post-graduates.

So far as the religion of the respondents is concerned, all of them belong to Hinduism. And coming to the caste factor it is revealed that eleven of them belong to the general category while 13 respondents belong to the other Backward Classes; eight of them belong to the Scheduled Castes and one belongs to the Scheduled Tribe. When we enquired into the place of education of the respondents, only three of them have studied in a city or town. And the rest 30 of them have had their education in the village level based educational institutions. So far as the occupation of the respondents was concerned, it was revealed that as many as 32 of them preferred to call themselves 'housewives' only and the lone respondents who accepted that she had some occupation, put it as agriculture. The same is the case with income status. Only one respondent mentioned that her income is below Rupees one thousand per month, which she received from agricultural activities. All of them are married including one widow.

Another significant factor that merits a special mention is that except two respondents, all others have been elected to Gram Panchayats for the first time. But as many as twenty one of them have been members of village Mahila Samiti, Self-Help Groups and have been active in the civil society activities.

We probed into the functions, responsibilities and duties of the women elected representatives in the Gram Panchayats. We found that they have been participating in the deliberations and meetings regularly. The majority of the members have one grievance that they do not receive official communication in time. And most of the time, according to the women representatives, tribal issues and procedural matters over ride the basic and substantial questions relating to development activities and welfare programmes. So far as the powers and position of women members are concerned even though they are at par with their male counterparts in terms of constitutional and legal status, the family responsibilities, house-hold duties, looking after the children and the aged, other social responsibilities of women consume a major chunk of time available to women. Even though their kith and kin appreciate their new public position and responsibilities they seldom allow them to spend more time outside the family domain.

While discussing the issues relating to workload and capability, we could find that women representatives did not shy away from their duties and responsibilities either. As we all know the 'Gram Sabha' is the basis and foundation of the edifice of the Panchayati Raj, but Orissa has a different story. There are 'Palli Sabhas' in Orissa which operate at the Panchayat ward level; unlike the 'Gram Sabhas' elsewhere in India that operate at the Gram Panchayat level. The Palli Sabha is a more compact and well-knit social structure, especially due to its size and nature. The women ward members, just like their male counterparts in other wards, preside over the meetings of the Pallia Sabhas and help the residents of the ward in arriving at decisions regarding the developmental activities to be undertaken in the ward under the auspices of the Gram Panchayat concerned.

So far as the main issues and problems of the people and the locality are concerned, the women representatives mentioned poverty, disease, lack of infrastructural facilities like approach road, safe drinking water, electricity supply and primary school etc. Even though a number of developmental programmes are being implemented with the help of financial assistance from the Government of India and State Government, due to operational and practical hurdles, the beneficiaries do not get the intended outcome. While discussing the remedial measures and solutions, the respondents subscribed to a number of steps including that of a more people friendly work procedure; simplified rules and regulations; more financial resources and financial autonomy; more interactions within the PRIs and the government functionaries operating at different stages of administration.

A majority of the women representatives of the PRIs were of the view that there is the urgent need of a comprehensive training programme for them because of their lack of experience and expertise in administration. From our discussion and interaction with the respondents, we would gather that most of them have very little information and awareness in relation to the provisions of the 73rd Amendment Act of the Constitution of India; the Orissa Acts relating to the PRIs; historical development of the local self government institutions in India and in the state; the planning process in India; specific schemes and programmes of central government and state government that are being implemented in the rural areas; issues and problems relating to resource mobilization and management in the rural areas; the activities under the MP Local Area Development Fund and the MLA's Constituency Development Fund, and last but not least, the bulk of laws, rules, regulations, circulars, notifications etc. pertaining to the working of the PRIs.

When we discussed the activity dimension of the working of the Gram Panchayats, most of the women representatives expressed the view that they arc not conversant with the details of the items or subject matters of the Eleventh Schedule of the Constitution of India. These matters mostly remain as subjects of academic interest. A few routine matters come up for discussion in their meetings. But issues like land reforms, rural industrialization or environmental protection and sustainability are seldom discussed.

It became clear from the present study that in spite of the constitutional provisions, legal frameworks and structural arrangements most of the women leaders in the Panchayati Raj system have not participated in the working of the Institutions effectively. They have played a very limited role in the policy formulation and decision-making stage. Their major interests revolve around the service functions of the Panchayati Raj Constitutions. Most of the women representatives, like their male counterparts too are more concerned with the implementation of government sponsored welfare schemes and development initiatives; but not with local level planning and resource management.

In the conclusion, it may be pointed out that there is the urgent need for regular and intensive orientation and training programmes for the women representatives. There is also scope for short-term workshops, exchange programmes and interface sessions consisting of women leaders, government officials, NGO functionaries, social activists and other stake holders in the rural areas. Women leaders have occupied the political space. It is time for them to consolidate their role, position and performance with the active support of the reinvented civil society.

References

1. Moitree Bhattacharya, Panchayati Raj in West Bengal: Democratic Decentralisation or Democratic Centralism, New Delhi, Manak, 2002.
2. B.B. Mohanty, 'Panchayati Raj in Maharastra and Orissa: An Overview', IASSI Quarterly, 21(3-4), January-June, 2003, pp. 92-128.
3. S. Kavitha, 'Koothambakkam Panchayat in Tamil Nadu: People's Participation at its best', Kurukshetra, 52(8), June, 2004, pp. 46-47.
4. Ella Louise Bell, 'Myths, Stereotypes and Realities of Black Women: A Personal Reflection' Journal of Applied Behavioural Science, 40(2), June, 2004, pp.146-59.
5. Mala Bhandari, 'Women in two work roles and Quality of their Life', Sociological Bulletin, 53(i), Jan. – April, 2004.
6. M.P. Boraian, 'Empowerment of rural Women Towards Reversal of Gender Relations', Indian Journal of Social Work, 64(4), October, 2003, pp. 521-32.
7. Snehalata Panda, 'Land Rights for Women', Social Welfare, 51(3), June, 2004, pp. 36-39.

8. Karunakar Patnaik, 'More powers to Panchayati Raj Institutions', Kurukshetra, 51(II), September, 2003, pp. 32-36.
9. S. Gohilavani, 'Empowering Women – a Sociological Perspective', Guru Nanak Journal of Sociology, 23(1), April, 2002, pp.19-32.
10. Bina Pradhan, 'Measuring Empowerment a Methodological Approach', Development, 46(2), June, 2003, pp.51-57.
11. Richard Vengroff et. al., 'Electoral System and Gender Representation in Sub-National legislatures: is there a national – sub-national gender gap?', Political Research Quarterly, 56(2), June, 2003, pp.163-73.
12. Kuldip Kaur, 'Gender Status in Panchayat: Issues and Problems', Guru Nanak Journal of Sociology, 23 (1), April, 2002, pp. 33-40.
13. Jayanti Alam, 'Gender and the Ideal of a Pluralist Society', Mainstream, No. 37, Dec. 25, 1999, pp.79-86.
14. C.L. Claridge et. al., 'The Environment, Development and Women: What is the Connection', Journal of Rural Development, 18(1), March, 1999, pp.1-27.
15. Shaukath Azim, 'Gender Empowerment – Where does India Stand?', Social Welfare, 48(2), may, 2001, pp. 9-11.
16. S. Dasgupta, 'Women Power: Beginning at the Lowest Level', Statesman, May 17, 2001, p. 8.
17. Jean F. East, 'Training Women for Leadership Development: An Empowerment Model', Regional Development Dialogue, 22(1), Spring 2001, pp. 66-76.
18. Anupama Roy, 'Community, Women Citizens and a Women's Politics', Economic and Political Weekly, 36(17), April 28, 2001, pp.144-149.
19. J.P. Singh, 'Indian Democracy and Empowerment of Women' Indian Journal of Public Administration, 46(4), October-December, 2000, pp. 617-30.
20. Murlidhar C. Bhandare, (ed.), The World of Gender Justice, New Delhi: Har-Anand, 1999.
21. Prabhat Dutta, (ed.), Major Issues in Development Debate-Lessons in Empowerment from India, New Delhi : Kaniska Publishers, 1998.

Women's [illegible] Panchayati Raj [illegible] (Delhi: Gyan [illegible]

8. [illegible], "Women power in [illegible] Panchayati Raj Institutions", Yojana, [illegible] September 2003, pp. 72-[illegible]

9. S. [illegible], "Empowering Women as [illegible] Sociological [illegible]", [illegible] April 2002, pp. [illegible]

10. [illegible], "Measuring Empowerment in [illegible]", [illegible] Development [illegible] 2000, [illegible]

11. Richard [illegible] et al., "Election [illegible]", Political Research Quarterly, [illegible] March 2002, pp. [illegible]

12. [illegible], "Gender [illegible] Empowerment [illegible]", [illegible] Journal of Sociology, [illegible] April 2002, pp. 39-44

13. [illegible]

14. [illegible] et al., "The Empowerment Development and [illegible]", [illegible] Development, [illegible] March 1998, pp. [illegible]

15. [illegible], "Gender [illegible] Empowerment [illegible]", [illegible] Social Welfare, [illegible] May 2001, pp. [illegible]

16. [illegible] 2001

17. [illegible], "Training [illegible]", [illegible] Rural Development [illegible]

18. [illegible] Ray, "Community, Women Citizens and a Women's Politics", Economic and Political Weekly, [illegible] April [illegible] 2001, pp. [illegible]

19. [illegible] Singh, "[illegible] Democracy and Empowerment of Women", Indian Journal of [illegible] December 2000, pp. [illegible]

20. [illegible]

21. [illegible], "[illegible] Women [illegible] in Panchayats [illegible]", [illegible] Empowerment from India, New Delhi: Kanishka Publishers, [illegible]

7

Political Empowerment of Weaker Sections: A Study of Municipal Bodies in Haryana

Rajesh Kumar

Introduction

Political participation is one of those terms which is very difficult to define because of its wide use in administration today. It is very often used to cover all the forms of action by which citizens take part in the operation of administration. Local government is defined, by Goulding, as the management of their own affairs by the people of the locality. In the words of Harris, it is a government by the people themselves through freely elected representatives. P. Stones defines local government as "local government is that part of the government of a country which deals with those matters which concern the people in a particular locality".[1]

Historical Perspective

It may be appropriate to attempt, in brief, the evolution of the municipal government in India. The origin of municipal government in India can be traced back to 1687 when a municipal corporation came into existence at Madras (now Chennai). A royal charter of 1720 established a mayor's court in each of the three presidency towns of Madras (Chennai), Bombay (Mumbai) and Calcutta (Kolkata). Later on, municipal administration was extended to district towns in Bengal in 1842, when the Bengal Act was passed which enabled the setting up of a town committee. In 1850, an act was passed for the entire country. The next step forward in this direction was taken in 1870 by the publication of Lord Mayo's resolution paving way for a measure of decentralization from the centre to the provinces which emphasized the idea of increased association of Indians in administration.[2]

A study of the Montague Chelmsford Report (1918) reflects that local government was fully representative and responsible and had total popular control on local bodies and the largest possible independence for these bodies from the outside control. Under the leadership of Lord Chelmsford and Mr. Montague, a bill was drafted and introduced in British parliament, which aimed at devolution of authority. Dyarchy was introduced in Indian provinces i.e., central and provincial and two parts-transferred and reserved subjects.

The Act of 1919 enlarged the role of local government in sphere of taxation coupled with more independence. Dyarchy system was in operation up to 1937 when the Government of India Act of 1935 came into force.

Municipal Government After Independence

After independence, a new era of democracy was started in India. The country adopted the federal system of government. A federal system stands for the decentralization of powers. The Constitution has allotted local government to the State List. Indian Constitution directs the State vide Article 40 to organize local institutions. The only reference to urban self-government is to be found in two entries in Seventh Schedule: Entry 5 of List-II (State List) and Entry 20 of List-III (Concurrent List).

In the backdrops of the above mentioned problems, inefficiency and ineffectiveness of the local bodies, late Shri Rajiv Gandhi, then Prime Minister of India, had expressed his desire in 1985 to take the country to 21st century and the politics and programmes of the local government were to be directed to this objective. After a long discussion, during the P.V. Narasimha Rao government in 1991 parliament passed the 74th Constitution Amendment Act, which came in operation in April 1993.

Political Empowerment in Municipal Bodies

Prior to the 74th Amendment to the Constitution there was no uniform pattern of organization of the municipal bodies in India. There were no similarities in size as it varied from state to state. The municipal bodies were regulated through the state municipalities Acts. They were composed of elected councilors, associate councilors and co-opted councilors. These municipal bodies were constituted from such date as was specified in this behalf by a notification of the state government. The total number of councilors varied from state to state. It was provided that if no person belonging to Scheduled Castes was elected, the elected councilors may co-opt one such member. There was also provision of women members to be co-opted, in case no woman member was elected. Similarly, members from amongst notified backward classes were also to be co-opted. There was no adequate procedure for representation to the weaker section of the society in municipal bodies in India as well as in Haryana. In this regard, just symbolic representation was given to scheduled castes, backward castes and women.

Political representation as a means to emancipate the backward sections of Indian society from the age-old bondage was not given recognition during the nineteenth century. Thus, the Government of India Act of 1858 and the Indian Council Acts of 1861 and 1892 did not recognize the special claim of the depressed classes.

The 74th Amendment Act provides for adequate representation to scheduled castes and women in municipal bodies, and provisions have been made for reservation of seats for all the segments of the society. The proportion of seats to be reserved for SC/ST to the total number of seats shall be the same as the proportion of their population in municipal area to the total population of that area.

Empowerment of Weaker Sections

The democratic values such as freedom, equality and social justice are emphatically stressed in the developing nations of the world. The term 'weaker section' has been defined differently by various authorities. The study group on the Welfare of Weaker Sections was of the view that "we should not however, be wrong if the agriculture labourers, small cultivators and village artisans also constitute weaker sections.[3]

Weaker sections consist of the vulnerable groups of society needing special care and protection. They are alienated section of the society. For the purpose of the present study the SCs and BCs as identified by the Government of Haryana are taken as the weaker sections of the society.[4]

Reservation in Municipal Bodies in Haryana

In every municipality out of the total number of elected members, the state government reserves some seats for the following categories:

Scheduled Castes

In every municipality seats are reserved for Scheduled Castes. The number of seats so reserved bears as nearly as may be, the same proportion to the total number of seats to be filled by direct election in that municipality as the population of the Scheduled Castes in the municipal area bears to the total population of that area. Such seats may be allotted by rotation to different constituencies known as wards in municipality.

Backward Classes

In every municipality one seat in municipal committees and two seats in municipal councils shall be reserved for backward classes and such a seat is allotted by rotation to different wards.

Scheduled Castes Women

Not less that one-third of the total number of seats reserved for scheduled castes are reserved for women belonging to the Scheduled Castes and such seats are allotted by rotation and by lots amongst the wards reserved.

Reservation of Office of Presidents

The office of president in the municipalities is reserved to the extent of five per cent for the scheduled castes and women by rotation and by lots in the manner prescribed under the law.

Total Number of Wards in Municipal Bodies in Haryana

As per data, total number of wards in all the municipal bodies were 1410 during the tenure of municipal bodies for the period 1994-99, which came down to 1357 for the period 2000-2004. Out of these 1357 wards of all the municipal bodies, since 29 municipal committees were abolished, total number of wards of all municipal bodies remained 991 for the year 2000-2004. The details of total wards for all categories of municipalities are given in Table – 1.

The Table 1 reveals that out of the total wards of all municipal bodies, there are 579 wards for general category (men) and 386 wards for women of general category during the period 2000-2004, as against 656 for general category (men) and 376

Table-1

Total Number of Wards in Municipal Bodies in Haryana (1994-2003)

	General		*Genereal (Women)*		*SC*		*SC (Women)*		*BC*		*BC (Women)*		*Total*	
	1994-99	2000-03	1994 99	2000 03	1994 99	2000 03	1994-99	2000-03	1994-99	2000-03	1994-99	2000-03	1994-99	2000-03
Municipal Committees	367	299	212	221	101	87	67	68	78	118	0	0	825	793
Municipal Councils	278	270	158	158	52	43	31	30	43	38	0	0	562	539
Municipal Corporations	11	10	6	7	2	2	1	1	2	2	3	3	25	25
Total	656	579	376	386	155	132	99	99	123	158	3	3	1412	1357

for women of general category during theyear 1994-1999. Further, there are132 wards reserved for SCs during 2000-2004 as against 155 in 1994-1999, out of total wards in all municipal bodies in Haryana. In addition to reservation to general category of women, SC women enjoy the reservation in 99 wards during 2000-2004 same as of the last term of the municipal bodies during 1994-1999 in the state.

Out of the total wards of all municipal bodies, there are 158 wards reserved for Backward Classes in 2000-2004 as compared to 123 wards during 1994-1999. The rural wards remained just three during both the periods.

Reservation of Wards for SC and BC

Reservations of wards for SC and BC in all municipal committees, councils and corporations have been presented in Table 2.

As shown in Table 2 in all municipal committees of Haryana, there were 823 total wards during 1994-1999, this number decreased to 793 during 2000-2004 due to abolition of 29 municipal committee in. Further, presently out of total wards, there are 77 wards and 54 wards reserved for SC men and SC women respectively during 2000-2004 as compared to 99 Wards for SC men and 64 for SC women during 1994-1999. So far as the reservation for BC is concerned, the table reveals that, during the first term of municipal committees (i.e. 1994-1999) there were 77 wards reserved for BC as against 90 wards during 2000-2004.

The reservation for SC women is in 33 wards during 2000-2004 as against the 31 wards in last term of the municipal councils i.e. in 1994-99. Table 2 further reveals that total number of wards reserved for BCs were 43 during 1994-99 which decreased to 42

Table – 2

Reservation of Wards for Municipal Committees, Councils and Corporation in Haryana (1994-2004)

	Total	*Wards*	*SC*		*SC (Woman)*		*BC*	
	1994 -1999	*2000 -2004*	*1994 -99*	*2000 -04*	*1994 -99*	*2000 -04*	*1994 -99*	*2000 -04*
Municipal Committees	825	793	99	77	64	54	77	90
Municipal Councils	562	595	52	47	31	33	43	42
Municipal Corporation	25	25	2	2	1	1	2	2
Total	1412	1357	153	126	96	88	122	134

Source: State Finance Commission, Haryana, Chandigarh,1994-1999 and 2000-2004.

during 2000-2004. In Municipal Corporation of Faridabad, there were total 25 wards during its first term (i.e. 1994-1999) which remained same in its second term as well. Out of these total wards, 2 and 1 are reserved for SC men and SC women respectively and 2 are reserved for BC. The total number of wards for each category remained same during both, first and second terms of the municipal corporation. The study reveals that it declined due to the delimitation of the wards in Haryana before the municipal elections held in April 2000.

Women Empowerment and Political Participation

Political empowerment of women implies the degree of equality and freedom enjoyed by women in shaping and sharing of power and the value given by the society to political role of women. The Indian Constitution guarantees political equality through adult franchise. However, actual working of the Constitution over the past five decades reflects that women, who roughly constitute 50 per cent of total electorate, have not been able to participate effectively in various walks of life including the political field. The lack of women's political participation can be attributed to various socio-economic constraints under our traditional social set up. The over-all situation of women political participation has not been very satisfactory. Women have not made much progress in spite of laws that guarantee equality of opportunities. Thus such a situation necessitated empowering of women.

In the following paragraphs an attempt has been made to review the women empowerment through 74th Constitution Amendment Act with special reference to the women participation through reservations in municipal bodies in Haryana.

Political Empowerment Through 74th Amendment Act

Through 74th Constitution Amendment Act, care has been taken to reserve one third of total seats to women in membership as well as chairmanship. In the municipal bodies, one third of reservation for women in urban local bodies has opened up new vistas for their participation in the municipal politics. This clearly indicates change in the traditional norm-which restricted free movement of women in the Indian societies. The Constitution Amendment (74th) providing one-third representation for women in municipal bodies as well as reserving of identical posts for chairpersons has been a step forward towards the political empowerment of women. Certainly, our social taboos and traditional societies raise certain doubts about inducting women into urban local bodies. It was also being felt that women would not come forward with their male counterparts and even if they come, they would not be effectively participating in meeting and would not have freedom of free decision making, so no substantial change could be brought about. Under the present study above-mentioned aspects have been analysed.

Women in Municipal Bodies in Haryana

The number of wards reserved for women and women representation in municipal bodies in Haryana has been given in Table 3.

Table 3
Number of Wards Reserved for Women

Municipalities	*General (Women)*		*SC (Women)*	
	1994-99	*2000-04*	*1994-99*	*2000-04*
Municipal Corporation	6	7	1	1
Municipal Council	158	158	31	30

(Contd.)

(Contd. Table 3)

Municipalities	*General (Women) 1994-99*	*2000-04*	*SC (Women) 1994-99*	*2000-04*
Municipal Committee	212	221	67	68
Total	376	386	99	99

Source: State Election Commission, Haryana.

The analysis reveals that there are total 386 wards reserved for women (General) during 2000-2004 as against 376 wards in 1994-99. Where as during 2000-2004, number of wards reserved for SC women remains the same (99) as during 1994-99.

Respondents' Perception of Women's Involvement in the Decision-making Process

A study was conducted in the State of Haryana during the period 1994-1999, so as to know and find out that as to what extent weaker sections have been empowered in the municipal bodies. During the course of the study sampled respondents were also asked to express their perception about the involvement of women in the decision making process. The perception shown by the respondents is summarized in Table 4.

The data show that out of the total sampled officials, 21 officials were of the view that involvement of women in decision making process is to a great extent, while 8 officials responded that involvement of women members in decision making process is to some extent, whereas 12 officials have responded negatively regarding this aspect. The analysis further reveals that out of total sampled councilors, 26 were of the view that involvement of women members in decision making is to a great extent, whereas 24 councillors stated that involvement of women in decision making process is to some extent and 9 councillors were of the view that there has been no involvement of women members in the decision making process.

Table 4
Officials' and Councillors' Perception Regarding Women's Involvement in Decision-making Process

		The	*Extent*	*Of*	*Involvement*
S.No.	*Sampled Respondents*	*To a great Extent*	*To some Extent*	*Not Involved*	*Total*
1.	Officials (N=41)	21 (51.24)	8 (19.50)	12 (29.260)	41 (100.00)
2.	Councillors (N=55)	26 (47.31)	24 (43.68)	5 (43.68)	55 (100.00)

Note: Figures in brackets denote percentage.

During the course of the study, sampled respondents were asked to give their views about the different aspects of reservation to SCs, BCs and women in municipal local bodies in Haryana. The study reveals that majority of the respondents, comprising officials and councilors, opined that SCs and BCs are actively involved in the meetings of the municipal bodies in Haryana. Further some respondents stated that reservation provided opportunities to the downtrodden, while a size of respondents favoured reservations on economic criteria, whereas very few advocated abolition of the reservation in municipal bodies.

Conclusion and Suggestions

India's experiment with protective, progressive or compensatory discrimination is a bold and unique innovation made by the founding fathers of our Constitution. Before independence little had been done for upliftment of the weaker sections of the Indian community. However, after independence, a number of provisions have been made and strategies and policies adopted for the upliftment of downtrodden section of the Indian society. Accordingly, provisions of reservations for Scheduled Castes, Backward Classes and Scheduled Tribes were made to give them representation in Central and State legislatures and in educational institutions owned and aided by the Central and State legislatures and in educational institutions owned and aided by the Central and State governments. Initially, provisions for reservation were made for ten years that have been extended from time to time and presently it has been extended upto year 2010.

Later on, it was realized that SCs, BCs and women should be given adequate representation in the local self-governments in India. Accordingly, 74th Amendment to the Constitution was enacted through which, reservations of seats were made for Scheduled Castes, Backward Class and women in municipal local bodies.

In Haryana in commensurate to new dispensation the municipal enactments were revised and the new Municipal Act 1994 and new municipal Corporation Act 1994 were passed to give adequate representation to weaker sections of society namely SCs, BCs and women.

Political empowerment of women implies the degree of equality and freedom enjoyed by women in shaping and sharing of power and value given by society to political role of women. The Indian Constitution guarantees political equality to women. The 74th Constitution Amendment Act, 1992 further enhanced the opportunities for their political participation in urban-local politics. Accordingly, one-third of the total number of seats, to be filled by direct election in every municipality have been reserved for women.

Such seats are allotted by rotation to different constituencies in municipal bodies. Further, there is a provision of one third seats of the total number of seats reserved for scheduled castes to be reserved for women belonging to scheduled caste.

Provision has also been made for reservation of offices of President of the municipal bodies. Out of these, five per cent of the women including those belonging to scheduled castes have been given representation as president in municipal bodies of all categories.

Empirical investigation reveals that reservation to women has raised the status of women in society after their election to municipal bodies. Majorities of women have been attending the meetings of municipal bodies regularly. However, in some cases load of domestic work, lack of communication by chairman and non-availability of escorts by family members have been the reasons for irregularity in attending meetings by the women. The study further reveals and confirms that the involvement of women in decision making process has increased to a great extent after 74th Constitution Amendment Act.

The provision of reservation of seats for weaker sections of society – scheduled castes, backward classes and women in urban local bodies in Haryana as per the Haryana Municipal Act, 1994 and its implementation as reflected in the previous two municipal elections held in 1995 and 2000 has been hailed as revolutionary in ushering in an era of genuine democracy at the grassroots level.

There is no denying the fact that their contributions to deliberations and decision making processes leaves much to be desired because of their lack of proper education, experience and training. But they will certainly improve in this regard with the passage of time and the national leadership will emerge from these sections of the society in due course as has been the case in respect of advanced sections of the society heretofore.

References

1. P. Stones, Local Government for Students, London, 1963, p.18.
2. Lord Ripon's Resolution, Gazette of India, Supplement, April to June 1982, p. 742.
3. P. G. Mishra, Gurvinder Kaur, Reservation Policy and Personnel Selection, Uppal Publishing House, New Delhi, 1990, p.14.
4. Sectional Village Community, Vol. II, Government of India Ministry of Community Development and Co-operation, New Delhi 1961, p. 57.

8

Participation and Development (A Case Study of Municipal Corporation, Shimla)

Pawan Kumar Banta

Since long, the virtues of participation have been pronounced and proclaimed. Much concern has been shown in recent years concerning participation and development. The Economics and Social Council has recommended that governments should adopt popular participation as a basic policy measures in national development strategy and should encourage the widest possible active participation of all individuals and national non-governmental organizations, such as trade unions, youth and women's organizations in the development process in setting goals, formulating policies and implementing plans. Keeping in view the above in this paper, the researcher has attempted to understand the phenomenon of participation and development with relation to Municipal Corporation, Shimla. The researcher wants to assess whether the participation by elected representatives/members of Municipal Corporation, Shimla has brought about any development or not.

Our attempt, therefore, is to first define participation and provide a viable parameters of development in which all the aspects of participatory development will be coached in. 'Participation' is one of the terms that are very difficult to define because, while it is widely used in today's language, the scope and meaning that are ascribed to often differ very widely. The term 'participation' is used to cover all the forms of action by which citizens 'take part' in the operation of administration. It is also understood in the sense in United Nations documents.

The word 'participation' is used broadly to refer to the role of members of the general public, as distinguished from that of appointed officials, including civil servants, in influencing the activities of government or in providing directly for community needs. It may occur at any level-from local village to the country as a whole. It may be in form of an advisory committee to a minister. It may also involve decision making as in the case of governing bodies of local authorities. It may even extend to actual implementation as in the case when villagers decide to implement a village self help project. The participation thus may involve (a) participation in decision-making, (b) participation in sharing the benefits, and (c) participation in monitoring and evaluation.

Participation in decision-making and implementation pertains to the 'inputs' of development projects, providing authority, information, labour, and other resources while people's involvement in benefits and evaluation of development activity concerns the 'output' of this.

Decision-making

Central point of this kind of participation are the generation of ideas, formulation and assessment of options, and making choices about them, as well as the formulation of plans for putting selected options into effects. Only for this reason a distinction may be made in three types of decisions (i) initial decisions, (ii) ongoing decisions, and (iii) operational decisions.

Implications

There are three main ways, through which people can participate in the implementation aspect of the project. They are: (a) resource contribution of the project, (b) administration and coordination efforts, and (c) programme enlistment activities.

Benefits

Three possible kinds of benefits can be expected from a project. They are: (1) material, (2) social and (3) personal. We would agree that participation in benefits is one of the more passive kinds of participation, it has such a long tradition in economic literature that it should not be overlooked. The only danger, perhaps in focusing of this kind of participation is that it can sometimes be quite high and lead observers to overlook the fact that participation in other important aspects of projects, such as decision making, has either not occurred or has been quite limited.

Evaluation

It is difficult to conceptualize how this kind of participation might be analyzed and measured. Direct or indirect participation can occur in relation to actual project centered evaluation if there is any formal review process. One would like to know who participates in it, how continuously, with what power to achieve actions or suggestions and so on. Possible participation in elections at local, regional or national level can provide some opportunities for favourable or unfavourable local evaluations to be led into policy process. Such inputs, however, are likely to be rather gross, reflecting simply dissatisfaction or satisfaction with what the project has accomplished.

In a democratic society, participation gives the ordinary citizen a means of voicing his position and of showing by his behaviours and actions that he is able to take on responsibilities. It gives the ordinary citizen a chance to show his willingness to carryout constructive public work and to demonstrate his good citizenship by other means than periodically exercising his right to vote.[1] Participation involves a factor of determination on the part of the person participating "participation means self-motion".[2]

According to some writers, however, participation should be understood in a narrow sense. It would consist in a convergent action by which the citizen takes part in accomplishment of administrative services, without however belonging to the governing as managing organs. It would then be situated at a more advanced stage of convergence than consultation, since the citizen does not confine himself to expressing an opinion on a possible or actual administrative measures, but participation directly in its accomplishment.

For our part, we prefer the former facet acceptance of participation, to give the notion a very wide meaning and to look upon, for instance, consultation, joint public and private agreement, cooperation and association simply as different ways of exercising it. They are chiefly distinguished from one another by the varying degree of intensity of citizen's efforts.

One proportion, however, be made. Any kind of citizen-intervention in administration does not necessarily appears to fit into the concept of participation. This is the case when it is improved by the administration authority without leaving the citizen any opportunity to avoid it, i.e. when it is forced as merely passive, it can no longer be described as participation. What then occurs is another process which English speaking potential scientist call 'mobilization'?

We have been laying great stress on the participation of citizens in the affairs of state since long. Analyzing the relationship between participation and social and human development, Aristotle has emphasized that participation in the affairs of state was essential for human happiness. It contributed for the "good of life" and led to the development and fulfillment of human personality. It has also been believed that public participation in public administration guards public interest. Participation of citizens in the affairs of state is essential for a modern welfare state. It is also necessary to ensure democratic, meaningful, and effective administration. Public participation is, thus, closely related to democracy and development.

The participants whose characteristics warranted specific attention are generally of four types, which require making distinction. Depending on the setting and the goals of the project, certain characteristics of participants would be more significant than others. We should distinguish (1) local residents, (2) local leaders, 93) government personnel, and (4) foreign personnel. Each of these set of persons can be sub-divided into a number of groups. Moreover, they can be further classified with regards to a number of important background characteristics which are known to be essential to the analysis of individual participation.

The first two sets of people are those who have local roots, whereas the last two are, to varying degree, outsiders. Local residents form a residual category. It includes a large and heterogeneous group made up of self-sufficient tenants of landowners, labourers, herdsmen, craftsmen, and so on. It is this group of people who are usually the target of urban/rural development project. Local leaders have a long run involvement in the areas in which they work. Usually they are people who are considered local elites, such as landowners, merchants and professionals.

The definition of local leader varies from area to area. Basically there are three types of leaders: (1) Informal leaders such as clan chief, religious figures, influential professionals and local notables, (2) Associational heads elected or appointed for a formal organization, such as a cooperative league president, the chairman of a voluntary association or the leader of a local trade union, (3) Local office-holders, such as headmen, mukhias, pradhans, chairmen of Zila Parishads, Mayors or tax collectors. Sometimes the nature of office makes it difficult to distinguish such local leaders from government personnel.

Government personnel are assigned to an area for a certain period. Even if they are from the local areas, their career rests with the bureaucracy at the center and their future is not usually determined by what happens in the areas. This being the case, they are subject to transfer. They are usually determined by what happens in the area. They usually have higher education and social status than do locals. It is important to look at the participation levels of those people to evaluate what role they may be playing in promoting, controlling or blocking project activity.

Some consideration should be given to foreign personnel. While often not important, they can at time play a crucial participatory role. Among them would be included foreign donor, employers, heads of private voluntary associations, missionary personnel, expatriates, or immigrants, who live and work at the local level. Which personnel background characteristics are important in a given situation depends on the circumstances and the kinds of participation possible.

People's participation, like employment, is also both means and an end but we are inclined to look upon it more an end in itself in social and political terms as it is the sine qua non of development, particularly at the local level. In addition, by people's participation – it may be spontaneous or induced, but certainly not 'coerced', for, that is not participation. Just as implementation is the touch stone for planning, people's participation may be looked upon as the touch stone of 'unified' or 'integrated approach to development'.

Development is a complex phenomenon comprising many dimensions – social, political, economic, administrative and so on. According to Esman, development is relative process of organizing and carrying out prudentially conceived and staffed programmes or project as one would organize and carry out military or engineering operations.

To Colim and Geigner, development means change plus growth. Weidner defines it as a process of growth in the direction of national building and socio-economic progress. Fred W. Riggs defines development in terms of "rising levels of autonomy or discretion (of social systems) in the sense of ability to choose alternatives, not of course, in the sense caution or moderation:" Development, thus, is a phenomenon which has got many dimensions.

Participation and Local Government in India

Pandit Jawahar Lal Nehru and Sardar Vallabh Bhai Patel, former lawyers in the early decades of twentieth century became municipal chairman in their respective cities. Subhash Chandra Bose, who declined a job in the ICS, he had earned through a tough competition, became the Executive Councilor of the Calcutta Municipal Corporation. There were many others who began their political career with the local government institutions.

This was because the local government institutions in accordance with a new policy of the British Raj, offered the first opportunity and freedom of decision-making to Indians. Desire for participation in political institutions turned out to be widespread in India after Independence that the state and central stage of politics got overcrowded. Local government institutions receded to an unimportant place because of the meagre power that they offered to incumbents. But this was because after the acceptance of the principle of adult suffrage, which, under the republican constitution of India, was to inform all political institutions of the country, was to be implemented in the areas of local government but because of the stupendous nature of the task, a clear cut policy was taking time to evolve.

Table I

Relationship Between Participation and Development

Time Phase	*National Policy*	*Local Feed Back*
1947-52	Participation	Development
1952-56	Development	Participation
1956-61	Participation	Development
1961-66	Participation	Development
1966-71	Development	Development
1971-76	Development	Participation
1976-80	Participation	Development
Since 1980	Development	Participation

National concern was re-focused on local government institutions in the wake of the need of associates by local people in the process of implementing the centrally formulated schemes of development under the Five Year Plans. This occurred in 1957. Table I represents a broad perspective summation of the reality relating to Indian experiments in the relationship between participation and development. The perception of Ashok Mehta committee, concerning the period since Panchayati Raj came into existence, confirms the formulation presented in the figures.

The analysis reflects that the story of local institutions has been a story of ups and downs and it seems to have passed through three phases: the phases of ascendancy (1954-64); the phase of stagnation (1965-69); and the phase of decline (1969-71). Local development and local participation have thus been very much connected to national policy in this regard. The 73rd and 74th Constitution Amendment Acts prescribe for uniform system of local governments in the country. They facilitate the democratic decentralization at the grass root level and provide stability through the mandatory elections within stipulated period of five years. All sections of the society including women are guaranteed due representations in the city government and setting up of District Planning Committees to be prepared by the Panchayats and Urban Local Bodies in the district and to prepare a draft development plan for the overall integrated development. These Acts provide for setting up of a Finance Commission every five-year to review, reserve the resources and help the local bodies to strengthen financially. The Indian society is primarily traditional and man-dominated but the country has been pioneer in giving the equal constitutional and social status to the women. This provision further affirms the commitment of strengthening the vulnerable classes of the society.

The emergence of woman power structure into Panchayati Raj and Municipal Institutions is a milestone in achieving socio-economic development in a positive direction. The framers of the legislation have to ensure that undue difficulties that may discourage them from participation in the political process of decision making are made away judiciously.

Municipal Corporation Shimla: A Brief History

Shimla one time summer capital of government of India and head-quarters of Indian army and now that of government of Himachal Pradesh is picturesquely "situated on several small suburbs of lower Himalayas at the mean elevation of about 7100 feet above the sea level. Its attitude is 36.6 N and longitude 77.3E. Easily accessible by road and rail it has bracing climate, cool bright refreshing days and crisp nights. It is one of the finest hill stations of the country with an area of 7.55 square mile. It was a dream of coolness in a very hot land, a lope of healthy rest from the burden of imperial office, a heaven of familiarity pinnacled above the alien dust of the plains, a solace of wounded and the desolate, the ill and the bored, a promise of fun and flirtation, above all a bitter-sweet memory of home-cuckoos and thrushes pones in the mist, honey-suckle and roses in the rain.

Once Shimla had passed under the direct jurisdiction of government when the first civic rules were formulated in the year 1829. The earliest houses, paths, and water reservoirs built by individuals were now brought within the general scheme of improvement of the town. Bentick, the governor-general, suggested two hundred square yard be utmost allowed to an individual for construction of a house. As a first step the boundaries of houses and the land attached to them were demarcated. A graduated ground tax, ranging from twenty to forty rupees, depending on the built up area, was fixed. The proceeds from the chowkidari tax were meant to defray the cost of policing.

In 1832, Bentick appointed a three-man committee to suggest measures for improvement of the town. The main problems, which confronted three members, Captain Kennedy, Colonel C.B. Stevenson, the quarter-master general of Subathu, and Mac Sween, a house owner, were how to improve the water supply and roads in Shimla.

Shimla's municipal committee was first introduced in December 1851 under the provision of Act XXVI of 1850. Shimla municipality shares the distinction of being the oldest in Punjab. All the members were elected originally. The chairman was also elected but afterwards the deputy commissioner was nominated ex-officio president and later on some ex-officio members were added, and many other changes were made. It was first constituted in 1852 according to the Government of India notification on December 15, 1851.

In view of pressure from house owners, a new constitution was framed in 1855. According to this, although the deputy commissioner was an ex-officio member of the committee, the municipal commissioners were all elected by house owners. In 1864, three ex-officio members were added to represent the interests of the government. During 1871, it was given the status of first class municipality, one of the six categories created by an Act in these were officials, seven to ten house owners, of whom three were Indians. The committee from a list of six submitted by the Deputy Commissioner chose three representatives of the summer visitors.

The first municipal board for Shimla was constituted by Punjab Government in 1876. It consisted of 19 members, 7 of whom were officials and 12 non-officials – out of 12 non-officials, three were appointed by notification. The remaining were appointed by selection from property owners. Out of latter nine, two were to be Indians.

In 1876 the Committee was once again reconstituted to ensure official control. The Deputy Commissioner served as ex-officio President, and committee was limited to five nominated members, two salaried government officials and two house owners. Shimla's private house owners rekindled the controversy on the unrepresentative constitution of the municipality in 1881. The attack of the despotic and arbitrary tendencies of the Shimla Municipal Committee was launched by Allan Octavian Hume and some other house owners. Between 1876 to 1883 the strength of the committee was same as reconstituted in the year 1876. Hume favoured an elected element in Shimla Municipal Committee though in a gradual process towards that aim. The Committee's recommendation were based, predictably on the concept of enfranchising interests and classes rather than individuals.

In Shimla, in June 1882, a memorandum of fourteen points spelled out the basis on which the new municipal constitution was framed, after the Ripon's Resolution of 18th May 1882, on local self-government in Simla. A seven member committee which included A.O. Hume, Edward Cullin, a lawer and J.Elston, a house owner was appointed by the government to draft a suitable constitution for the Shimla Municipal Committee. By September 1882, the committee had submitted its recommendations. Despite four dissenting notes, the Committee favoured a wholly elected Municipal Committee. The Municipal Committee was consisted of thirteen honorary members, including the President, who were elected by the Committee and had three years term. One third members were to retire each year. All the voters had to be residents, property owners and tenants, consisting of two wards - station and bazaar wards.

The first elections held in 1883, changed the complexion of Municipal Committee. A.O. Hume was elected president. In 1890, the Punjab Government after consulting the Government of India, decided to fix the number of the members of the board at 10 instead 13 and it was stated that in the future out of those 10 members, 6 members to be elected and 4 nominated to represent interest of government.

In 1891, the committee was reconstituted to consist of four nominated and six elected members. Of the latter three seats each represented the two wards. The Indian representatives from bazaar ward were non-controversial, virtually ciphers who did not understand English. In 1883, the Municipal Committee passed a resolution saying that, "with a view to the expenditious dispatch of business a majority of the committee shall decide what matter are proper and necessary to be explained in the vernacular to the Indian members." However, it seemed 'inexpedient' to appoint Indian members to a subcommittee even for the special inspection of the Bazaar, and they were doubtless induced to cast their votes in favour of Government resolutions. With such a composition it was possible for Government to effectively control municipal functioning. In 1884, two permanent committees, one for finance and other for executive and general affairs, were appointed. From time to time various ad-hoc committees were set up to enquire into complaints, the construction of large buildings one of the four wards into which towns divided. The ward commissioners were authorized to grant permission on the spot for routine or trivial matters, reporting them for formal confirmation by the Municipal Committee.

Subsequently during 1900, the elected seats were reduced to five. Again in 1907 it was reconstituted with just seven members. Its unfortunes never looked up and remained dominated by the government officials since then. The nominations were also made on choose basis and managed a large number of services. In 1906, the façade of elections was removed and for reasons affecting the 'public interest' the Municipal Committee was reconstituted to consist of seven nominated members, of whom only four were ex-officio Government nominees. The experiment with a completely elected members bequeathed a lasting mistrust of democratization.

Subsequently, it was decided that Municipal Committee should be consisted of 10 members including the President, all of whom were to be elected. The right of election vested in the members of the committee alone. The Punjab Government increased the number of members to 12 of whom three to be elected and nine appointed by name.

This system continued upto 1953. Election during 1953 to 1960 was held on the basis of this system. During 1962, the Punjab Government raised the number of members to 19(13 single and 3 double member constituencies) according to the population of the town. Out of these 19 members three members were to be from scheduled caste. The general elections to the Municipal Committee, Shimla were held on 6th November, 1960 and notified by the Punjab Government. The committee took oath of allegiance on 8th December 1960. Civil Surgeon, Shimla, Executive Engineer, Shimla Central Division and Shimla provincial Division, respectively and Adjutant General, Western Command, Shimla were appointed as advisors.

As a result of reorganization of Punjab with effect from 1st November 1966, Shimla along with other hilly areas was merged in Himachal Pradesh. The development of this town and its suburbs and management of municipal affairs therefore, engaged the attention of Himachal Pradesh Government. The Government felt that concrete steps were necessary and this could be done if there was a separate legislation for this purpose. As a result of Himachal Pradesh (Development and Regulations) Act was passed by Himachal Pradesh Legislative Assembly, which received the assent of the President of India on 20th June 1969. Consequently the erstwhile Municipal Committee, Shimla was dissolved on 27th June, 1969 and replaced by Corporation consisting of one administrator and ten nominated members, out of which one each was to be woman and scheduled caste. Upto the constitution of the Corporation, the Deputy Commissioner, Mahasu, was appointed as officer-in-charge to perform the functions of the corporation. The Municipal Corporation came into being from 1st September 1970 vide Himachal Pradesh Government. Shri R.K. Anand, IAS was appointed as Administrator.

Election and Constitution

Municipal Corporation, Shimla had to wait for no less than twenty five years in the Independent India to have an elected body.

This too was done on the intervention of courts. The elections were held in 1986 after successive governments avoided to get themselves involved in the institution of local self-government. Elections scheduled for 1963 did not take place, and in 1966, the Punjab Government superseded the committee on the charge of incompetence, misappropriation of powers and nepotism. A court order reinstated the committee in 1976, however fresh elections were not held in view of the Himachal Pradesh (Development and Regulations Act, 1968, and the committee was converted into corporation totally manned by nominated members. In 1986, elections were again held, and a band of councilors with a Mayor, shared power with the corporation, and the mayor did not enjoy a majority support. Earlier the Municipal Corporation, Shimla functioned under the control of the Commissioner, who was a Government servant belonging either to Indian Administrative Services or Indian Police Service as per practice. The Assistant Commissioner, who belonged to the Himachal Pradesh Administrative Service, assisted the Commissioner. There was no governance at the local level. These elections were held due to the judgment of High Court of Himachal Pradesh to hold elections. It was on the petititon filed by Shri Om Prakash Sood and Shri Yoginder Lal Sharma, the enlightened citizens of Shimla.

The High court of Himachal Pradesh ordered the Government to hold election by 31st March, 1986. The election was delayed because of winter and was ultimately held on 5th May, 1986. The Himachal Pradesh Government divided Municipal Corporation, Shimla into 21 wards and of which three wards were reserved for scheduled castes.

Since only when one woman was able to get elected in this election, Government of Himachal Pradesh under section 6 of H.P. Municipal Corporation Act, 1979 nominated Smt. Ram Piari to the Municipal Corporation, Shimla and local M.L.A. was coopted as associate member. In order to provide adequate representation to minority communities, the Government of Himachal Pradesh nominated Brig. Samuel Joseph Mukand, Mumtaz Ahmed Kazmi and S. Nirmal Singh to Municipal Corporation, Shimla.

A Mayor who is assisted by a Deputy Mayor heads the corporation. The terms of the Mayor and the Deputy Mayor was two years and six months. Shri Adarsh Kumar was elected first Mayor of the Municipal Corporation, Shimla on 9-6-1986 and Shri Narinder Singh Thakur as Deputy Mayor.

Next elections to municipal corporation were due in the month of May 1991. However, the Government could not conduct the election as scheduled. Citizen Forum on 24th May 1991, thus approached the Hon'ble Hich Court of Himachal Pradesh to ask the state government to conduct the election. The Hon'ble High court ordered the Government of Himachal Pradesh to conduct the election by 30th November 1991.

Government of Himachal Pradesh wanted some more time for the revision of electoral rolls and for delimitation of the wards in view of new census figures. Ultimately the Hon'ble High Court of Himachal Pradesh ordered for the conduct of the elections by May, 1992. As a result of this the election to Municipal Corporation, Shimla was held on 24th May 1992. The election was conducted in 20 wards only. In one ward, election could not be conducted due to the death of one of the candidates. All twenty seats were captured by the Congress party. The Bhartiya Janta Party, ruling party of the state, was completely routed. Three wards were reserved for scheduled castes. The Government of Himachal Pradesh under the provisions of the Municipal Corporation Act, 1979 nominated three members from Sikh, Muslim and Hindu religions.

In pursuant to the 74th Amendment to the Constitution, the old Himachal Pradesh Municipal Corporation Act, 1979, was replaced by new Himachal Pradesh Municipal Corporation Act, 1994. In the year 1996, the Government of Himachal Pradesh extended the municipal limits to adjoining rural area, which included Tara Devi, Chakkar, Chora Chowki, Tutoo, Dhalli, Kasumpti, Vikasnagar and New Shimla, etc. in order to provide better civic amenities and planned development. After delimitation of wards and expansion in area of the Municipal Corporation, the number of wards were increased to 25 from 21.

The elections to the corporation were held on 22nd May 1997. The Governor of Himachal Pradesh under section 4 sub-section 3 of Himachal Pradesh Act, 1994 nominated Shri Adrash Kumar, MLA Shimla assembly constitutency and Shri Charanjiv Lal Kashyap, MLA from Kasumpti assembly constituency as associated members of Municipal Corporation, Shimla. They were replaced by Shri Narender Bragta and Shri Roop Dass Kashyap new MLA's from Shimla and Kasumpti assembly and constituencies in the year 1998 after formation of new assembly.

The Governor of Himachal Pradesh under section 4, sub-section 3 of Himachal Pradesh Municipal Corporation Act, 1994, nominated Shri Deepak Sharma, S. Baldev Singh and Smt. Bimla Kashyap as councilors with no voting right.

Keeping in view the disparity between the core municipal area and newly developed fringes, Government of Himachal Pradesh trifurcated the Municipal Corporation, Shimla into three separate Nagar Panchayats namely, Dhalll, New Shimla, (Kasumpti) and Totu so as to provide better administration and efficient municipal services.

After delimitation of wards and area of the Municipal Corporation, number of wards was decreased to 24 from 25. The latest elections of the corporation were held on April 2002. The

Congress Party captured the Municipal Corporation, Shimla again routing to then ruling party in the State-Bhartiya Janta Party.

Local member of Legislative assembly was coopted as associate member to the Municipal Corporation. The Governor of Himachal Pradesh nominated one woman, one Sikh and one Hindu to the Municipal Corporation, as councilors they have no voting right.

With the change of government of the state, the ruling Congress party replaced the nominated councilors with their own persons. But the councilors nominated by previous government filed a petition in the Hon'ble High Court of Himachal Pradesh and got the notification stayed till the final decision of the petition.

Longest Term as Mayor

Whereas duration of term is one year. Shri Adarsh Kumar the first Mayor of Municipal Corporation, Shimla has created a record of longest term as Mayor. He was elected Mayor on 9-6-1986 and resigned as Mayor on 11-10-1996 after he was elected to Legislative Assembly of Himachal Pradesh. His total term was 10 years four months and two days. He was also elected as Chairman of All India Mayor Council in the year 1996.

According to Municipal Corporation, Shimla (facilities for Mayor) Rules, 1986, the Mayor is entitled for an honorarium of Rs. 350 per month. The mayor is also entitled to a sum of Rs. 500 if he occupies his own house and reimbursement of rent upto Rs.1000 per month on the production of receipt if he hires accommodation for his residence. For the discharge of his functions as mayor, he is provided with a car at the cost of the corporation for use with in the jurisdiction of the Municipal Corporation, Shimla. For outside journeys outside Shimla city the Mayor is entitled to traveling allowance and daily allowance at the highest rate admissible to the grade I officer of Himachal Pradesh. The Mayor is also entitled to incur an expenditure of Rs. 500 per month as official entertainment. The Mayor gets free use of telephone in his office and residence and is not charged for any official trunk calls and local calls for the office and upto 2000 local calls per month from his residence telephone.

According to the Municipal Corporation Shimla (Honorarium for Deputy Mayor) Rules, 1986, the Deputy Mayor is entitled to an honorarium of Rs. 350 per month. He is not entitled to facilities like residence, telephone, official car, etc. The meeting of the Municipal Corporation is generally held every month. Every member who attends meeting gets Rs. 30/- per day. The meeting is held generally for a day or two in a month.

In the year 1996 the government of Himachal Pradesh revised the honorarium to the Mayor, the Deputy Mayor and the councilors to Rs. 2400, Rs. 1500 and Rs. 1200 respectively per month, along with telephone facility. Subsequently the government of Himachal Pradesh again raised the rates of honorarium to the elected representatives. The Mayor, the Deputy Mayor and the Councilors can now draw Rs. 2700, Rs. 1800 and Rs. 1500 respectively per month along with telephone facilities.

Result of Participation

In the above, we have discussed election, constitution, and what can be called as the cost of democracy at local level. Now we shall discuss what results this participation has brought about and what development has been made. We will assess whether after the assumption of office by the municipal councilors, the corporation has been able to provide more social services that are effective and have been able to maintain the environment in a better way or not.

The new municipal corporation took oath on 29th April, 2002. In the present paper, we will discuss the participation and development only with reference to municipal corporation, Shimla which functioned from 3rd June 1992, i.e. for one decade together.

Shimla was designed to cater to a population of approximately twenty-five thousands souls, but its population has increased to 1,42,161 according to 2001 census and has 21,023 number of inhabited housed with 19.55 sq. km. area. Being famous tourist resort its population during summer days swells to approximately one lakh fifty thousand and town receives a continuous and unending streams of tourist throughout the year. Beside this due to pressure of population on the land, some influx of rural population has also been noticed. All these factors and growth of the population has over strained the essential services like water supply sewerage and sanitation. The size of urban population as also the increase in it has serious repercussion on the civic infrastructure and services. Shimla town has experienced in recent years deterioration in the standard and quality of life. The availability of basic services had declined and sizeable population is without access to such services. The town has not only grown congested but high rising concrete monsters raised heads in the most sought after areas in the town. The efforts of the British rulers, to make Shimla the most beautiful British town and their insistence on the retention of hill architecture, has no meaning for people, nor for the officials administering in the town is located in a highly seismic area and unplanned growth could lead to great danger in future.

Though the first sinking was reported in 1942 in the Lakker Bazaar area, the municipal corporation, Shimla failed to provide any concrete plan to avoid recurrence. In the subsequent years and particularly after 1956, creeping movement or sinking of land was also reported from several parts of the town. However, the cracks and sinking of area were more noticeable and more dangerous around the Ridge. The team of experts submitted a comprehensive plan and pointed out that lack of proper drainage facilities and the lack of vegetation and the growth of technically ill planned buildings in the area were responsible for the damage. The constant sinking of Ridges has been an unending topic since 1918.

Unfortunately, little heed has been paid to various recommendations and sinking, though on lesser scale, is reported almost every year. The Municipal Corporation of Shimla to top it all constructed a major commercial center – Padam Dev, near the most affected area. Fresh surveys were carried out and it was stated that the area falls under loose zone. The Central Road Research Institute in its report had attributed the reasons of damage to the enmasse movement in the mantle of slopes. It pointed out that sound bed rock had not been affected but "the other factors responsible for the slope failure were the inadequate design of the walls, movement of heavily loaded trucks. On roads which cause damage to the underground water pipes, frost – action increase in overburden due to excavation of loose fill and loss of dine material, the subsoil due to seepage of water. However, the corporation has already decided to abandon the project of construction of lift from Rivoli bus stand to Ridge on the recommendation of team of the experts from Roorkee University. But in case of this commercial complex, the recommendations of the experts unfortunately have remained ignored. Some half-hearted attempts have been made but the experts are of the opinion that concerted action is called for. The absence of vegetation and the huge pressure on the drainage system are among the reasons cited for taking immediate steps to avoid any catastrophe.

It is also interesting to note that practically no improvement has been made on sewerage system and water supply in the town since 1893. The system has certainly been extended to some areas which were not connected but the main town has the same sewerage and water pipelines which have outlived their life. Fragment leaks are noticed causing insanitation and un hygienic conditions. Partly due to heavy leakage and partly due to large population, the water supply system in the town is in doldrums.

However, the decision of OPEC to provide financial assistance of rupees forty crore to the municipal corporation for sewerage project, has removed the major hurdle. As per the agreement a steering and monitoring committee has already been constituted. The natural drains and nallahs have clogged and have become a favorite dumping ground. During the sport of building activity in the town, the waste or unused building material was also dumped in nullahs which have caused insanitation and the slush water generally gets spilled out causing damage to nearby buildings. There has been substantial number of 'safai majdoors' but the sanitary conditions in the town are worse then ever. With the security of services guaranteed and political backing, the safai mazdoors now constitute a formidable force and the corporation can not take any harsh decisions against them. On several occasions in the recent years, the corporation had to taste their wrath. During their strike the corporation watched helplessly as they struck work for period ranging from a week to a fortnight and put the water supply and sewerage system out of gear. At one time the corporation had to seek the help of the armed forces to ensure the water supply.

Domestic, commercial and hospital wastes generated in Shimla have become one of the major pollutants causing considerable damage to the ecology and threat to human health. NORAD project has been launched to address this problem.

The image of corporation in the public mind is that of inefficiency, maladministration, delay and corruption. Such an image and poor functioning of the corporation has further accentuated the indifference of citizens even towards the affairs of the corporation. On the working of present councilors there are divergent opinions ranging from highest praise to the lowest condemnation. Those who praise their work say that these councilors are doing their best under the present circumstances. They are sparing no efforts to provide better services to the people and to beautify Shimla within the limited resources they have at their disposal. Those who criticize say that these councilors are doing nothing. They are only after their perks. They are helping only the rich and not the poor. They are busy in getting their own work and that of their own relation done through the municipal authorities. The councilors and the Mayor were unanimous in pointing out the following difficulties in achieving the objectives of development. Firstly, they do not have sufficient resources to execute various schemes/projects, which require immediate execution. Secondly, they do not have sufficient powers to carry out the functions assigned to them.

Despite the above-mentioned constraints, the municipal corporation has succeeded in completing many projects. It has solved the problem of drinking water at many places in the city except the Ridge Lakker Bazaar. The list of the projects completed by the corporation over the last decade is as follows.

1. Construction of shopping complex, Lakker Bazaar, Shimla
2. Construction of Padam Dev Complex near the Ridge
3. Construction of Nand Lal Verma Commercial Complex, Lower Bazaar
4. Construction of Daulat Ram Chauhan Complex, Lakker Bazaar.
5. Construction of Parking and shopping complex, Auckland School
6. Construction of temporary sheds for Tibeten refugees near Rivoli Cinema

7. Rain Shelters at Bemloe, 103 Tunnel, Phagli Tara Hall Bhariari Khalini Sanjauli, Deve
8. Shopping complex at Bioleangang and Kanlog
9. Construction of Shopping complex at Middle Bazaar Shimla
10. Construction of remodeling shopping complex at Lower Bazaar Tunnel
11. Type I Quarters, two Blocks of 8 quarters each, at Ladakhi Mohalla.
12. Beautification of the Ridge at providing railings benches and lights
13. Checking of leakages in the Lower Bazaar tunnel
14. Parking near high court
15. Construction of shops at the old place of Rick show Dhara at Chota Shimla
16. Provision of railings/street lights on the roads of city.
17. Maintenance of corporation building
18. Completion of NORAD Project
19. Maintenance of Nullahs/Drains
20. Parking at Yoda Niwas
21. Beautification of Tourist Spots at Chedwilk Fall and Gem
22. Tarring of various roads on yearly basis
23. Starting of door collection of house hold wastes
24. Introduction of single window system
25. Various other schemes under EIUS and NRY
26. Above all electrification of various heritage buildings

To sum up, the achievement of the corporation can briefly be stated follows. Sinking problem in Shimla has been solved, sewerage system has been introduced in many areas, railing and light have been improved on the roads and streets to raise the income of the corporation, new shopping complexes have been constructed and tax income has been doubled. The corporation has further identified following ambitious projects to be completed in the near future:

1. Construction of rest house near Gurudwara Area, Cart road.
2. Construction of marketing complex at Subzi Mandi & Anaj Mandi.
3. Construction of ropeway from Ridge to Jhakhoo.
4. Various other schemes/projects.
5. Construction of Lift from Rivoli to Ridge.
6. Construction of fly over near St. Edward School, Shimla.

The list is quite impressive, it may take four to five or more years to complete the projects. However this speaks of the ambitions and aspirations of the Municipal Corporation. The following table shows that the corporation has raised its civic infrastructure comprehensively during 1996 to 2002.

Civic Infrastructure with Municipal Corporation, Shimla

Years	*Roads K. M.*	*Streets K. M.*	*Street Lights Points*	*Public Toilets*	*Water Supply KiloLitre per day*	*Drains*
1996	50.48	75.07	3173	101	15400	—
2002	162.48	40.58	4749	114	—	121.89

Source: State Finance Commission report – 1996-2002.

At present Corporation has created following infrastructure to cater the needs of the population and tourists:[3]

1.	Residential Houses	654 Nos.
2.	Shops/Stalls	874 Nos.
3.	Sheds	187 Nos.
4.	Car Parking	3 Nos.
5.	Water Pump (main lines)	65 kms.

6.	Water Pipe (branch lines)	110 kms.
7.	Sewerage Line	18 ksm.
8.	Sewerage Plants	5 Nos.
9.	Septic Tanks	10 Nos.
10.	Storage Tanks Water	32 Nos.
11.	Rest House	One
12.	Town Hall	One
13.	Labour Hostel	One
14.	Working Women Hostel	One
15.	Cutting and Tailoring Centre	One

Present Study

The questionnaires were given to the elected representatives. Maximum councilors told that they have made a great development after assuming their services in the corporation and reminding municipal authorities again and again for various services to a great extent. As far as interference in day to day work of municipal corporation was concerned the councilors who were supported by the party in power in the state were unanimously of the opinion that they did not make any interference. However the councilors who had their affiliation with the opposition party pointed out that the councilors supported by the party in power in the state were making unnecessary interference in the day to day working of the municipal corporation employees and the councilors. All were of the view that by providing the reservation to women, scheduled castes etc., on rotation basis, which is an attempt to improve their socio-economic status, the main thrust of this provision has lost the idea behind it. Since the reservation of particular ward will be for only one term, and the work culture on the part of elected councilors is lukewarm and also missing will be the aspect of nursing the constituency.

During the course of the research every interviewee also highlighted some major problems. These were scarcity of water, menace of encroachment, solid waste, menace of polythene etc. The corporation despite its best efforts could not contain the ever rising eyesore problems. Despite repeated encouragement received from time to time in various public interest petition or otherwise the corporation could not combat nuisance. The permission granted on the bazari is making the problem a complex one and is posing grave danger in congested localities. It is a source of annonyance to general public. Discarded polythene bags and wrappers have been posing serious threat not only leading to the degradation of environment, chocking of nallahs but also to the cattle population and resultantly to human beings. Most of the residents are in the habit of throwing house hold garbage packed and filled in polythene bags indiscriminately down hill on hill slopes, back lanes, vacant spaces and in the drains, resulting in blocking of the nallahs, are hampering the free and proper working of the drainage system. Dumping of polythene waste in the forest areas is major source of the degradation. The State is one of the first states to enact the H.P. Non-Bio-degradable Garbage Control Act, 1995. Recently the state of Himachal Pradesh has banned the use of recycled polythene bags.

The councilors were also found concerned to the domestic, commercial and hospital waste generated in Shimla which has become one of the major pollutants causing considerable damage to the ecology and threat to human health. To address the problem of solid waste, the corporation has evolved a scientific disposal of waste through the financial assistance from NORAD (Norwegian Agency for Development and Cooperation) on by- pass road near drain – is not conducive as it is creating nuisance to the passersby. The corporation has also introduced the system of house-to-house collection of garbage on private participation on fixed charges on monthly basis. On the other hand the main criticism of the corporation was water supply. The corporation has failed to provide water for twenty-four hours instead of only one shift. Duration of supply to consumer in different locations of the town varies from 20 minutes to 60 minutes.

The failure of urban basic services like water, transportation and waste management can be attributed to high cost of operation and management, lack of financial resources, crippled organizational delivery mechanism, overlapping institutional arrangements, multiplicity of laws that govern the improper pricing services, lack of coordination among the government bodies, improper policies or strategies adopted for achieving the goals framed.

Partly due to political reasons the corporation is unable to use several power vested in it. During the Raj Days the house owners were required to paint the roofs of their houses at least once in two years. At the expiry of the period the corporation used to get the paint done and charge a penalty besides the cost of painting from the house owners. The corporation still has this power but does not use it. A high powered committee of government decided that a plan for the face lifting of the town should be given top priority. It was proposed that the plan would include removal of dirt from outside the buildings, painting of roofs and windows, repair of down pipes, repair of roofs. It was also decided that after a plan of enforcement for each building has been made by Municipal Corporation some assistance could be provided by the Deputy Commissioner who could distribute this work to the Magistrates who could persuade the people of the area to undertake the improvement. However it noted that unfortunately nothing tangible has been done in this direction. Municipal Corporation has sufficient legal authority to enforce this type of improvement.

The Himachal Pradesh Municipal Corporation Act, 1994 suffers from the following drawbacks in the areas of functional and financial decentralization and popular participation of civic affairs of Municipal Corporation, Shimla:

1. There is overlapping of functions between Municipal Corporation, Shimla and functional departments of state government i.e. Town Planning Department and Housing Board which are functioning for urban planning and housing respectively.
2. Some development programmes are out of the pale of the corporation, for example augmentation of water supply. The sectoral programmes also create confusion at the local level, as responsibilities are not clearly defined. The administration is fragmented and overlapping.
3. Additional responsibilities and functions are bestowed on the corporation, but without earmarking additional resources (human and financial). The absence of a financial decentralization will simply lead to worsening of civic problems.
4. Little attempt has been made to improve the revenue base of Municipal Croporation, Shimla. A practice of waiting for the State Finance Commission to recommend municipal fiscal reforms may not be healthy. The newly created local political structure will lose credibility to perform.
5. There have been confrontation in Municipal Croporation between the executive and deliberative wings in the past. However, the fact that some confrontations never led to any statement of unresolved crises, speaks well for the cordiality of atmosphere and amenability to reason. However, some conflict has reached a flashpoint with the councilors who have decided to ask the government to recall the commissioner.
6. Municipal Corporation Shimla though elected, enjoys a limited autonomy and the State Government has reserved wide powers with regards to its administration. The existing

excessive State control is generally negative rather than corrective in its approach.

7. The State Government knows that the existing and potential revenues of the Corporation as well as transfer of resources from State Government are not sufficient to meet the development need of the Shimla town. This conclusion did not force the Government to look for an alternative strategy in raising resources in the Act. The Act does not visualize the corporation for having an independent policy to look for avenues to finance various utilities in the town. A limited autonomy is offered to the Corporation in the form of auctioning of municipal properties subject to the approval of the State Government in exceptional cases.

Unless the functions are devolved, the financial powers cannot be contemplated. But at the same time, if the finances are not made available, the functions cannot be carried out. It is true that for making a real decentralization system, some functions and sources of income enjoyed by the state government must be transferred to the municipal corporation. The transfer of half bites cannot achieve the purpose for which the 74th Amendment was made.

Suggestions

On the basis of the above discussion it can be pointed out that the elected representatives are making the best efforts for the development. There are constraints which need to be examined in order to take appropriate steps if the pace of the development to be accelerated. These include:

1. Undertaking the second round legislative exercises by the State Government to precisely describe functions, sources of finances, matching of functions and finances, revenue, sharing and intergovernmental transfer rules and a municipal

accountability systems, keeping in view the special national and international importance of Shimla city.

2. Making distinction between functional responsibilities of Municipal Corporation, Shimla with non-buoyant sources of revenues cannot be expected to discharge the same obligations as the larger ones in the absence of corrective inter-governmental transfers.
3. Development of model alternatives regarding the mix: (i) local taxes (ii) assigned (state) taxes along with well-defined and precise formulae for revenue sharing and (iii) inter-governmental transfers. One to one matching between functions and revenue sources should be attempted.
4. There have, indeed been confrontations in the Municipal Corporation, between the executive and the deliberative wings. In order to avoid such conflicts it is suggested that either the system of Mayor-in-Council be introduced or the real executive powers should be vested in the Mayor.
5. The elected representatives who are doing a creditable work in providing better services to the people have done only a fire fighting exercise. They should make long term development plans for the development and beautification of the city and should also try to harness and mobilize new financial resources for development.
6. The elected representatives due to their over occupation with tightening of nuts and bolts are not in a position to devote time for long-term planning. Moreover, since they have to cater to the demands of various pressure groups in the city, they fear from taking hard decisions. At times their approach and vision tend to be myopic. Dedicated bureaucracy, which has no stakes in the public can come to the rescue of the elected representatives in such a situation. Some professional compulsion should be added to the recommendations of the Strategic Planning Group.
7. The municipal employees are not happy about their working conditions. They are also worried about their future in the

corporation. The elective representatives should try to understand their personal problems, grievances and apprehensions. They should approach the State Government for meeting various demands of the employees in as much as it is with competent and satisfied workers that we can hope to achieve the desired development.

8. Any strong or sound policy frame work that will be conceived in future for the urban development of Shimla city should formulate the problem of demand that expands more rapidly than the supply. Its applicability should be tested in ground as hill topography of the town may pose an inherent limitation to the design and implementation strategy of the development proposal(s).

9. Shimla should see a perceptible shift from the conventional Master Plan concept, which is based in favour of physical land use plans and the land of an important constraint in the town. So any plan that aims for sustainable development should take into account a coordinated physical, spatial and economic planning. The critical linkages that exist between the investment proposals and the resource availability should be examined. An appropriate agency to monitor regularly the implementation plan should be explored.

10. The success of development plans, irrespective of what it is and how big it is, have strong social and political implications. No plans can be successfully implemented without public private participation so there is a need for participatory work and awareness programme to mold the public to follow in the line of sustained practices and participation to enable the bodies to perform their functions in proper fashion. This would be beneficial both from the financial and environmental angle.

Conclusion

The study reaches to the conclusion that the elected representatives to the Municipal Corporation, Shimla were making great efforts for development. They were reminding the Municipal Corporation authorities again and again for various services to be provided to the local people and thus working as "watch dogs" of democracy in the Shimla city. There were some personnel problems of municipal employees, which needed to be addressed in the interest of development. The financial resources at the disposal of the corporation are meagre. Its liabilities are increasing day by day. The state government should give liberal grants-in-aid in view of the special national and inter-national importance of the city known as Queen of Hill stations.

Though there exists complex problems in almost every sector of urban services programmes, few services like water supply, sewerage and solid waste needs immediate attention from the planners, managers and policy makers. The corporation should prioritize the 'Integral Urban Waste Management' as the future action area. The solving of problem in Shimla would mean full stop to urban plight that is increasing day-by-day, amelioration in the insanitary conditions that exists to improve the health and environment benefits. Pursuing these exercises have subsequent benefits like financial, which is, tangible and environmental, the intangible.

The second state finance commission had careful consideration of the suggestions made by the urban development department, government of Himachal Predesh and after the impact of notification issued by the state government for delegation of functions to urban local bodies including Municipal Corporation Shimla, the Commission is of the view that:

1. Developmental schemes be transferred along with supporting staff and resources
2. Schemes transferred to urban local bodies should be in the state of the art technical existence. Sufficient financial

support be made available after proper assessment for renovation or augmentation.

3. Cost of services being provided to the people should invariably cover at least running and maintenance cost of the service.

Functional clarity and strengthening of Municipal Corporation, Shimla, its finance and management should occupy the centre-stage of the follow-up action on the conformity legislation. The ways to improve municipal functioning will have to include among other things, the rational allocation of responsibilities and finances, levels of government, incentive-penalty structures to enhance local efforts to raise revenue and improve the responsiveness of service providers, minimization of waste, adoption of efficient practices and promotion of policies that enhance local initiative. Municipal reforms need to be addressing these issues systematically. We have to make zealous efforts to strengthen the Municipal Corporation, Shimla. Let us all remember what A. De-tocqueille has said, "local institutions constitute a strength of nation. A nation may establish a system of free government but without local institutions, it cannot have the sprit of liberty. Local meetings are liberty what primary schools are to science; they bring it within the people's reach. They teach men how to use and enjoy it". It is a fact that a system of democratic form of government for its success requires local self-governing institutions. Lord Bryce had rightly said, "the best school of democracy and the best guarantee for its success is the practice of local self-government".

References

1. Soysal, Mumtaz, "Public Relations in Administration: The Influence of Public on the Operation of Public Administration, Excluding Electoral Rights", Central Report to XIIth International Congress of Administrative Sciences, Paris, 1965, Burssels, IIAS, 1966, pp. 46-47.

2. Decentralization for National and Local Development, United Nations Publications, New York, 1962, Series No. 6211 H. 22 paragraph 97.
3. Mishra, S.N., Kaushal Sharma and Neena Sharma, "Participation and Development", (New Delhi: N.B.O. Publishers, Distributors (1984), p.15.
4. Mishra, S.N., "Participative Management and Rural Development", (New Delhi, Mittal Publications, 1992), p. 2.
5. Gautam, Padam Nabh, "participation and Development: A Case Study of Municipal Corporation Shimla" Unpublished Research Paper-1995, p.1.
6. Soysal, Mumtaz, *op. cit.*, p. 47.
7. Glovanni, Sartori, "Concept Misformation in Comparative Politics", 'American Political Science Review', Vol: LXIV, No.4, Dec. 1970, 1050-52.
8. Esman, Miltaon J., "The Politics of Development Administration", in Montgomerry and Siffin (eds), Approaches to Development Politics, Administration and Changes (McGraw Hill, New York, 1962, p. 95).
9. Colim, Gerhard, and Theodore Greiger, "Country Programming as a Guide to Development, In Development of the Emerging Countries, as Agenda for Research (Brookings Institutions, Washington, 1962), p.47.
10. Riggs, Fred W., "The Idea of Development Administration", In Edward W. Weidner (ed) Development Administration in Asia, (Duke University Press, Dureham, 1970), p.8.
11. In 1964 Nehru died. In 1964-66, Lal Bahadur Shastri was the Prime Minister. Mrs. Gandhi took over on the death of Lal Bahadur Shastri in 1966. But she acquired pre eminence in policies as prime minister only in 1969. The Mehta Report formulation takes these deaths a cut-off point in the history of panchayati Raj. This all the more illustration how macro level changes affect local level development.
12. Buck, Edward J., "Shimla: Past and Present", (New Delhi: Summit Publication, (First Published 1904), First Indian Reprint-1979), p.1.

13. Barr, Potand and Desmos, Raj, "Shimla – A Hill Station in British India", (Delhi; B.R. Publishing Corporation-1978), p.7.
14. Kunwar, Pamela, "The Political Culture of Raj" (Delhi: Oxford University Press 1990), p.16.
15. Banta Pawan Kumar, "Personnel Administration of Shimla Municipal Corporation", Mimeo-1987, p. 102.
16. Hunter, W.W., "Lord Amherest and British East Wards to Burma", (London: Oxford University Press, 1889), p.198.
17. Act XXVI of 1850 of Punjab Government.
18. Gautam, Padam Nabh, "Administrative History of Shimla Municipal Corporation", An Unpublished Research paper, July 1981, p.3.
19. Banta, Pawan Kumar, "One Hundred Fifty Year of Civic Administration in Shimla City – Tiny Bits of England" in U.B. Singh (ed) Revitalized Urban Administration in India, (Delhi, Kalpaz Publication-2002), p.353.
20. Banta, Pawan Kumar, "A Study of Municipal Corporation, Shimla with Special Reference to 74th Constitutional Amendment Act", Submitted to Indian Institute of Public Administration, New Delhi, 1999, p.15.
21. Kamwar, Pamela, op. cit., p.112.
22. Gautam, Padam Nabh, "Municipal Corporation of Shimla: A Monograph by Punjab University", Patiala, 1983, p.8.
23. Sharda, Sarita, "Finances of Shimla Municipal Corporation: A Analytical Study" Mimeo, 1983, p.55.
24 Pubby, Vipin, "Shimla: Then and Now" (New Delhi: Indus Publishing House, 1988), p.96.
25. Banta, Pawan Kumar, "Municipal Corporation Shimla, (Lucknow: Journal of Public Administration, Vol: 6, No.1 to 4, Arial 90-March 91), p.12.
26. Bhasin, Raja, "Shimla: The Summer Capital of British India" (New Delhi: Penguin Book India Pvt. Ltd., 1992), pp. 166-167.
27. Puby, Vipin, op. cit., p.119.
28. Gautam, Padam Nabh, "Participation and Development", A study of Municipal Corporation Shimla", Mimeo, 1995, p.5.
29. Second State Finance Commission Report 2002, p.15.

30. Banta, Pawan Kumar, "A study of Administration of Municipal Corporation with Special Reference to 74th Constitutional Amendment Act," Ph.D. Thesis, 1999, p.401.
31. Report of the Himachal Pradesh 2nd State Finance Commission, 2002, p.17
32. Ibid., p.32.
33. Lipman, V.D., "Local Government Areas, 1934-1945"(London: Oxford University Press-1974), p.1
34. Singh, Mohinder, "Democratic Decentralization in India after 73rd Amendment Act: Some Issues and Challenges", Paper submitted for seminar held in H.P. University, Shimla, Unpublished, 2001, p.1.

(Footnotes)

1. Soysal, Mumtazz, op. cit., p.47
2. Glovanni, Sartori, "Concept Misformation in Comparative Politics" 'American Political Science Review', Vol: LXIV, No 4, Dec. 1970, 1050-52
3. Banta Pawan Kumar, "A study of Administration of Municipal Corporation with Special reference to 74th Constitutional Amendment Act", Ph.D. thesis, 1999, p.401.

9

Municipal Government in Assam (A Case Study of the Palasbari Municipal Board)

Jogendra Kr. Das

Introduction

In the present paper an attempt has been made to briefly deal with the municipal governance in Assam with special reference to the Palasbari Municipal Board. The approach of this study is largely historical and sociological. Methodologically, the study is based partly on primary data and partly on exploring documents. We have also consulted secondary data such as published books, government records, official records of the Palasbari Municipal Board and published journals. We largely rely on independent variables, however dependent variables such as self perception and attitudes of the Board office bearers and some local distinguished personalities have also been counted for the purpose. Data have been collected through field investigation.

In terms of the independent variables the study has the following objectives:

1. To present a pen-picture of the nature of urban development and urban local governance in Assam
2. To sketch a brief history of Palasbari
3. To outline the genesis and growth of the Palasbari Municipal Board
4. To analyse the procedure of elections
5. To analyse the distribution of power and social bases of the members
6. To discuss the infrastructure, management, role-achievements
7. To look into the staffing pattern
8. To find out the problems and future prospects
9. To draw a logically tenable general conclusion and suggestions.

In the present study, we deliberately avoid theoretical problems and discussions because of time and space constraints. For the same reason, however, we admit that the present micro work may suffer from inherent limitations because of non-availability of dependable data.

Urban Government in Assam

As per 2001 census, out of the country's total population of 100 crores, a slightly less than 27 crores people dwell in India's urban areas. This implies that one out of every four Indians is an urban dweller. However, the process of urban development in India was lethargic and it was started only after the 17th century industrial revolution that too, on the aegis of the British rule as a hidden agenda of their colonial exploitation. Whatever may be the case, urbanization is an integral part of the process of development which is an indicator of industrialization, commercialization and modernization. A transformation from an agricultural society to an industrial one occurs along rural-urban dimensions. A shift from rural to urban society brings about changes not only in the economic structure but also in social relationship and cultural profiles. In common outlook, urbanization means migration of population from village to urban environment. Urban development also connotes provision of basic facilities and services in urban areas and regulation of growth. These facilities and services may be listed as water supply, drainage, sewerage, urban housing, electricity, transportation, road construction, maintenance of market, health and sanitation and many more planned and systematic ones. Since the subjects relating to urban development figure in the State List, it is the state government that decides which specific subjects be devolved upon local government for performance.

Generally, the brunt of urbanization in India has been borne by Municipal Corporations, Municipal Councils or Boards. Hence, urban areas are governed by urban local bodies of various types – the Municipal Corporations, Municipal Boards, Town Area Committees, Notified Area and Cantonment Boards etc. The state government defines their functions, responsibilities and the power of resource mobilization.

In the specific context of Assam, the Municipalities or the Municipal Boards are guided by the Assam Municipal Act, 1956 as amended in 1994 (Assam Municipal Amendment Act, 1994). The Government of Assam may constitute any town, together with or exclusion of any area in the vicinity of any such town as 'Municipal Board' under the Assam Municipal Act, provided that such a town has a population of more than 10,000. A town committee may be constituted under the Act, with a population of less than 10,000.

In Assam, the process of urbanization accelerated during the last 30 years though industrialization in modern sense, is yet in infancy. In every census, new urban centres are identified. The moderate rate of urban growth in the state is mainly due to the corresponding moderate acceleration of modernization rate which is interwoven with slow process of industrialization. But the fact is that the agents of modern material culture are fast expanding to even the remotest agrarian areas, which reduced the gap between urban and rural living standard. But still we must admit that the ideational (non-material) cultural lives are lagging behind the fast moving technology in the state.

Today, the small business and trade centres having well communication and transport accessibility where 75% of the male working population engaged in non-agricultural activities with a population of even less than 5000, with 260-400 density per sq. km., small township has grown up and the government recognizes these centres as urban centres by creating Municipal Board (MB), Town Committee (TC), Census Town (CT) and Out Growth (OG) etc. in the state for the management and development of these areas by decentralizing powers to each local urban body.

In Assam, the total population as per 1991 census was 2,24,14,322 of this while rural population being 1,99,26,517 the number of urban population was 2487795. We find the rural – urban difference being 1,74,38,732 which reflects natural predominance of rural dwelling in the state.[1] As per 2001 census (provisional) the total population of Assam is 2,66,38,407, an increase of 4,22,405 people over the 1991 census The rural population is 2,32,48,994 while the urban dwellers are 3,38,9413. Thus, the gap between rural – urban living was 1,98,59581 in 2001. We find that while the urban population of Assam was 24,87,795 in 1991, the number rises to 33,89,413 in 2001, an increment of urban population by 9,01,618 as of now.[2] This however, reflects a moderate rate of migration of rural people to urban centres for seeking jobs.

After observing the urban population trend, it is necessary to look into the number of towns and cities in the state of Assam where urban local governments have been constituted. As per the Assam Municipal Act of 1956, subsequently amended in 1994, a municipal board may be constituted where the population is 10 thousand or above. A town committee may be constituted where the population is less than 10 thousand, while a Census Town may be constituted with a population of 5000 or less. A Municipal Corporation may comprise a population of 5 lacs or more, while a metropolis may comprise a population of 10 lacs or more.

As per census report, of the total of 131 urban governments in the state, there are 25 Municipal Boards, 52 Town Committees, 53 Census Towns and 7 Out Growth.[3] Assam has only one Municipal Corporation – the Guwahati Municipal Corporation, constituted in 1974 as per "The GMC Act, 1969". Except in Morigaon and NC Hills district, all other districts have at least one municipal board each. Nagaon district has the highest number of MBs, i.e., 3, while Karbi Anglong has 6 TCs, the largest number. The largest number of CT being constituted in Kamrup is 7.

The census data highlight that Palasbari though very old, is the smallest Municipal Board in Assam, both in size and population containing only a meager 4,741 population.[4] This number is even less than the existing town committees of Assam barring Dokmoka T.C. of Karbi Anglong and the Howraghat TC (KA) containing 4670 and 4659 population respectively. According to 1991 census the size of the Palasbari Municipal Board is only a very microscopic 1.03 sq. km. while the size was 2.67 sq. km. in 1971, a rapid decrease of 1.64 sq. km. in 10 years. The size is gradually declining due to severe and continuous erosion. Palasbari MB, which is our prime focus, however has a tragic past history for its present dilapidated condition which needs a closer scrutiny.

A Brief History of Palasbari Municipal Board

The old historically famous town, a very crucial and growing commercial centre of Assam, Palasbari was totally obliterated, it had grown to its credit to be absolutely collapsed in the far-flung and lies in the sandy river bed of the mighty Brahmaputra 50 years back and now in oblivion. Palasbari had a very rich commercial heritage and was having more potentialities to grow into a great city, unfortunately drowned in the Brahmaputra with ceturies old resources and habitats and the destruction was almost completed by 1959 when it was in the brunt of reshaping in the line of urbanization with the newly constituted Palasbari Municipal Board in 1954.

Palasbari was a predominant business and trade centre and in fact, was one of the leading wholesale markets of Assam. A moderate township had developed during the last part of the 19th century. The town was thickly populated and initially was rich in forest, agriculture, timber, *Muga Silk, Paat,* Jute and other commercial goods. Later, as a result of rapid development of non-agricultural economy its environment was in the offing. The inherent enriched infrastructure, trade and marketing feasibilities and transportation advantages, virtually attracted the big Indian business to it and as a result, internal migration from Rajasthan, Gujarat, Bihar and Bengal was started in the 19th century. The *Marwaris* are the dominant migrants to Palasbari and have strong grip over commercial and trading capital. But significantly, they do not flaunt their superiority in language and culture of this area and have only indirect and tacit role in its municipal politics.[5]

Palasbari as a town predominalty inhabited by caste Hindu Asamiyas,[6] had all the potentialities, infrastructures, civic amenities like schools, hospitals, oil storage, markets, colonies, communication channels, government offices, non agricultural inputs, play ground, burial places, water supply facilities and all and had become the communication linkage and gateway of Northern and Southern banks of the district of Kamrup including Gauhati. Prior to 1962, when Saraighat bridge was inaugurated, it was not only the connecting link of North and South Kamrup rather it was the main trading and business channel between Gauhati (Guwahati) and Calcutta (Kolkata) and had become a hinterland of Indian big business and the British colonial rulers. Frequent trade shipping between Palasbari and Calcutta had enhanced the urban status of the town. It is assumed, Palasbari would have become a great city and a merger with Guwahati had it not been in the trap of erosion some five decades back. It is very depressive to note that this nascent, enriched and up-growing township covering a vast area of not less than 8-10 kms. radius had been washed away and totally destroyed within years following severe erosion swallowing all human efforts, habitats, fertile lands, houses, high-rises, civic built ups, properties and enriched ecology.

Today, original Palasbari town is in the heart of the vastness of Brahmaputra and it has become a barren sandbank lying on northern bank of the river. The original site and location of the Palasbari town *vis-à-vis* the Brahmaputra river can be gleaned in the map, and the outrage and mass destruction of erosion in 1954 can be observed in the photographs.[7] The town was vanished and perished by 1959 and its people had shifted elsewhere. Majority of Hindu natives were shifted and settled at Mirza and the *Marwari* business strata had established residential and business houses at Uparhali later naming as Bijoynagar. Seven *Marwari* families had settled down at Fancy Bazar and two families at Pandu. Bengalis, *Biharis* and others are scattered everywhere. However, a section of the native inhabitants of this illfated town remained at the outskirts of old Palasbari. Though the newly settled area is also known as Palasbari, it is just a periphery and consists only a fifth of the original. Yet Palasbari still clutched at the remnants of its past glory with its old, but now weak Municipal Board. Hence, Palasbari is divided into three parts – old outskirts – that is Palasbari, Mirza and Bijoynagar.

Palabari had village status up to 1918 and gradually developed all necessary prerequisites to be recognized as a town.

The village was originally comprising of altogether eleven *paras* stretching over 1.5 sq. mile.[8] The name of these paras were Ojapara, Satudharpara, Balapara, Dewapara, Nowabari, Janarpar, Satupara, Gandhipara, Charalpara and Deuriapara. However, in later years the township had crossed the historically specific boundary and assumed far and wide dimensions.

Palasbari was multi-caste, multi-racial and multilingual town. Caste Hindu *Asamiyas* were the dominant groups including the scheduled castes. Very significantly, there was no tribal domiciled and Muslims were also very microscopic. Besides, the migrants from Rajasthan, there were migrants from erstwhile East Pakisthan (now Bangladesh) and West Bengal called the '*Mosai*'and *'Sarkar'* , *Mandals* from Koch Bihar, the Biharis, *Mutias* and Gujarati migrants. The only Muslim family and the *Marwari Jains* gave multi-religious status to Palasbari. These migrant-groups contributed much towards the richness of composite culture and language of this part of Assam. In fact, it was an excellent example of human assimilation and conglomeration largely through the media of business, trade and commercial exchange followed by cultural and linguistic contact and social interactions resulted in the growth of a town. Constant trade and business cooperation, economic interactions and exchanges helped in the development of this area in the line of modernization. In spite of having some leading centres like Boko, Chhaygaon and Rani, Palabari has grown spectacularly to have an urban setting.

The map of old Palabari demonstrates all necessary prerequisites of a town. First, the ecology, folk-urban continuum and dimension and geographical environment including climate were congenial. Second, inland transportation to Bengal and shipping business was advantageous. Third, the 37th National Highway went through it which connected it with the rest of the state. Fourth, the Palasbari-Loharghat road established good communication link with Meghalaya. Fifth, population was also adequate for the growth of a township and non-agricultural activities were also predominant. Road and inland transportation were feasible which made it easier for import and export of commodities and commercial goods and services.

The leading contributors of the growth of Palasbari as a commercial centre and transforming it into a town were the *Marwaris, Mosais, Biharis, Mutias, Mandals, Sarkars* and other migrants and the native indigenous people had extended active cooperation and involved in such business and helped in the growth of the township. It is known that the Marwari trading giants and merchants were keen to adapt with *Asamiya* society, culture and language, though basically profit was their chief motive of investment. The later Rajasthani *Marwaris* had constructed the Palasbari market, schools and some other built ups on the line of North Indian architecture. This market was known as *Kayar Gola*. They also established a Marwari Dispensary, *Hanuman Mandir* and a big *Jain Mandir*. A guest house was constructed in 1954. There was only one primary school established at the dawn of the 19th century. In 1920 the R.B. High School was established. The school was originally donated by Rid Karan Balchand Cheraugi. But later in 1977 it was provincialised. Jogesh Tamuli was the first Head Master. Students from far and wide including north Kamrup studied in this premier institution. In 1960, it was shifted to the present site at Mirza.

Though erosion was started in 1933, it launched its final mission in 1954 to destroy Palasbari altogether, which totally ceased the developmental process and its urban growth has been exclusively retarded. The nascent Palasbari town came to end, but the central and the state Government remained as silent spectators, indifferent and reluctant to save it from the trap of erosion. Though the government proposed to establish a planned town at Mirza, unfortunately, the then Finance Minister of Assam Matiram Bora had tacitly withdrawn the allotted money and transferred the scheme to Nagaon.

Genesis and Growth of Municipality at Palasbari

Embracing centuries old heritage and glory, spearheading the process of development, Palasbari got township status in 1918. The colonial government after monitoring the commercial and business importance and future potentialities, was pleased to form the first ever Town Union Committee at Palasbari following the relentless efforts of Kaliram Boruah and good will of Manik Ch. Baruah. Meanwhile, the density of population was considerably increased at that time and the demographic structure and composition was also qualitatively transformed into diversity. The conjectured population in 1918 was 3,800 or more.[9]

The first Chairman of the Palasbari Union was late Kaliram Baruah, the then Mauzadar of Chayani Mouza. There is no record of the other members of the union. Since 1918 the Palasbari Union had taken up egalitarian measures for the upliftment of the town and mobilized resources to meet the Union expenditures. Between 1918-37, the Union took up developmental and progressive measures to provide civic amenities such as street lamp, water supply, drainage, construction and repairing of roads and bridges and cleaning public places. The provision of tube-well was made in 1922 throughout the town for drinking water. The Union first appointed sweeper from a "*Bongalia*" community to remove carcasses and night garbages and cleaning the markets. The Bonsfor community sweepers also cleaned the latrines and urinals.

The formation and elections of Palasbari Union was not regular. In 1924, Purna Ch. Paul was nominated as Chairman to the Union. He was an Assamese caste Hindu and was belonging to "*Kumar*" sub-caste. Record is not available as to the formation of Palasbari Union and later Town Committee upto 1944. The Palasbari Union was replaced and transformed into Palasbari Town Committee (PTC) in 1937. In 1944, Narendra Nath Baruah was elected Chairman and in 1947 Abhay Ch. Thakuria was elected as Chairman. Late Dharmeswar Das had then taken over the charge as ad-hoc Chairman. He remained in office in between 1950-53.

During early fifties, the population of Palasbari had grown into more heterogeneous form than before. The number of Rajasthani migrants increased. The total number of *Marwari* population was approximately 3000 or more. The conjectured density of population in 1954 was 450 and above per sq. km. and the total conjectured number of population was 15,000 or slightly less.[10] Trade and business of the town was extended and internal migration rate also increased. We have already indicated that Palasbari was not an industrial town and was basically a commercial town. In the early part of the fifties the trade of *Eri, Muga, Pal* and Jute commodities were fast expanded and specifically, jute were exported in huge quantities from Palasbari to various parts of the country via Calcutta. Timber trade was also gaining momentum and the range of other economic activities were enlarged. Viewing the on going resourcefulness and for systematic management, the Government of Assam had brought Palasbari under municipal governance creating the Palasbari Municipal Board (PMB) in 1954. Late Gondho Ram Kalita was the first elected Chairman and Dhiren Ch. Kalita was the first Vice-Chairman. This committee enjoyed full term of four years and continued up to 1958. But the tragic fact was that before the newly constituted Municipal Board started functioning systematically to built up this town, Palasbari had fallen in death trap following devastating erosion.

The election to the municipal board was irregular. Since its inception in 1954, municipal elections were only held in 1954, 1967,

1972, 1978, 1992 and in 1997 respectively.[11] Ad-hoc committees were formed in 1958, 1963, 1967, 1985 and in 1986 respectively.[12] The last municipal election was held on 16.6.1997. After completion of 5 years term on 19.8.02, the present board has been functioning on ad-hoc basis as per government order. No election is held uptill now.

Distribution of Power and Social Bases

Though old Palasbari was eroded, yet its political machinery, the PMB is not abolished and is still functioning though in weak manner. Though it loses credibility and competence to some extent, to function properly in the absence of its old jurisdiction and resources, it has still been working by distributing the shares of power to the people in the outskirts of the parent area.

Though the boundary of the present Palasbari is relatively very small, marginal both in size and population, yet the entire area is subdivided into 10 wards for operational convenience and each ward sends one representative to the Board through secret ballot on the basis of adult universal suffrage.

It is worthwhile to mention that we do not get necessary records of members, either elected or nominated to the Palasbari Unions and Town Committee between 1918-53. However, we have got the information of the Chairman. During these 35 years (1919-1953) altogether 5 Chairmen were either elected or nominated. Out of these 3 were Kalitas, one S.C. while the other was OBC. The first chairan was graduate while the others were matriculates.

From the available data, it appears that since 1918 to 1971, no woman was elected to the Board as member. In 1972 Rajani Bala Das was elected and in 1985 Junu Das was nominated to the Board. But the situation was changed from 1993 onward. The Constitution 74th Amendment Act transformed the pattern of representation to the urban local bodies. According to this Act, 30 per cent of the total seats shall be reserved for SC/ST and for women.[13] The PMB has also managed to seek SC and women representation in it and as a result four women were elected to the Board in 1997. Thus, we can infer that women take part in the decision making process in the Municipalities.

TABLE – 1

Caste Distribution in the Palasbari Municipal Board (1954-1997)

Caste/Office Bearers	*Members*	*Chairman*	*Vice-Chairman*	*Total*
Brahmin	01(1.4)			01(1.3)
Kayastha	02(2.8)		01(10.00)	03(3.2)
Kalita	22(31.00)	1(10.00)	06(54.00)	28(31.5)
Keot	05(7.00)	01(10.00)		06(6.5)
OBC	29(41.00)	08(80.00)	02(18.00)	39(42.4)
MOBC	02(2.8)			02(2.1)
SC	08(11.2)			08(8.7)
Marwari	01(1.4)		02(18.00)	03(3.2)
Bengali/ Gujarati	01(14)			01(1.3)
Total	71(100)	10(100)	11(100)	92(100)

Source: Primary data generated by the investigator.

The figures in parentheses indicate percentage to total.

Observing the history of representation, we find that Late Dharmeswar Das had either been nominated or elected as chairman to the Board for 7 consecutive terms since 1953 except in 1986 and elected as a member in 1978. He remained Chairman upto 1992.

The nature of distribution of power in society by the Board can only be understood in terms of the variables such as caste, education, religion, income and possession of properties (economic status). We fail to collect data on economic background of the members. The distribution of caste can be observed in Table 1.

The data demonstrate that of the total of 71 members between 1954-97 the OBC groups find the largest representation constituting 41 per cent. Next to the OBCs, the Kalitas find 31 per cent of the total membership. The SC has only 11.2 per cent representations. The Brahmins have an extremely microscopic representation, while the representation of Kayastha, Keot, MOBC, Marwari, Bengali and Gujaratis are negligible. The data show that the OBCs also have claimed 80 per cent chairmanships in the Board possessing overwhelming dominance in totality between 1954-97. However, the Kalitas have dominated the post of Vice-Chairmanship constituting 54 per cent. Thus we find that since its inception the PMB has been dominating by the OBCs constituting 42.4 per cent followed by the Kalitas constituting 31.5 per cent. The educational background can be observed in Table 2.

The analysis reveals that the position of chairmanship was exclusively held by the persons having qualification of intermediate stage constituting 90 per cent followed by only one graduate. The position of Vice-Chairmanship was dominated by non-matrics, constituting 45.5 per cent followed by intermediates (27.3 per cent). We find that the membership of the Board was also largely claimed by the non-matrics constituting 38 per cent followed by matriculates constituting 35 per cent. There were no illiterates and only a few were barely literates. The position of P.U./H.S. level and graduation was negligible. Thus the PMB was dominated by the non-matriculates and intermediates, and the highly qualified persons seem to have little or no attraction to be member of the Board. Occupationally, the Board was dominated by businessmen, traders, landlords (small and medium) and social and political workers. It

Table – 2

Educational status of the members and Chairpersons of the Palasbari Municipal Board (1954-97)

Positions/ Level of Education	*Illiterate*	*Barely literate*	*Non-Matric*	*Matri-culation*	*PU/HS*	*Inter-mediate*	*Graduate*	*Total*
Chairman	-	-	-	-	-	9(90)	01(10)	10(100)
Vice-Chairman	-	-	05(45.5)	02(18)	02(18)	03(27.3)	01(9.2)	11(100)
Members	-	05(7.2)	27(38)	25(35)	6(8.5)	06(8.5)	02(2.8)	71(100)
Total	-	05(5.4)	32(35)	27(29.3)	6(6.5)	18(19.5)	4(4.3)	92(100)

Source: Primary data generated by the investigator.

*The figures in parentheses indicate percentage to total

is difficult to know the economic status of the members and chairmen because of the non-availability of authentic data. However, it is learnt that the members and chairpersons were economically sound.

Role of Political Parties in the Elections

We have no sufficient data at hand regarding the role of political parties in the municipal elections. The elections were contested at the individual level and not on party banners upto 1985. The Board, nominated in 1986, was however largely dominated by the Congress (I) when the party secured eight seats while the AGP secured only two seats.[14] In the next elections held in 1992 again the Congress (I) swept away the municipal poll securing eight seats while the AGP secured two seats. However the Board formed in 1997 was exclusively won by the AGP.

Intrastructure, Management and Role

Since the total obliteration of the original town, area in the PMB jurisdiction has been marginalized and people also lost confidence in it. The low-density of population, decline of trade and business and decline of larger number of people depending on non-agricultural activities make it a very weak municipal government. Fees and market collections are very scanty. Due to wanton financial crunch and non-availability of income generating sources, the Board has to struggle hard for its existence. It has one small office at Palasbari with poor infrastructural facilities. In the absence of slaughter house, dead animals are disposed of in the Brahmaputra. However, water supply provision is adequate in Palasbari. Every household has own tube-well. The Board fails to take steps to provide maternity house, guest house, vaccination, burial ground, parks, gardens and all.

However, the Board looks into the maintenance of streets and roads and their improvements. Ghats, wells, channels, drains, latrines, public urinals within the municipal areas are constructed. Streets, markets and toilets are cleaned by municipal sweepers. Relief is being given in times of flood scarcity and in other natural calamities. The Board has constructed a road, one concrete bridge and also has done a lot for the development of the market. The acute financial crisis renders the Board helpless to work for the betterment of the urban dwellers. Even the Board has failed to pay the monthly salary of its employees for the last 20 months. The government of Assam has not paid the motor vehicles tax to the Board for the last four years, nor it releases any grant. Usually all expenditures have been incurred from various taxes, house rents, licence fees, market collections and sale proceeds of daily market etc. But this earning is not adequate to meet the huge expenditures. The Board submits the annual budget estimates before the government every year including the planned expenditure details. But the budget is remained chronically untouched by the government as is reported. During the financial year 2002-03 the PMB submitted a budget amounting to a total of Rs. 60,38,923.00 covering its own sundry sources. The Board has to receive grants from the state government. It is very depressive to note that even the Board has a huge arrear of money to receive from its own sundry sources amounting to a total of Rs. 47,55,79.00. Had the Board received the amount both from the arrear sector and from the government, it would have been possible to expedite the developmental works and to make up the large amount of deficits.

Recently the PMB has prepared a plan and applied to the government for the realization and spearheading its unfinished works. The planning includes low cost sanitary latrine, construction and repairing of markets, construction of public toilet, cremation ground, construction of dwelling houses under Ambedkar Abas Jojona, gravelling of interior roads and bridges, self-employment generation schemes for educated youths and many others amounting to a total of Rs. 79,23359.00. But despite repeated efforts being made by the Board, this amount has not yet been released.[15]

Field investigation reveals that the PMB got Rs.3,87,620.00 during 1998-2001 from several heads of the government. The amount was reportedly spent in the construction and repairing of flood damaged roads. In 1999 the Board received Rs. 1,25,000 from the MLA fund and it was spent on the construction of bridges. Besides another grant of Rs. 2,31,000.00 was released from the MLA fund in 2000 for the total electrification of all the roads of the municipal area. But very depressively, this task has not been performed uptill now and the entire amount reportedly is lying unused at the ASEB office of Mirza.[16]

Staffing Pattern

At present the PMB has 6 grade-iii employees, 5 grade iv employees and 6 part-time sweepers. There is one Head Asstt., one Asstt. Engineer, one Tax Daroga, one Office Asstt., one supervisor, one Moharrior, office peon, Tax collector and a Tube-well operator. The part-time sweepers are working on fixed pay while the rest are permanent. Monthly salary payments are made from its own earning sources. The Board has codified the service rules, regulations and conditions of its employees in 1997. There is no sub-committee so formed to plan and expedite the works of the Board, though, generally, big municipalities work through sub-committees in modern times.

Concluding Observation and Future Prospect

The above discussion reveals that though a lot of urban centres have been identified by the government, the process of urbanization in Assam is extremely lethargic and the growth rate is also slow. In Assam though the government has set up Municipal Boards, Town Committees in several urban centres, these urban bodies fail to function properly in the absence of positive attention.

The government does not allocate necessary fund for urban development. Those urban bodies which have sufficient market collections and adequate earnings from their own sundry sources somehow function, but these having poor earnings are struggling hard for their existence. As information obtained from municipal sources, at present, the Barpets MB, Howli T.C., Barpets Road M.B., Jorhat M.B., Tezpur M.B., Dibrugarh M.B., Silchar M.B., Tinsukia M.B. and Karimganj M.B. are to some extent working as urban government because of adequate market collections. But the financial conditions of other municipalities are poor and become victim of government's apathy.

But the financial condition of Palasbari Municipal Board is probably the worst for which its move to urban road is extremely slow and the board's activity has become marginalized. The above discussion reveals that before its matured growth as a modern town it was vanished but still the PMB remains in its outskirts and hardly working rather in a narrow confinement. Therefore, Palasbari needs a closer and fresh attention. In order for survival of this old Municipal Board the present jurisdiction and its boundary must be expanded.

We have indicated earlier that after erosion Palasbari was sub-divided into three adjacent parts – Palasbari, Mirza and Bijoynagar. As most of the original inhabitants were shifted to Mirza and Bijoynagar, Palasbari lost its size and population. Therefore, it may be advantageous for proper functioning of the MB and for rapid growth and future development of the town, these three sister parts need to be united and merged together with its historic Palasbari Municipal Board. Unless a merger is taking place, one cannot find a bright future prospect and good management of this urban body. However, public opinion needs to be formed in order to avoid the status-quo. The present chairman suggested that the municipal office maybe shifted to Mirza. The Central

Government has released a grant of Rs. 90,00000.00 to Palasbari M.B. for the provision of supply of pure drinking water. The constructed water tank has a capacity of 2 lakhs litres, but Palasbari needs only 40,000 litres a day. The remaining 1 lac 60 thousand litres of drinking water may be supplied at Mirza. The entire amount is not spent in the water supply provision, which needs to be reckoned with.

We assume that Palasbari still has sufficient potentials to grow as a prosperous modern big town if the merger takes place. While understanding the self-perception of the PMB on this issue, the Board invariably suggests merger of Palasbari with Mirza and Bijoynagar, in times to come. In addition to a possible merger and unification, both the Central as well as the State government should immediately take appropriate measures to stop further erosion of the Brahmaputra, so that natural history as was occurred 50 years back, does not repeat itself to create the second great tragedy with respect to this potential town, Palasbari.

References

1. Census of India, 2001, Provisional Population Total, series
2. *Ibid.*
3. 'Out Growth' is generally means a natural development of a big town or city, here it means a suburb of the present town having all urban characteristics.
4. Government of Assam, Statistical Hand Book of Assam, 2002, Directorate of Economics and Statistics, Assam, Guwahati, pp. 6-13
5. See for a detail discussion on Marwari domiciled in the State of Assam (i) Das, J.K Society and Legislature" A Study of Social Background of the Eighth Assam Legislative Assembly", Unpublished Ph.D. thesis, Gauhati Unv.,

   ICSSR Documentation Centre, New Delhi, 1995. Also see for a discussion of Social groups of Assam Vis-à-vis Asamiya nationality

Question (ii) Das, J.K. "Society of Assam: A Study of Groups, their Structures and Status", Indian Journal of Politics, AMU, Vol. XXXV, Nos. 1-2, Jan-June, 2001, pp. 85-103.

6. The term "Asamiya" is used to mean the 'Asamiya' speaking population of Assam. Our usage covers the Asamiya speaking groups of Palasbari.
7. These Photographs of old Palasbari were published in the Souvenir, Golden Jubilee issue, Palasbari Rash Mahotsava, Palasbari, 1996, pp. 11-14. The Map of old Palasbari was also published in the same journal, it is a revised version of this map prepared by Prabin Ch. Das. The present Map is compiled by Prof. Homeshwar Das of D.K. College.
8. See Choudhury, Bhabani, 'Palasbarir Itihashat Abhumuki', Souviner 1996, *ibid.* p.4.
9. *Ibid.*, p.11-12.
10. *Ibid.* p. 10. The present Palasbari Municipal Board informs the investigator that in 1965 the scheme or a planned town at Mirza was prepared and the process was started. But because of opposition from quarters, the then Sarat Sinha government had abolished the town planning scheme in 1972 even after a gazetted notice being served, published and issued by the government, in this regard.
11. Palasbari Municipal Board Office Record.
12. Palasbari Municipal Board Office Record.
13. Ibid. The record of 1958 Ad-hoc committee was not found.
14. See for detail discussion on urban local government in India, Maheswari, S.R. "Local Government in India", L.N. Agarwall publication, Agra, pp. 178-240. The constitution 73rd and 74th Amendment Act was extracted in this book.
15. Palasbari Municipal Board Office Record.
16. Information obtained from the present Chairman of Palasbari Municipal Board.

10

Role Conflict Among Elected Woman Representatives in Urban Local Government

U.B. Singh

Women who constitute half of the human race can certainly play a key role in influencing the cause of history as well as shaping the destiny of mankind. Since time immemorial women are being treated as inferior human and their position is looked down as general subordination to men irrespective of the position they hold in and outside their family. Generally in almost all the societies, women play most important roles towards family starting from childhood, through motherhood till the late stage of life. From generation to generation they help not only propagation and continuing hereditary lineage but also a conscience factor for social structure and an adhesive for family semblance. Irrespective of their contribution to family and society, they were looked down upon through ages.

But recent years have brought great change in the life of women all over the world, influencing their attitudes, values, aspirations, ways of feeling and acting for effective participation in all walks of life.

One of the main enduring consequences of the recent social evaluation for women has been their emancipation from their traditional bond ethos both legally and politically by the virtue of various acts and statutes.

Now women have expanded the role of housewife into dominant, mature feminine role. Urbanisation, education and employment which were the contributors of social evaluation have provided them with new avenues to express and assert themselves. The changed social milieu along with new wave of modernization has altered roles and relationship drastically. Indian urban women have come out of the four walls of their homes in search of economic gain as well as fulfillment of their personal hopes and desires. By coming out of their homes in gainful employment and social participation they have added new roles to their old roles of mother and wife.

Being subjected to the dual demands of home and work, which are often antagonistic in nature, the working mother is liable to experience role conflict. In addition to the biological function she has to perform and the culturally defined roles in which she has to act, she is confronted with responsibilities and duties connected with her employment/profession. The dual responsibilities not only overload her but may be so incompatible that they cannot be performed properly. Having less time and more cogent demands of dual roles the working women experience more and more role conflict.

While analyzing the roles of women it is important to focus on the general status of Indian women. The social status of women in India is comparatively lower than many other countries of the world. Though Constitution of India guarantees 'Equality of Status' to women, they do not enjoy full equality in the society. The vast majority of women are illiterate, underpaid, exploited and disadvantaged. They have been suppressed to inferior positions in society, completely dominated by men. But in urban areas with the spread of education and increase in the number of working women outside their homes, the situation is gradually changing. Women have risen above socio-cultural tradition and well defined roles of housewife and gradually evolved into dual and more self fulfilling roles of working woman and a housewife. The major contributing factors for such a change are better education, changing socio-cultural values and need for supplementary income due to inflation. But despite these changes Indian society remains 'Male dominated'.

Women in India: A Profile

In India the plight of women is no better than that of women in other developing countries. Despite the honour and reverence accorded as deities, the general reality speaks otherwise. In a patriarchal society like India, the unfounded belief that only man is the bread winner, the male child gets the best of the limited facilities and resources within the family and the girl child runs the risk of being aborted.

The sex ratio is an important social indicator to measure the extent of prevailing equity between males and females in a society at any given point of time. According to census of India 2001, the sex ratio stands at 933 for country as a whole (1991 census recorded 927 females per 1000 males) which is a welcome improvement. The table below indicates the sex ratio of total population in selected states in the country.

With regards to literacy rate the population of literates for country as a whole in 2001 worked out to be 65.38 per cent. The corresponding figures for males and females are 75.85 per cent and 54.16 per cent, thus showing male and female literacy rate gap of 21.69 per cent. The table below shows literacy rate and sex in selected states.

Table I.1
Sex Ratio (2001)

State	*Sex ratio (females per 1000 males)* 1991	2001
Uttar Pradesh	876	898
Uttaranchal	936	964
Bihar	907	921
Jharkhand	922	941
Orissa	971	972
Chattisgarh	985	990
M.P.	912	920
India	927	933

Source: Provisional Population Tables, Census of India 2001, Series 1, paper 1 of 2001, statement 10, p. 02-03.

Despite the fact that women are massively involved in almost all sectors of economy their activities as producers are not reflected in National Income Statistics, thus making their contribution unrecognized and invisible. Human Development Report (2003) has highlighted that $11 trillion worth of unpaid or invisible economic activity is performed by women world wide. In fact they contribute more than half of the wealth of nations, yet they are denied economic, social and even political and legal rights and privileges that such a valuable contribution is entitled.

Table I.2
States by literacy rate (sex-wise) (2001)
(Percent)

Statos	*Persons*	*Males*	*Females)*
Uttaranchal	72.28	84.01	60.26
Chattisgarh	65.18	77.86	52.40
Orissa	63.61	75.95	50.97
M.P.	64.11	76.80	50.28
Jharkhand	54.13	67.94	39.38
Uttar Pradesh	57.36	70.23	42.98
All India	65.38	75.85	54.16

Source: Provisional Population Tables, Census of India 2001.

Constitutional and Legal Rights of Indian Women

In India, during both pre and post Independence periods, various enactments have been legislated for protection and upliftment of women. The framers of the supreme law of the land realized the unequal status of women and assured that women get equal rights. The preamble to the Constitution itself secures to all Indian citizens 'Justice' – social, economic and political, 'Liberty' – of thought, expression, and 'Equality'- of status and opportunity. It further resolves to promote among all citizens 'Fraternity' assuring the dignity of the individual.

The Constitution in Articles 14, 15 and 16 guarantees the principle of equality as fundamental rights.

Art. 14 – Equality before law

Art.15 – Prohibition of discrimination on grounds of religion, race, caste, sex or place of birth

Art.16 – Equality of opportunity in matters of public employment.

Apart from the various Constitutional rights several enactments have been passed for protection and upliftment of women. Some of the major social enactments relating to women are:

- Hindu Marriage Act, 1955
- Hindu Succession Act, 1956
- Hindu Adoption and Maintenance Act, 1956
- Women's and Children's Institution (licensing) Act, 1956
- Dowry Prohibition Act, 1961
- Medical Termination of Pregnancy Act, 1971
- Family Courts Act, 1984
- Indecent Presentation of Women's Act, 1986
- National Commission for Women, 1992
- National Commission on Human Rights, 1993
- 73rd and 74th Constitution Amendment Acts, 1992
- Women Empowerment Policy, 2001

In addition to the constitutional provisions and enactments, the Five Year Plans have also focused on women development which has contributed greatly on the upliftment, development and empowerment of women in all sectors.

Women in Politics

Political rights of women are right to vote, to contest elections, to hold political office and to vote in legislature. Equal participation of women in political life plays a pivotal role in the process of their advancement, development and empowerment and also strengthening the role in governance and decision making structures at all levels.

Historically women have played a very significant role in the growth and development of parliamentary democracy in India. They have held important positions both in the legislature and government. Their contribution to the growth and development of parliamentary procedures and practices are in no sense less significant than their male counterparts.

A study of Indian history indicates that women of royal families besides being expert in knowledge of science and arts, used to learn politics and warfare. They were housewives as well as secretary to their husbands. Kautilya has mentioned in 20th chapter of his book 'Arthshastra' that women were main part of Mauryan courts. Manu has not found any difference between men and women in administration. Although since, olden times women belonging to privileged class have been providing active assistance to their husbands in politics, common women had no entry in the administrative set up, only women of royal families used to participate.

Indian women's involvement in politics in the modern era started in the late 18th century. Although British imperialism profoundly influenced the political engagement of both elite and non-elite women, its impact on the character and the purpose of their engagement was very different. During the freedom movement, many women leaders actively participated and strongly advocated the protection of women's interest and their rights. Prior to 1926 women could not become the member of any assembly. From 1926 only nominated women could become member of legislative assemblies but they had no voting rights.

In 1935 when new Indian Act was framed, women also started demanding privileges on par with men, but their demand was given a deaf ear. In 1937 elections, women contested from reserved seats. Only 41 seats were reserved for them in whole of India. Smt. R.B. Subharayan became the member of state council and Smt. Renuka Ray became member of central legislative council. But overall in pre-independence era women have no political privileges.

In Independent India, the Constitution after guaranteeing equality to women in all spheres, left their political representation to their own willingness, opportunity and support. Several committees on local self government advocated reservation for women representation at grass root level as no initiative was seen to encourage their participation at high levels of legislature, which was thought exclusive domain of elite class. Balwantrai Mehta Committee (1957) suggested a token co-option of two members in rural local bodies. The Committee on Status of Women in India was set up in 1971 to look into all aspects of women's status in India with a special focus on their political participation. The committee recommended separate women panchayats at the village level. To make women's political right more functional and to give them more opportunities to participate in the formal political places, the Committee recommended that political parties fix a quota for women candidates. It also proposed allotting a block of seats to women in municipal councils. The committee recommended the setting up of permanent independent commission on women at both state and national levels.

The National Perspective Plan for Women was drawn up as a long term action blueprint for 1988-2000 but women's groups pointed out several short comings in its approach, coverage and methodology. National Commission for Women set up in 1992 has initiated planning process involving women and protecting their interests. However the 73rd and 74th Amendment Acts become the watershed for women's political empowerment at the grassroot political institutions and providing for not less than one-third of seats reserved for women in rural and urban local bodies in the country.

Representation of Women in Legislature

The Constitution of India has granted women equal rights but in practice these rights have no meaning due to their poor representation in legislative bodies. Even after five decades of functioning democracy women's participation and role in political life has been low.

Table I.3
Women's Representation in Lok Sabha

Year	*Total Seats*	*No. of women Members*	*Percentage*
1952-57	489	14	2.8
1957-62	494	18	3.6 (60.0)
1962-67	494	30	6.0 (50.0)
1967-71	520	31	6.0 (44.8)
1971-77	520	20	3.8 (24.4)
1977-80	542	19	3.5 (27.1)
1980-84*	529	28	5.3 (19.7)
1984-89	542	42	7.7 (25.6)
1989-91**	523	23	4.4 (13.6)
1991	536	39	7.2 (12.0)
1996	543	40	7.3 (6.7)
1998	543	43	7.9 (15.7)
1999	543	49	9.02 (17.3)
2004	543	44	8.01 (12.4)

Source: Election Commission of India

*Elections were not held in 12 constitutencies in Assam and in Meghalaya

**Elections were not held in J & K and Punjab; figures include women elected from Punjab during by elections in 1992.

Figures in parentheses denote percentage winning of woman candidates.

During 1952 to 1996 representation of women in Lok Sabha shows their per seat candidature as low as 0.30 per cent. The ratio of women candidates have been computed as 3.2 per cent. During 1952-1999 in Lok Sabha on an average there were 31 women members in the House of 528, constituting 5.95 per cent. The most populated state of Uttar Pradesh sent only 6 members accounting for 19.35 per cent. Women representation from U.P. was recorded highest (9 members) in 1996, 1998 and 1999. In 2004 general elections seven major political parties put only 133 women candidates which was little more than one-tenth of their total candidates.

Table I.4

Women's Representation in Rajya Sabha

Year	*Total Seats*	*No. of women Members*	*Percentage*
1952	219	16	7.3
1957	237	18	7.6
1962	238	18	7.6
1967	240	20	8.3
1971	243	17	7.0
1977	244	25	10.2
1980	244	24	9.8
1985	244	28	11.4
1990	245	24	9.7
1991	245	38	16.5
1992	245	17	6.9
1994	245	20	8.1
1996	245	18	7.3
1997	245	18	7.3
1998	245	18	7.3

Source : Election Commission of India.

Women's representation in Rajya Sabha during 1952 to 1968 demonstrates that women members as an average comprised 8.8 per cent only. The table below shows that even in Rajya Sabha where there is indirect election and members come through nomination there has been low representation of women.

The status of representation of women in state legislatures has also not been upto the mark. During 1952 to 1997 average representation of women in state legislatures was recorded just 4.0 per cent. In the state of Uttar Pradesh the average number of women members during 1946-47 to 1996 has been computed as 15 members constituting 3.80 per cent of the House. In the U.P. State Assembly elections of 2002, 341 women contested out of which only 26 got elected. Thus the success rate has been quite low.

Women in Urban Local Government

The interest in women in local governance has recently developed at global, national and local levels and providing some statistics on women's representation in politics world wide to help put people's concerns into perspective. It is seen that development of women's movement at local level, operating through the processes of civil society where women have worked individually and collectively in autonomous women's groups to further their cause and raise awareness of women's continuing disadvantageous position has not yielded desired results.

The number of women in politics at local level prior to 1993 has been very small and their influence negligible. The insignificant presence of women at these levels was an important indicator of two basic facts: one that women who are planted at the top often lacked the kind of training required for effective participation, secondly the society was unable to accept women in politics, particularly at the grass-root level. Due to their secondary status and low esteem, most of them were denied entry in political decision making.

The 73rd and 74th Amendments to the Constitution have provided one third reservation of seats for women in grassroot governance. The participation of women in local self institutions is considered essential not only for ensuring political participation in the governance but also for realizing the developmental goals of urban and rural development. Participation of women in these local bodies involves: (i) women as voters, (ii) women as member of political parties, (iii) women as candidates, (iv) women as making planning, implementation and monitoring and evaluation of programmes, (v) women as member of various committees, core groups, associations, task force etc. The emergence of women power structure into panchayats and municipal institutions is a milestone in achieving socio-economic development from different quarters.

The 74th Constitution Amendment Act 1992 has served as a major break - through towards ensuring women's equal access and increased participation in local government. This Act ensures constitutional guarantees to safeguard the interest of urban local self governments to enable them to function as effective democratic and self governing institutions at the grassroot level. The Amendment provides for reservation of one-third of elected seats for women at level of local government in urban areas. There is also identical reservation for women at the post of chairpersons of these local government units.

The 74th Constitution Amendment has ushered a new era in the democratic process of the country by not only providing constitutional status to the municipal bodies but has also provided an enabling environment for women to directly participate in local self government and has brought women to the forefront and centre of local development. Involvement of women in the political arena and in decision making roles are an important tool for empowerment as well as monitoring standards of political performance at local level.

As a consequence, a very active role for women in local governance is envisaged as compared to governance at the state and national levels in India. These provisions have provided great opportunities and challenges to women in India, particularly in the field of local government. This is of great significance, since this grass root level participation has considerably broaden the base of women's participation in politics at city level.

In the state of Uttar Pradesh, 223 women Presidents were elected in municipal institutions in 1995. Similarly 4243 women ward members were also elected. Moreover women represented more than one-third share in Nagar Palika Parishads and Nagar Panchayats. Women have been elected against their reservation for the weaker sections i.e. Scheduled Tribes, Scheduled Castes and other Backward Classes as well as general castes. Women's representation in case of Chairman/President was reported least in Nagar Nigams (27.27 per cent) and slightly higher than mandatory in Nagar Palika Parishads (33.38 per cent) and Nagar Panchayats (33.41 per cent). Similarly women as corporators/ members had much higher share in Nagar Panchayats (37.49 per cent) and Nagar Palika Parishads (35.77 per cent) while just one third (33.61 per cent) in Nagar Nigams. There was no representation of ST (either male or female) as President/Mayor, while a few members of the community were elected as representatives.

After creation of Uttaranchal in 2000, tribal population in the State has reduced to nil. Majority of the tribals are concentrated in hilly region. Presently a group of tribals are found scattered in Sonbhadra, Gonda and Bahraich districts.

After municipal elections held in 2000, only 189 women were elected as Presidents/Mayors and 3928 women belonging to different segments of society were elected as representatives. A comparative scenario has been depicted in Table I.5.

Table I.5

Reservation of Seats in Urban Local Bodies (2000 Municipal Elections)

	Nagar Nigam	*Nagar Palika Parishad*	*Nagar Panchayat*
Chairman/Mayor	11(11)	193(226)	416(444)
Numbers	-	-	-
S.C. Women	-	8(8)	20(21)
S.C.	1(1)	17(15)	40(42)
S.T. Woman	-	-	-
S.T.	-	-	-
O.B.C. Women	1(1)	19(20)	39(40)
O.B.C.	2(1)	38(40)	77(80)
Women (General)	2(2)	29(46)	68(88)
General	5(6)	85(93)	172(175)
Total women	**3(3)**	**56(75)**	**127(145)**
Percent	27.27	29.01	30.52
Corporator	830(830)	4909(5744)	4782(5074)
S.C. Women	40(40)	243(313)	263(439)
S.C.	66(66)	336(391)	457(324)
S.T. Women	-	- (3)	-(5)
S.T.	-	-(3)	-(7)
O.B.C. Women	62(64)	404(607)	447(517)
O.B.C.	111(111)	761(928)	566(806)
Women (General)	177(174)	1109(1134)	1083(947)
General	374(375)	2056(2465)	1966(2029)
Total Women	279(278)	1856(2057)	1793(1904)
Percentage	3361(33.49)	35.77(35.81)	37.49(37.60)

*Renukoot (Sonbhadra), Nagar Palika Parishad and Loni, Sikanderabad (Bulandshahar), Nagar Panchayats are not included in this table.

* Figures in parentheses denote 1995 scenario which includes Uttaranchal

Source – State Election Commission, Uttar Pradesh.

The reservation of seats for women in municipal bodies shows that it has tremendous implications not merely in terms of number of women entering the public arena and holding public office, but also in terms of social, economic and political impact that these reservations have had for the total system.

Women in local government need to develop their capabilities to play their rightful roles in the development process. The role of political representatives at local level is demanding, needs time to gain experience and to understand the rules, regulations and procedures governing the administrative bureaucracy with which they now have to work-often quite closely in urban service delivery system.

Review of Literature

A number of studies, surveys and research have been carried out by social scientists, development experts and academicians. These studies and research focus on various dimensions and aspects of women's empowerment, upliftment, development and welfare. There is scarcity of literature on role conflict among women representatives in local bodies and political institutions. Though plenty of pertinent literature on women's role conflict is available which, focuses more on working women in urban settings. The women's liberation movement, particularly constitutional and legal provisions (enactments) followed by conferences and conventions has created interest of many educated elite on the issue of proper roles of men and women in India. Role Conflict is considered as single phenomenon having both psychological and sociological consequences. But attention is strictly focused on one type of consequence that is behavioural conflict resulting from the prevalent inconsistent norms within the role system.

Kapur (1960, 1984) dealing with a number of working housewives highlights the issues like role conflict and adjustment. She further presents multidimensional problems of working women in various professions.

Kundu (1999) finds that role conflict varies according to levels of education, economic earnings and social position. Similarly Hemlatha and Suryanarayan (1983) state that working women's problems are greatly influenced by factors such as age and socio-economic status, huband's treatment, children's age and their numbers, family size and type, nature of work etc. They experience that positive attitude of family members towards women's employment help them a great deal to carry on both the roles successfully.

The working mother's role is widely regarded as a classic conflict situation. Potentially conflict has been suggested from a variety of sources. The diffused nature of role and overload of work are two known sources. Such sources are dealt by eminent scholars like Chakraborty (1978), Rama Kapoor (1969), Kala Rani (1976), Orden and Bradburn (1968) and many others. Arora et. al. (1963) observe that strains are felt by all the working women since their husbands do not help in house-keeping. The attitude of family members and their nature of co-operation are crucial for the role adjustment of a working wife. This has been discussed in detail by Powell (1963), Kala Rani (1976) and Hoffman (1963).

These studies no doubt focus on role conflict among working housewives, however no study is directly related to role conflict among working women representatives in unit of democratic governance and decentralized planning. Although positive discrimination has been advocated and being considered for development planning and administration, women's representation in the unit of urban local bodies due to the provision of reservations has enhanced the possibilities of potential role conflict. Hence the present study deals with various dimensions of role conflict among women representatives in urban local bodies, so that conflict may be reduced and women's role may be enhanced for effective functioning of these urban local bodies. This maiden study concentrated on role conflict among women in politics, seeks to highlight women's role in functioning of local bodies and problems and challenges being faced by them.

Scope for Role Conflict

The differential role of women over the history has been mainly based on role conflict. The level of role conflict has been a major determinant of status of women in Indian society. The recent revolutionary measure (in the form of 74th Amendment to the Constitution) is a harbinger in setting the role of women in different sectors – social, political, administrative, ethical, aesthetic, environmental etc.

A woman representative has multidimensional roles to perform. As a housewife, she holds the traditional status of a mother, wife, sister, daughter, daughter-in-law and as people's representative has to perform for the fulfillment of people's aspirations and expectations. Therefore as compared to their other counterparts in society, these women representatives (woman in politics) have to perform two sets of roles i.e. traditional or prescribed as a woman in a male dominated Indian society and an achieved or ascribed by acquiring political status. As such a woman as a role occupant finds now lesser time for family. Her role is now divided into two sets of role for family and for society.

This leads to a constant and continuous phenomenon of role conflict. In case of any biasness, the effectiveness of constitutional provisions may be prejudiced. A woman representative has therefore to make a balance between the two roles for a harmonious and peaceful life and effective role in decision making. There is need to judiciously distribute time to strike a balance in those conflicting roles. The factors causing conflict are numerous. The level of education, family background, social traditions and customs, prevailing environment, level of mutual understanding, economic status of family, women empowerment movement and programmes, healthy competition are some of the major determinants influencing role conflicts among women representatives. The influence of these factors and their impact is the major concern of this academic endeavour.

A number of studies have been undertaken to study the role conflict among women in employment sector but none has touched the political aspect. So in this maiden study an attempt has been made to highlight the problem of role conflict among women representatives in urban local government.

Objectives of Study

It is basically considered that education is a channel to awareness, which creates role dynamism and facilitates change in role perception. How a woman judiciously and elegantly perform the set of roles under conflicting demand and work stress has to be studied thoroughly. The way for striking a balance in picking roles on priority basis and their order of performance, has to be dissected minutely. Hence the study concentrates on and attempts to examine various related issues. The main objectives of the study were:

- To trace the background of women entering into political role
- To highlight the change that occurs in status and position of women representatives
- To measure the degree of change in status and the extent to employment of new roles to the existing traditional ones

- To examine the nature and degree of conflict between various roles
- To identify the determinants of role's selection and performance in order of merit
- To focus the stabilizing and destabilizing forces responsible for affecting the status achieved
- To assess the long run consequences on family and children
- To highlight the conflict oriented abnormalities and consequences on adjustments within and without family and self
- To measure the social benefits in terms of service to society
- To analyse the family and social variables to determine role, status and role conflict.

Hypotheses

Political activeness integrates on with a higher status, greater role for society, disintegration from family by curtailing role towards it with increase in role conflict and status factor. Higher the level, higher the status and independence, higher the conflict and lesser degree of association with family and feministic role and vice-versa. In this backdrops, present study was designed to verify the following hypotheses:

(i) Higher the level of interest of women representatives in local governance, higher respect in political circle and more in role multiplicity

(ii) Higher the level of interest in new role, higher the freedom and independence and acquiring more decision making power in the family

(iii) Higher the level of interest in local governance, higher the freedom, more the conflict, more the egalitarian relationship and more the ego clash

(iv) Higher the interest in politics, greater the role performance towards society and more the social work

(v) Higher the level and interest in ascribed role, more the freedom, lesser the attachment to tradition and more the empowerment with increase in modernity.

Universe of the Study

The state of Uttar Pradesh has been selected for the purpose of the study, as by virtue of being the most populous one and also enjoying the status of having the second largest number of urban local bodies in the country. In Uttar Pradesh more than four thousand women participate in decision making in urban local governance. There are three municipal carporations (out of 11) headed by woman mayors. About 184 women are chairing the municipal boards and nagar panchayats. In addition as a consequence of 74th Amendment to the Constitution about 3900 women are representing different city wards. Thus about 4114 women are playing vital role in the grassroots level institutions in the state. Hence the state provides a broad perspective for indepth study of such nature.

The sample of the present study was selected purposively, because urban local government units having women representatives were taken up for In-depth study. Therefore, all the municipal corporations having women mayors were selected. The other two types of urban local bodies i.e. Nagar Palika Parishads (municipal councils) and Nagar Panchayats were selected on regional basis. For this purpose the state was divided into four regions viz. Eastern, Central, Western and Bundelkhand. 25 per cent of Nagar Palika Parishads and Nagar Panchayats headed by women representatives from each region were taken up randomly for this study. In addition 25 per cent of women representatives were interviewed. Thus in all 1000 women representatives were contacted and interviewed. In addition and for substantiating the responses, 100 officials of urban local bodies and 200 family members of the main respondents were also contacted and interviewed.

Sources of Data Collection

Both primary and secondary sources were used for data collection. The primary data were collected through personal interview and by mailed questionnaires while secondary data were collected through books, reports, journals etc.

For collecting primary data, following types of structured questionnaires/interview schedules were developed and used:

(i) Questionnaire for Women Representatives

(ii) Questionnaire for Officials

(iii) Questionnaire for Family Members

Thus, an attempt has been made to substantiate the responses of elected representatives with the views from municipal officials as well as from the family members of elected women.

Methodology

In the present study questionnaires as well as interview schedules were used for collection of data. For fetching primary data a comprehensive questionnaire covering various aspects of roles of women representatives was developed and administered. Questionnaires were also mailed to women representatives. Most of the women representatives were personally contacted and interviewed to get a better insight into the various aspects of the study.

Limitations

The study is mainly based on the responses received through personal interviews, observations and discussions with women representatives with their family members and also with the officials. The views collected through primary sources were supplemented by data reproduced through secondary sources including books, reports etc. The findings have been derived on these counts.

II
PROFILE OF THE UNIVERSE

Municipalities Studied

Although the study centres around the elected women representatives, it was thought proper to fetch the views of their family members and urban officials as well. With a broader aim in view, while selecting the units of urban local bodies, it was attempted that all the geographical regions – eastern, western, central and Bundelkhand were represented. In addition urban local bodies being headed by male chairpersons were also selected and views of elected representatives (councilors) belonging to those municipalities were also taken into cognizance. It was necessary for bringing balance in study as views of women in different scenarios had been collected.

The elected women councillors in female headed municipalities may not have the similar circumstances to face than that of in the municipalities being headed by a male. With this aim in view, five Municipal Corporations, 37 Municipal Councils (Nagar Palika Parishads) and 45 Nagar Panchayats were selected. These included five municipalities with male as chairman. All other urban local government units were headed by female presidents. Jhansi is one Nagar Palika Parishad which has been elevated as Nagar Nigam and thus Council has been dissolved and Administrator appointed. Hence the formerly elected women members were interviewd. Out of total coverage 18 municipalities were from Central region, four from Eastern region, 11 from Bundelkhand

and 41 are from the Western region. This is in commensurate to the urbanization pattern in the State. Eastern and Bundelkhand regions are least urbanized and the Western part is most urbanized, hence more urban centres and the largest number of municipalities. Hence the skewed selection.

Socio-Economic Profile of Women Representatives

The socio-economic environment of an individual greatly influences the attitudes, values, socialization, participation, efficacy, status and position. The differential role of women is the major cause of role conflict. The socio-economic profile like age, marital status, number of children, family type, education, parents'/ spouses' background etc., of women plays a very important role in the performance of their roles and related problems. Hence in order to study role conflict among women representatives in urban local government, it is important to analyze their socio-economic profile which has an impact on their role performance and the problem of role conflict.

In the present study women representatives from Nagar Nigams, Nagar Palika Parishads and Nagar Panchayats were selected randomly which included both elected and nominated members.

Age and Family Status

In dealing with the problems of women councillors the factors of age and marital status play a very important role. The roles and responsibilities of women vary significantly in different periods of their life. The personal profile (age and marital status) of universe is compiled in following table.

Among the women representatives interviewed maximum respondents were found to be between the age group of 25 to 40 years. It is because of this age factor that they are active, dynamic, enterprising, hardworking and sincere. As regard their marital status absolute number of respondents (83.75 per cent) were married while 15 per cent were widow.

Table II.1
Personal Profile

(Percentage Distribution)

Age/Marital Status	*Married*	*Unmarried*	*Widow*	*Divorcee*	*Total*
25-30 years	18.75	-	-	-	18.75
30-35 years	18.75	-	1.25	-	20.00
35-40 years	17.50	-	1.25	-	18.75
40-45 years	10.00	-	1.25	-	11.25
45-50 years	12.50	-	7.50	1.25	21.25
50-55 years	5.00	-	1.25	-	6.25
55-60 years	-	-	1.25	-	1.25
Above 60 years	1.25	-	1.25	-	2.50
Total	83.75	-	15.00	1.25	100.00

Since most of the women representatives are in the younger age group and are married, they have a major responsibility towards their family and home and are likely to have more familial work load. Managing both family and municipal responsibility becomes really tedious for them as both roles are quite incompatible in nature and is the major reason for role conflict. Contrarily women councilors who are middle aged or above have comparatively lesser problems because by their age. Most of them become free from their basic family responsibilities and are quite stable in their married as well as - family life hence they face lesser work related conflict and are able to devote more time to their municipal role.

Table II.2
Family Structure

(Percentage Distribution)

Type of	*Nuclear*	*Joint*	*Extended*				*Total*
Family	51.25	48.75	-				100.0
Total Members	1-5	6-10	11-15	16-20	21-25	26-30	
of Family	37.50	42.50	13.75	2.50	2.50	1.25	100.0

As regards family structure, the data (Table II.2) reveal that more than half (51.25 per cent) women respondents live in nuclear family while remaining (48.75 per cent) are a part of a joint family. Those living in nuclear family have lesser obligations to fulfill while women in joint families face more adjustment problems as there are greater demands and expectations from different family members. One positive aspect related to joint family is that women representatives get help from other family members both in household as well as in performing official functions. The size of family also contributes a lot in emergence of role conflict. It is found that women councilors having small families (37.50 per cent) are found to be more satisfied and are able to manage both the roles effectively. Further women living with in-laws have many more social complexities than the women living in nuclear families consisting their husband and children.

Family consists of children of various age groups. And children are major responsibility for a married woman and also the major cause of concern and worry for those who work outside their home. Age of children is one of the important factors that may encourage or discourage a mother's involvement in other roles.

Table II.3
Children

(Percentage Distributions)

Major >18	*53.75*	*Minor <18*	*62.50*	
Number of Children	0-5	6-10	11-15	Total
Response	87.50	11.25	1.25	100.0

The data depict that every six out of ten women respondents (62.50 per cent) have minor children while more than half (53.75 per cent) women have only major children. With regard to number of children majority of (87.50 per cent) women respondents have children less than five while every tenth woman has more than five children.

Because of prevalence of traditional outlook regarding division of labour within the family, it is the mother who remains in charge of young children even if she is involved in any other profession. It is observed that women representatives having minor and more number of children experience maximum role conflict because they have a major responsibility towards children and have to devote more time and attention in managing their children. While women representatives who have grown up i.e. major and lesser number of children experience comparatively lesser role conflict.

The analysis reveals that maximum respondents belong to the general category (45 per cent) followed by backward (40 per cent) and Scheduled Castes (15 per cent). With regard to religion an absolute number (77.59 per cent) of women are Hindu while about one fourth (21.25 per cent) are Muslims. These observations indicate that representation of women in local bodies is coming from all castes and sections, which is a positive sign indicating equal opportunity of representation and participation by all segments of society.

Table II.4
Social & Religious Stratification

(Percentage Distribution)

Class/ Religion	*Hindu*	*Muslim*	*Christian*	*Sikh*	*Others*	*Total*
General	37.50	6.25	-	1.25	-	45.00
Backward	26.25	13.75	-	-	-	40.00
S.C.	13.75	1.25	-	-	-	15.00
Total	77.50	21.25	-	1.25	-	100.00

Educational Qualifications

Education plays a very important role in building up the mind, personality and perception of an individual which has an impact on the performance of his/her roles. Even in the political role it is observed that those having good education level are able to participate, socialize and perform better than those who are less educated or illiterate.

The analysis highlights that a little more than one-fifth of elected women are just literate. They can read and write and have no formal educational qualification. Every sixth woman possesses a certificate of High School and an identical number as that of Intermediate. Similar number of elected women has post-graduate degree and a little less than that have the degree of graduation. Every twentieth elected woman has either M. Phil or Ph.D. Degree.

This shows that a blood of educationally qualified women is in fusing into local political arena. Those who were probably illiterate initially made an effort to learn at least to read and write and they are now literate. Such a situation reflects that educational level of elected women is quite good.

Table II.5
Education Level

	Just literate	*Middle Class*	*High School*	*Interme -diate*	*Gradu -ate*	*Post –gradu -ation*	*M.Phil/ Ph.D.*	*Total*
Percen-tage	22.50	7.50	16.25	16.50	15.00	16.25	5.00	100.00

It is clearly evident that women with good and high education are entering into their new avatar as people's representatives. Such educated women representatives are able to perform better and participate actively in municipal affairs.

It is observed that those women councilors who are just literate and have low education level are found to be unclear about their role and functions as representative and so are more dependent on their husband and other male family members for a helping hand in discharging their official duties. Low education and ignorance about municipal functions create low self esteem and lack of confidence among elected women.

It was further attempted to analyze the extent of literacy on the basis of place of birth of the women representatives.

It is clear from the analysis that level of literacy is directly related to place of birth. The women having borne and brought up in urban or semi-urban areas are educationally higher than those borne in rural areas. It is also observed that more than one third (35 per cent) women representatives have their root in villages and little less than one-fourth (23.75 per cent) in semi-urban and the highest number (41.75 per cent) in urban areas.

Table II.6
Place of Birth and Literacy level

(Percentage Distribution)

Education/ Place of Birth	*Rural*	*Semi Urban*	*Urban*	*Total*
Literate	17.50	2.50	2.50	22.50
Middle Class	2.50	2.50	2.50	7.50
High School	8.75	3.75	3.75	16.25
Intermediate	3.75	7.50	6.25	17.50
Graduate	1.25	3.75	10.00	15.00
P.G.	1.25	3.75	11.25	16.25
M.Phil/Ph.D./B.Ed.	-	-	5.00	5.00
Total	35.00	23.75	41.25	100.00

Employment

Nature of employment has a bearing on role conflict, hence the elected women were asked to reveal their employment pattern. The employed and professionals were further asked to divulge the nature of their employment. The responses (Table II.7) are quite revealing. About one third of elected women are employed as teacher at different levels. Identical numbers of women are engaged in allied sectors. Little less than one-fifth are involved either in clerical jobs or working as officers.

Table II.7
Employment Pattern

(Percentage distribution)

	Employed	*Self-employed*	*Professional*	*Industalist*	*Full time Politician*	*House wife*	*Total*
Response	1.25	5.00	1.25	0.50	15.00	77.00	100.00

Interestingly, highest number of women representatives is found to be house wives followed by a good number (15 per cent) as full time politicians. Negligible numbers of women are professionals. Self employment reflects that the male counterparts are performing business activities in the name of women or these women help their husbands in doing business activities.

Table II.8
Category of Employment

Category	*Clerk*	*Officer*	*Teacher*	*Others*	*Total*
Percentage	16.66	16.66	33.34	33.34	100.00

The elected women practicing as full time politician are those on whose behalf the male counterparts are doing politics. As regards reasons for seeking employment, the responses are quite clear. Two-thirds of elected women are working for earning additional income to the family and equal number wants to make use of their education, hence employed. The women working for obtaining good status in the society are probably clamoring for mental satisfaction and independence. This reflects the inherent tendency of educated women to have an independent and individual social personality.

Table II.9
Reasons for Employment

(Percentage Distribution)

Financial help	*Good status*	*Good Contacts*	*Utilise Education*	*Total*
33.34	16.66	16.66	33.34	100.00

As regards income level, eight out of ten elected women representatives are found earning a monthly income of less than Rs. 10,000.00. About one fifth are adding more than Rs. 10,000/ - per month to their family income. Surprisingly the elected women who are employed are found least interested in making their career in politics.

Table II.10
Income level

(Percentage distribution)

Income level (Rs)	*<5000*	*5000-10000*	*10000 15000*	*15000-20000*	*Total*
Response	26.66	52.52	9.62	11.20	100.00

Head of the Family

Heading a family means bestowed with power of decision making in the family. Surprisingly, the traditional system of male dominance prevails even after women earning independent income and performing political role. It is observed that majority of the families of women councillors are headed by their husbands. Every eighth family is headed by parents or in-laws. It is significant that every tenth family is headed of woman representative herself but this includes mostly those women who have lost their husband and in-laws and are widows.

Table II.11
Head of the Family

(Percentage Distribution)

Head	*Self*	*Husband*	*Parents*	*Others*	*Total*
Response	11.25	73.75	12.50	2.50	100.00

It is seen that in case of husband being the head of the family, he dominates in all matters and all family decisions are taken by him though claimed to be in consultation with his wife.

At this juncture it was thought imperative to get more information about head of the family, i.e. husband of elected women. The data reflect that more than half of the heads of family of elected representatives are self employed and business man. It signifies that the elected woman belonging to such a family is also either self employed or doing some petty business. In real sense they do not have their own independent business but they term the employment of their husband as their own. In the circumstances, woman representatives might not feel illegal to allow their male counterparts to perform their new role as politician.

Since status of the family is determined by the occupation and income of the head of the family, it is seen that maximum women representatives belong to family having good or high status but most of them do not have political background.

The income of the husband is also an important determinant of the status of the family as well as extent of conflicts in role performance by women councilors. It is observed that where husband's income is high, the family problems are less and there are less chances of conflict between husband and wife in relation to financial matters and this influences their role performance as well.

Table-11.12

Employment Pattern of Husband

Husbands Employment	*Employed*	*Self Employed*	*Professional*	*Businessman*	*Politician*	*Agriculture*	*Retired*	*Total*
Response	22.50	24.00	3.75	44.75	1.25	1.25	2.50	100.00

In sum, the respondents of the study belong to different strata of society. The representative character of respondents assimilates various facets of society, numerous familial characteristics and personal traits.

III

CONCEPTUAL FRAMEWORK

Role Conflict: A Definition

Role is the functional aspect of structural concept status. The position that a person occupies in a society through tradition, customs or achievement is called 'status', a symbol for recognition. As a result of this status, one is expected to discharge certain functions called 'roles'. Role has two elements, one is expectation from society as a whole and other is from the individual for fellow members. Role is a dynamic aspect of status and changes according to change in status. One person may have several status, as a son, as a husband, as a father etc. Every status has role associated with it. One has to discharge several roles according to one's status. There are many factors such as sex, age, kinship, wealth, education, power, courage, occupation, business, intellectual abilities etc. which determine status. Status and role influence directly as well as indirectly the emotions, sentiments, feelings, thoughts etc. of individual and in turn of society.

While discharging various roles attached to one's status achieved or bestowed, one becomes selective because of importance of roles and often, get perplexed in differentiating the roles, because of difference in prescription of such roles. Thus there arises a conflict about the roles to be performed in priority and intensity basis. The degree of conflict varies from person to person and even get complexes when status increases and multiplies.

The model of women's status and role shows the various roles that a woman has to perform which are quite conflicting in nature so incompatibility among these roles creates role conflict.

The term 'role conflict' is generally used by sociologists and social psychologists to denote the problem situation which arises due to simultaneous occupancy of two positions by an actor, i.e. problem that arises due to role incompatibilities. Role conflict is a state of incompatibility which occurs when there is a mismatch between thought and action, acceptance or rejection of mutually exclusive events of equal importance, simultaneous requirement of presence in two opposing situations, expectations of interacting actors, conceived notion and fact about any event, object or person and when potential antagonism leads to cognitive personalization.

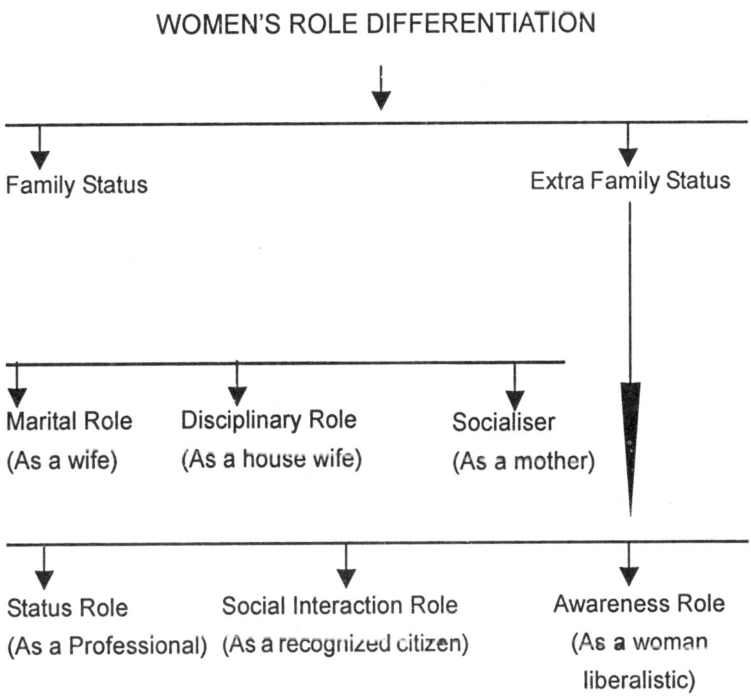

Source: Kundu, 1999.

Degree of conflict depends on personality, dispositions, beliefs, attitudes, characteristics, life style, moods and positions in social ladder. When two or more roles are to be fulfilled simultaneously which are contradictory or of mutually exclusive expectations the role conflict becomes even more pronounced. That is what happens when a woman has to perform simultaneously roles of a housewife and an employee or a professional. Due to different personality dispositions and personal characteristics, the role conflict may be accentuated. In other words the attributes of the actor may determine the degree of felt conflict.

Source of Role Conflict

The source of role conflict can be broadly classified into two groups:

1. Inter-role conflict
2. Intra-role conflict

A. Inter-Role Conflict

As the word suggests it is conflict between two or more roles of different kinds as :

1. Conflict due to diffused nature of roles

Since the employment of middle class women is a new thing, no fixed pattern or redefinition of role of women in terms of the changed context have yet been achieved. Neither working wives nor their husbands or other relatives nor society in general are clear and definite about their roles. Women's role and position at present are, therefore not clearly defined and thus this situation leads to role conflict (Chakraborty, 1977, Menon, 1964, Mahajan, 1966, McKinnon, 1964, Nevill & Demico, 1975, Raja Gopalan, 1963, Wardwell, 1952).

2. Conflict out of Incompatible Expectations

Women of today are assuming different roles besides the role within their homes. In the role relationship term, a married working or a professional woman is a wife, mother, daughter-in-law, neighbour, worker, subordinate, peer and so on. She has to play all these roles i.e. traditional roles and modern role of work/ professional, simultaneously and expectations of these roles and demands might lead her to conflicting situations because of their built-in-antagonism. According to Halahan and Gilbert (1979) "women in dual – career, marriage are experiencing higher role conflict than their spouses since they are now actively involved in adding a role (i.e. professional) which may require attitude and behaviour that are in consistent with those of their more traditional roles i.e. parent and spouse.

(i) Family relation and employment

In the inter role situation, family relation is of significance (Dahlstrom, 1917, Powell, 1963, Hoffman, 1961, Sullerat, 1971, D'souza 1968, Kala Rani, 1967, Singh, 1972, Nevill & Demico 1975a, 1975b). Since married women are a member of a family, their decision to work or refrain from work depends upon the views and the needs of their husband and other family members and presupposes a series of practical adjustment, some degree of cooperation and support for the role ideal by the husband and the family members. Presence of in-laws and size of family are some of the contributing factors in the role conflict among working women.

(ii) Attitude of husband and employment

The attitude of husband is often a decisive factor in his wife's decision to take up a job. Whereas a favourable attitude of husband towards his wife's employment facilitates her career choice, unfavourable attitude of husband hinders her employment. Hence the attitude of husband is one of the major role conflicting factors (Blood & Hamblin, 1958, Blood, 1963, Bailyn 1970).

The negative attitude of men can be attributed, in part to their general family ideology and opinion of social prestige. There is a serious risk of conflict and tension in the marriage, particularly when the wife's employment/profession creates a change in earlier habits (Dahlstrom, 1967, Nischal, 1975). Wife's work participation can create a potential status problem for husband. Arora et. al. (1963) concludes that traditional attitudes of husbands always produce role conflict among working wives.

(iii) Husband's Cooperation in household chores and employment

A working wife cannot manage effectively the household job and employment if her husband does not extend his help in the household work (D'Souza 1968, Kapur, 1974, Dhingra, 1972, Tripathi, 1967, Kala Rani, 1976). Dhingra (1972) found that almost half of the married

women of his sample were experiencing substantial difficulty in carrying out their household duties of their wife role adequately, including the care and attention given to the husband, along with their jobs. Conflict is felt among those working/professional women who need and expect help from their husband but do not get assistance in carrying out these responsibilities. Satyanand (1973) found that "husband was still quite not prepared to relinquish his patriarchal privileges."

(iv) Employment and mother role

The number and age of children are directly related to role conflict in working women (Bhatty & Bhatty 1972, Desai 1963, D'Souza, 1968, Dahlstrom, 1967, Hoffman, 1962, Order & Bradburn, 1968, Suchdev, 1974, Singh, 1972, Weller 1968). Family life in general and children in particular are highly salient factors of high overload.

Vasantha Kumar (1964) has found that strains of work at home and office coupled with lack of household amenities and vanishing domestic help have contributed to the experience of role conflict among working women.

3. Time as a factor/function of Role Conflict

As a traditional rule, a married woman is responsible for the larger share of house work. This also applies to working married woman. A married woman has to manage in terms of time both the household and the job responsibilities. Different activities attached to different roles require definite amount of time in a day. The limitation of time always produces role conflict among working women (Bhatty & Bhatty, 1971, Chakraborty, 1977, Dahlstrom 1967, Hoffman, 1963, Kala Rani, 1976, Rapoport and Rapoport, 1969).

Goode (1960) indicates that while meeting different expectations and obligations attached with different roles, women experience conflict due to time, place or resources. This type of conflict according to him is conflict of allocation.

B. Intra-Role Conflict

It is a conflict which arises from a number of sources within a specific role. These are:

(i) Expectational discrepancy as a measure of self-role conflict

Following Rotter's (1970) expectancy theory we can assume that working women develop certain expectations from job and family. These expectancies from job/profession may be of economic or personal gain. Similarly, while playing different roles of a wife or mother, a woman may develop expectancies that she may be treated by her husband as an equal or true partner or she may be given full respect and protection. When the fulfillment of her expectancies are not to the amount of ideal-self, she feels frustration. In other words the extent of discrepancy between the two i.e. the amount of held expectancy and the amount of the fulfillment of expectancy may be an index of psychological deficit which may lead to role conflict. The above facts have been supported by Hall & Gordon (1974) and Kapur (1974). Kapur (1974) found a vast gap between what privileges as an earning member of the family and woman expected and the privileges she in reality enjoyed – the gap affected the family and emotional adjustment of the working woman.

(ii) Behavioural discrepancy as a measure of self role conflict

Behavioural discrepancy is also an index of role conflict. Such conflict is very common in working woman's day-to-day activities. With the multiplicity of roles, her behaviour becomes complex in terms of expected and actual conduct (Kala Rani 1976). How much care or time they should pay on different role activities poses a great difficulty before the working women. Therefore a gap between their ideal-self and real-self related proper enactment of role is always maintained. Hence, they experience conflict. Kala Rani (1976) has confirmed this relationship by stating that the role conflict among working women is due to behavioural discrepancy.

Role conflict situations may arise from a variety of circumstances and the contents in which the role is performed will be an important determinant. Whatever may be the nature of conflict the consequence is always unhappiness and suffering. Conflict keeps people far from each other and everyone loses other's help and assistance without which it is not possible to run a smooth life. It is not that only the focal person suffers everyone directly or indirectly associated with the focal person is affected with the conflict, the consequence of which is always harmful. But conflict can be resolved through a number of ways. By adopting any one or more measures depending upon the situation, conflict can be resolved in order to make proper adjustment in every sphere of life.

Adjustments

The situation on role conflict and role strain tends support to the fact that tolerance level of the strain might bear some relationship with personality of the role players (Sinha, 1973). If the conflict is deeply felt, it may reflect in lack of adjustment either in family, in social and emotional life (Burchard 1954, Cousia, 1951) or in job setting (Kahn, 1964). The adjustment process also by its inherent nature involves active coping with internal and external stressful conflicts, frustration, etc. The individual has to respond in such a way that he becomes more adequately and more effectively related to self and environment (Phadke & Kulkarni, 1977). Investigations suggest that working wives are less adjusted than housewives. Chakraborty (1977) and Kapur (1969) find that highest number of working mothers experience role conflict because of their limited physical capacity and energy and stigma.

Status of a woman in family is regulated by the factor of her engagement or gainful economic activities. Change in status changes her roles. Because of her elevated status, she commands respect and receives better treatment than others. But the impact of employment can be seen from varied angles. The changing pattern from joint family to nuclear family, neglect of obligation towards home and children, avarice to observe traditional norms and customs, difficulties and annoyance in maintaining general decorum of family are some consequences. There was a change in relation between man and woman. Family bonds changed from traditional to non-traditional in structure and nature. Because of availability of lesser time, they shifted their household responsibilities and redistributed them among in-laws and others.

Employed women want to establish egalitarian relationship with their husband. Ego clashes, inferiority complexes which arise out of higher education, economic independence, freedom of movement and association with other male members in course of employment creates tension in the family. So whatever women perform other than prescribed by the culture and tradition does not change her status rather castigates it. Though education has attributed new roles to women, broadening roles with traditional family centers around feministic roles. The status given by employment creates new roles for a woman. Discharging of different roles depends upon their perception of these roles in their changing outlook. There arises conflict situation in selecting the roles that are to be discharged on priority basis.

The construct of role conflict involves a number of dimensions which are affected by a host of personality, social, familial and background variables. The present study is designed to examine some of them. Though various studies have been done on employed women but no study is directly related to role conflict among elected women, particularly in units of democratic governance and decentralized planning. The present study deals with various dimensions of role conflict among women representatives in urban local bodies and seeks to highlight their adjustment probiems and challenges being faced by them.

IV

ADJUSTMENTS AND CONFLICTS IN FAMILY

Problems and their specific solutions are always rooted in the socio-cultural context of the society concerned. Hence the problems of elected women representatives need to be examined at micro-level from a socio-cultural perspective. It is equally important to find out how they adjust themselves to the problematic situations in order to lead a happy maritai life.

Adjustment refers to "the state of accommodation which is achieved in different areas where conflict may exist in marriage". Lock and Williamson have defined marital adjustment as "the presence of such characteristic in a marriage as a tendency to avoid or resolve conflicts, a feeling of satisfaction with the marriage and with each other, the sharing of common interests and activities and the fulfilling of marital expectation of the husband and wife".

Green states that the "target of adjustment in a marriage are habits, attitudes and values of the spouses. Satisfaction in marriage depends upon the degree to which the spouses interact with each other are recognized, respected and satisfied. But conflicting expectations of marriage constitute a problem in adjustment......"

Hence, adjustment includes all those actions which tend to bring about functional changes in a relationship. Adjustment is a process rather than a stable phenomenon which means there is continuous interaction between the spouses, an interaction determined by the institutional specifications of the relationship, by the nature of the partners themselves and by the quality of relationship between them.

Thus in married life both the 'intra personal' and 'inter personal' relationships are liable to affect marital adjustment. In this process both husband and wife as well as all other family members, are supposed to extend their helping hand in order to strengthen the bond. This may lead to establish a harmonious relationship resulting in adjustment in the conjugal life.

Women in India whatever may be their status, visualize themselves primarily as mothers and housewives and consider the traditional role as the most significant one. Whatever they do or achieve is an extension of this primary (wife/mother) image. She imbibes life, gladly sacrifices everything and because of their sacrificing and forgiving nature, she is able to adjust better in adverse situations than her counterpart i.e. man.

Status within the Family

Family is the most important place that determines status and role. In olden days in the traditional middle class and upper middle class families, women had practically no role and their whole life had been spent within the family. With the change of time, family and home still hold their position as the focus of their activities, though to a considerable extent a woman has outside roles. Any change in their position will no doubt affect the members of the family. Decision making in the family is a critical element in the status of family members, since it involves allocation of resources and the distribution of roles within the family. The role of women in the decision making process can be assessed by considering her influence on all the family decisions.

Earlier, we have seen that every seventh family is headed by a woman. This trend, of course, is not much encouraging but positively indicates initiation of granting some status to woman in a male dominated traditional society like ours. Such a social status may provide a firm base for sustaining other roles including political one granted under the aegis of the supreme law of the land.

Table IV.1
Decision Making Power

(Percentage distribution)

	Self	*Hus-band*	*Both/ Jointly*	*In-laws Parents*	*Total*
Family Budgeting	10.00	30.00	45.00	15.00	100.00
Purchase of Assets	17.50	27.50	50.00	5.00	100.00
Rationing	18.75	27.50	52.50	1.25	100.00
Schooling of Children	21.25	22.50	55.00	1.25	100.00
On social relation	13.75	33.75	50.00	2.50	100.00
Average		**16.25**	**28.25**	**50.50**	**5.00**

It is observed that maximum decisions in family matters are taken jointly both by husband and wife. Decision relating to family budget, purchase of assets, rationing, schooling of children and social relations are mostly taken jointly. But comparative analysis suggests that husband has major say in respect of family decisions (Table IV.1)

With regard to spending of family income, it is revealed that husbands spend maximum family income. Though joint spending is observed but the income of both husband and wife is controlled by the husband (Table IV.2). Such a situation is not a healthy indicator. Male dominated society should transfer some financial powers to the better half of the society. Economic empowerment may achieve its aim only when women enjoy great financial powers.

Table IV.2
Spending Powers

(Percentage distribution)

Self	*Husband*	*In-laws/ Parents*	*Both*	*Total*
15.00	43.75	7.50	33.75	100.00

Adjustments at Home

A woman councilor has to meet the expectations and obligations corresponding to her various roles within the family whether nuclear or joint. In addition she has also to perform her political role, which lies outside the family purview. The political role compels the woman to step out of the limited spheres of the house and thereby makes her over burdened with work load. The political role demands very social and active life outside home, hence she has to adjust herself both at home and outside in order to avoid conflicting situations and run a smooth family life.

For effective management of household work women may require some helping hand. It may be from within the family or without in the form of domestic help. It is found that a little less than half of the elected women employ servant for domestic help out of which about one third have part time servant and the remaining have full time servant. The remaining half who do not engage any servant have to manage all the household responsibilities themselves (Table IV.3). Management of entire household responsibility by themselves, most of the time overburdens them and creates stressful situations.

Table IV.3
Domestic Servant Available

(Percentage distribution)

Yes	*No*	*Yes*		*Total*
		Part Time	*Full Time*	
48.75	51.25	38.46	61.54	100.00

For proper management of household as well, saving time for other roles, modern time saving amenities can play a very important role and may prove very beneficial for women in managing household work effectively. Most of the respondents have many of the modern time saving amenities like pressure cooker, mixer/grinder, LPG stove, scooter/car, fridge, washing machine. These devices greatly help them in saving time and managing work inside and outside effectively (Table IV.4).

Table IV.4
Availability of Modern time Saving Amenities

Pressure cooker	*Mixer Grinder*	*LPG stove*	*Scooter/Moped/Car*	*VCR/VCP/VCD*	*Kitchen Oven*	*Refrigerator*	*Vacuum Cleaner*	*Washing Machine*
100.00	65.00	100.00	77.50	56.25	40.00	66.25	11.25	33.75

Table IV.5
Managing Household Responsibilities

(Percentage distribution)

	Servant	*Husband*	*Jointly With Husband*	*Jointly With Sister (in laws)*	*Jointly With Servant*	*Self*	*Daughter In-law/ Daughter*	*Total*
Cooking	5.00		2.50	7.50	18.75	61.25	5.00	100.00
Serving food	3.75	1.25	3.75	7.50	12.50	67.50	3.75	100.00
Purchase of Crokery	10.00	46.25	12.50	7.50	7.50	11.25	5.00	100.00
Washing Clothes/Utensils	21.25	1.25	2.50	11.25	5.00	53.75	5.00	100.00
Cleaning house	16 25	1.25	2.50	6.25	11.25	51.25	11.25	100.00
Nursing sick children	3.75	1.25	7.50	6.25	3.25	72.50	5.00	100.00
Caring In-laws/Parents	45.00	1.25	20.00	5.00	5.00	18.75	5.00	100.00
Helping Children in Study	-	1.25	46.25	7.50	2.50	38.75	3.75	100.00
Average	**13.71**	**7.68**	**12.68**	**7.34**	**8.25**	**45.38**	**5.46**	**100.00**

In respect of management of household responsibilities like cooking, purchase of crockery, washing clothes, caring of in-laws, cleaning of house, helping children in study etc. majority of the elected women manage it themselves. For effective management of these household responsibilities they often take help from husband or in-laws and servant (Table IV.5). Management of household responsibilities often creates conflicting situations as the women councilors have to devote large amount of time and energy towards municipal role also. Hence management of dual responsibilities often overburdens them and creates conflicting situations.

Table IV.6
Familial Duties Neglected

(Percentage distribution)

	Always	*Freque-ntly*	*Some time*	*Rarely*	*Never*	*No Hus-band*	*Total*
Husband	16.25	23.75	18.75	22.50	2.50	16.25	100.00
Children	11.25	15.00	31.25	30.00	12.50	-	100.00
Family	23.75	8.75	31.25	32.50	3.75	-	100.00
Average	**17.08**	**15.83**	**27.08**	**28.33**	**6.25**		

In connection with primary duties towards husband, children and family, elected women feel that their husband, home and children often get neglected because of their new avatar in the form of political role in municipal field and consequently raised status in society for which they have to devote more time. A little less than one-fourth of elected women feel their husband frequently gets neglected. The identical number of women in political role find their children sometimes neglected and family rarely neglected. But they are of the view that in spite of the dual burden they try their best and are able to perform their family duties most of the time (Table IV.6). They however, confess that in any case their family is neglected, knowingly or unknowingly. In the same breath they feel that such a neglect is compensated by gaining a status in the society.

As regards management of time, it is observed that for majority of elected women children are the priority, followed by office work and household works. They are found sparing very little time for their own hobby and recreation (Table IV.7).

Table IV.7
Distribution of Time

(Percentage distribution)

	Most time	*More time*	*Little*	*No Husband, In-laws*	*Total*
For Husband	57.50	26.25	-	16.25	100.00
For Children	78.75	21.25	-	-	100.00
For In-laws	28.75	27.50	1.25	42.50	100.00
For House Work	58.75	42.50	6.25	-	100.00
For Office Work	75.00	18.75	6.25		100.00
For hobby/ Recreation	1.25	12.50	86.25	-	100.00
For Society	21.25	65.00	13.75	-	100.00
For shopping	-	20.00	80.00	-	100.00
For friends	-	15.00	85.00	-	100.00
For Self	-	6.25	93.75	-	100.00

But the women are not at all repentant about their time spent on various activities. Overall observations reveal that women feel satisfied with the time they give to various roles both in the family and outside (Table IV.8).

Table – IV.8
Satisfaction with Time Allotted

(Percentage distribution)

	Yes	*No*	*No Husband, In-laws*	*Total*
Husband	82.50	1.25	16.25	100.00
Children	98.75	1.25	-	100.00
In-laws (Parents)	56.25	1.25	42.50	100.00
Brother/Sister (in-laws)	98.75	1.25	-	100.00
Relations	98.75	1.25	-	100.00
Neighbours	97.50	2.50	-	100.00
At office	100.00	-	-	100.00
Society	96.25	3.75	-	100.00
Official obligations	100.00	-	-	100.00
Ward/Town	96.25	3.75	-	100.00
Self	93.75	6.25	-	100.00
Average Satisfaction	**92.62**	**2.17**	**5.11**	**100.00**

The analysis depicts that women representatives in spite of their dual role responsibilities try to fulfill their familial responsibilities and duties towards husband and children. They spare required time for their children and husband. Children always approach them when there is a need. Due to her raised status in society and family, husband frequently asks for her suggestions and takes decision, in consultation with his wife. The elected women are found making both the ends meet successfully. They always try to fulfill their family obligations along with discharging their role as people's representatives. At initial stage, they feel some problem of adjustment but due to passage of time they succeed in allotting time for each work and family members also extend helping hands (Table IV.9).

Table IV.9
Time Use

(Percentage distribution)

	Always	*Freque-nltly*	*Some time*	*Rarely*	*Never*	*Total*
Children approach	37.50	15.00	25.00	12.50	10.50	100.00
You dine with husband & children	12.50	52.50	18.75	13.75	2.50	100.00
Move with husband	22.50	48.75	21.25	5.00	2.50	100.00
Your husband takes decisions with your consultation	3.75	56.25	6.25	13.75	20.00	100.00
Asks for your suggestions	15.00	60.00	10.00	8.75	6.25	100.00
Approaches you when in grief	53.75	6.25	26.25	8.75	5.00	100.00
Observes time punctuality in works	3.75	10.00	56.25	21.25	8.75	100.00

Adjustment and Conflict with Husband

Adoption of the demands of dual career life style requires much flexibility as well as willingness to experiment and innovate by both the partners. Indian society has all along being guided and guarded by traditions, is now getting ready, of course at snail's pace, to accept women in many new roles.

A woman has to fulfill the demands and wishes of different members of the family because of the role she plays and the status she occupies. Acquisition of an additional role and status by a married woman is likely to induce a change in her role and expectations in relation to her husband and other family members. She is found making every effort to bridge to new roles and responsibilities with her traditional roles. However often the politician wife becomes tensed and confused because of the clash between her changed attitudes and traditional attitudes of her husband and family members.

Men picture an ideal woman as "a modest, shy, submissive, reserved and untouched". This stereotype seems to lead to marital frustration and disappointments which ultimately finds expression in marital disharmony of the working women. Combining the two roles is not an easy and smooth task especially for those who remain outside due to their active social and political life.

It requires not only additional physical strength but also psychological adjustment to the changes brought about by this combination. The moment the wife commits herself to work outside home, the husband feels that he loses a part of his wife's active support. The time and energy a wife can give to the emotional, social and physical needs of her husband are lessened.

These problems are even more pronounced in case of women councilors as they have greater responsibility towards society. Being representatives of the people in urban areas they are expected to devote more time towards the problems of urban citizens.

She has responsibility towards her husband as well as towards society. She tries her best to overcome the difficulties in handling both these roles to run a smooth political as well as family life. But if the husband is being influenced by the traditional female role, irrespective of the wife's political commitments and status, does not cooperate and resent to share household work with wife and if wife has less time for home management, the marital life is likely to be affected resulting in tension and conflicting situations.

There are different areas of conflict where the women representatives have to make adjustment with their husbands. Most of women representatives experience dispute with their husband on various issues. Though women representatives found their husbands cooperative, as they support them in their new role, because of their stereotypical attitude towards women role, more often husbands dispute with them.

Since women in political role have active social life, they have to interact on regular basis with officials and other municipal male members as well as citizens and hence they have to be more social and open which most of the time is not liked by their (conservative) husbands and other male members of the family. Male members of the family some times instigate husband against wife. It is observed that dispute with husband is mainly related to the freedom of the wife due to her new political role. As a people's representative she has to be out of the home more frequently which husband most of the time does not appreciate and wants more attention of wife towards home and family. With their new role women representatives are now becoming modern in their views and attitudes which have its effect on their behaviour as well. This change in behaviour and attitudes as a result of their modernity is not always appreciated by husbands who have stereotype image of women.

Hence the major reasons of dispute with husband are freedom due to new role (36.25 per cent), modernity (33.75 per cent), social liaison (26.25 per cent), on family tradition and decorum (12.50 per cent), on their negligence of family (48.75 per cent) (Table IV.10).

Table IV.10
Dispute with Husband

(Percentage distribution)

	Yes	*No*	*Some time*	*Total*
Over your new role	12.25	29.00	58.75	100.00
On your freedom	45.50	23.25	31.25	100.00
Negligence of family	58.75	32.75	8.50	100.00
On your spending	12.50	47.50	40.00	100.00
On family tradition/ decorum	16.50	54.25	29.25	100.00
On your modernity	43.75	18.25	38.00	100.00
On your behaviour	4.50	27.25	68.25	100.00
On social liaison	31.50	13.25	55.25	100.00
Average	**56.95**	**30.69**	**12.36**	**100.00**

Contrarily, in case of women representatives who were deliberately brought in politics by their husband and who work just as rubber stamps for their husband have lesser chances of dispute with their husband and husband also has lesser grievance because wife devotes full time at home and the entire official/municipal work is done by the husband or other male members of the family.

As regards reaction of husbands on joining the wife political role, a little more than one-third of the husbands appreciate their wives joining politics (39.75 per cent) because women have been able to acquire this new role due to support of their husband. About half of the women representatives discharge their official functions with the help of their husband. In many cases it is found that women only confine themselves to attending board meetings while the rest of the official works are handled by the husband. Hence in these cases husband seems to be very supportive (47.50 per cent) and cooperative.

The women having support of their husbands on their joining politics feel that in most cases they have been brought into politics by their husband. But few women representatives who have come in politics on their own for personal independence and status feel that their husbands most of the time do not appreciate their joining politics. Their number is quite less. The women in political role feel that their duties towards husband and family some times get neglected despite their best effort to fulfill the requirements at both the fronts. They always keep family, children and husband at top

Table IV.11
Response of Husband

(Percentage distribution)

	Always	*Freque-ntly*	*Some time*	*Rarely*	*Never*	*Total*
Like your joining politics	39.75	26.50	22.00	8.25	3.50	100.00
Grievance	30.00	6.00	29.00	30.25	4.75	100.00
Get support from husband	47.50	17.25	26.75	6.00	2.50	100.00
Help in official function	60.00	12.50	18.00	6.00	3.50	100.00
Neglect of your duties	18.25	13.25	32.00	14.75	21.75	100.00
Average	**30.10**	**15.10**	**25.55**	**13.05**	**7.20**	

priority and politics comes later on (Table IV.11). The husband is always helpful in performing the official responsibilities. The women getting full support from their husbands and appreciated by their husbands for their new role are the one who are assisted in performing the role. Thus many of these women are dummy. The political role has just been imposed upon them by virtue of new dispensation and the husbands are playing the real game. Such a situation makes the mockery of the Constitution and can not help bring empowerment of women. In spite of constitutional obligations, women in many places are like puppets in the hand of their husbands.

In connection with quitting politics under the pressure of husbands, a little more than one fourth women express that their husbands want them to quit the politics and devote more and more time on feminine role as against a little less than one-third who feel otherwise. The husbands favouring quitting the politics have many reasons including lack of sufficient time for husband, inadequate time for children, family tensions and less time for caring the family (Table IV.12).

Table IV.12
Reasons for quitting Politics

(Percentage distribution)

	Yes	*No*	*Some time*	*Total*
Not given more time to him	43.00	26.25	30.75	100.00
Not attending his parents	7.50	52.75	39.75	100.00
Not proper family care	12.00	30.25	57.75	100.00
Not caring children	44.00	17.75	38.25	100.00
Family tensions	30.50	19.25	50.25	100.00
Average	**27.40**	**29.25**	**43.35**	

Adjustment and Conflict in Managing Children

The responsibility of up-bringing the children lies on the mother whether she is people's representative or full time housewife. However mothers who have to work outside face difficult situations both at home and outside at work place. They make various adjustments despite their inconvenience. It is often found that mothers willingly sacrifice or subordinate their interests for the betterment of their children. The so called male chauvinism still prevents men to participate in house hold activities. Freedom of women due to other role outside home creates tension in the existing authoritarian family structure and relationships. While playing the role of mother various factors play major role in creating tensive situations and causing conflict.

The women representatives having large number of children (above 6) and minor (below 18 years) experience maximum role conflict because they have a major responsibility and have to devote more time and attention towards managing their children. While women representatives having less and grown-up children experience lesser role conflict.

Table IV.13 A
Care of Children

(Percentage distribution)

Servents care	*In laws/ Parents care*	*Husb- and Care*	*Neigh- bour*	*Sister Care*	*Relat- ion Care*	*On their own*	*Total*
15.00	18.75	20.00	3.75	1.25	3.75	37.50	100.00

The analysis reveals that mothers, who have proper child care arrangements while they are out to fulfill municipal functions, are found to be less tensed and experience lesser conflict. It is found that in their absence the responsibility of children is mostly left to in-laws and husband. Those having grown up children do not have any problem while those women having young children and living in nuclear family experience maximum conflict as they have to leave their children either in servant's care or have to find some other way for childcare. However, more or less elected women are found satisfied with the care their children get (Tables IV.13A& B)

Table IV.13B

Satisfaction with Children Care

(Percentage distribution)

Proper Care	*Improper Care*	*Neglected*	*Total*
75.00	15.00	10.00	100.00

Surprisingly, children of majority of women representatives do not like their mother's joining politics. They always have grievances and want more time and attention of their mother. The grievances of children become a major reason of conflict for women councillors as they have lesser time due to dual role responsibility. The elected women with grown up children always get support from their children and their children help them in performing municipal role (Table IV.14). A large number of women respondents feel that they rarely neglect their duties towards children but many a times due to dual responsibility at home and also at municipality they get lesser time for children. Many of the women are found satisfied with the time they spare for their children. Those with younger children are however highly dissatisfied. Time factor is found to be a major reason for conflict among the women performing political role.

Table IV.14
Children's Response

(Percentage distribution)

	Always	*Freque-ntly*	*Some time*	*Rare-ly*	*Never*	*Total*
Like mother joining politics	18.75	15.00	31.25	25.00	10.00	100.00
Grievances	22.50	12.50	25.00	21.25	18.75	100.00
Support Mother	18.75	5.00	28.75	37.50	10.00	100.00
Help in official function	18.75	6.25	33.75	28.75	12.50	100.00
Neglect duties	16.25	15.00	28.75	27.50	12.50	100.00
Satisfaction with the time given	15.00	6.25	38.75	33.75	6.25	100.00
Average	**18.37**	**10.00**	**32.04**	**28.96**	**11.66**	

Adjustment and Conflict with In-laws, Relatives and Neighbours

Family does not mean only husband, wife and children; it also includes in-laws, parents, brothers, sisters and other relatives. Married women have a major responsibility towards their in-laws. In-laws are expected to show cooperation and sympathetic attitude towards women who work outside home, especially those having active political and social life. It is found that their attitudes differ in terms of varying expectations. Sweet relations become bitter when expectations turn to demands. Women representatives actively involved in municipal functions at times find difficult to fulfill the demands and expectations of in-laws which leads to frictions and conflicts.

Most of the women representatives are able to muster support frequently from their in-laws. They also like their joining politics. However, in-laws of elected women are found to have a lot of grievances against them. The major grievance of in-laws relates to the neglect of duties towards them and little time and care given. The attitude of in-laws towards their daughters-in-law's new role and adjustment problems and grievances are major reasons of tension causing role conflict among women representatives. (Table IV.15)

Table IV.15
Responses from In-laws

(Percentage distribution)

	Always	*Frequently*	*Some time*	*Rarely*	*Never*	*Total*
Like your joining politics	21.75	34.50	36.75	3.50	3.50	100.00
Grievances	32.25	4.50	41.15	20.25	1.75	100.00
Get support from In-laws	16.75	34.75	33.75	3.75	11.00	100.00
Help in official functions	6.00	3.50	36.25	34.50	19.75	100.00
Average	**19.20**	**19.32**	**36.98**	**15.50**	**9.00**	

The relatives and neighbours also play a very important role in the adjustment pattern of working women. The data analysed in Table IV.16 show that most women representatives get support from relatives and also get help in discharging official functions. Women respondents feel that their duties towards relatives do not get neglected most of the time so there are lesser grievances. Similarly neigbours also provide them support and help. (Table IV.17).

Table IV.16
Response of Relations

(Percentage distribution)

	Always	*Frequently*	*Some time*	*Rarely*	*Never*	*Total*
Like your joining politics	60.00	6.25	25.00	7.50	1.25	100.00
Grievances	47.50	2.50	13.75	25.00	11.25	100.00
Get support from relatives	50.00	8.75	33.75	6.25	1.25	100.00
Help in Official functions	12.50	5.00	20.00	43.75	18.75	100.00
Neglect your duties	70.00	2.50	10.00	15.00	5.00	100.00
Average	**48.00**	**5.00**	**20.50**	**19.50**	**7.00**	

Table IV.17
Neighbours Response

(Percentage distribution)

	Always	*Frequently*	*Some time*	*Rarely*	*Never*	*Total*
Like your joining politics	57.50	13.75	10.00	7.50	11.25	100.00
Give full support	37.50	26.25	21.25	11.25	3.75	100.00

The women representatives feel that due to their elevated status in the society they are now more respected by relatives and neighbors and always get their help and support.

As regards grievances of family members, elected women feel that some times they get aggrieved due to the grievances from family members and this creates a lot of tension which has an impact on their mental health and also on performance of their roles. (Table IV.18)

Table IV.18
Feel Aggrieved

(Percentage distribution)

Yes	*No*	*Don't care*	*Some time*	*Total*
14.28		2.04	83.68	100.00

The data (Table IV. 19) depict satisfaction of women representatives with their family. They feel that most of the time family members understand their problems, appreciate them and try to make adjustments with them. But despite this there are lot of grievances and conflicting situations within the family, which women councilors have to handle in order to maintain a balance between both the roles.

Table IV.19
Feeling with Family

(Percentage distribution)

Fully satisfied	*Satisfied*	*Indifferent*	*Very happy*	*Total*
57.50	30.00	5.00	7.50	100.00

In respect of prioritizing their different roles, women in political role rate their roie of house manager as first (31.25 per cent), followed by mother's role (25 per cent), political role (25 per cent), and wife's role (21.75 per cent) (Table IV.20). In spite of fixed suitably in their present role as people's representative they still give top priority to their familial role i.e. as house manager, mother, wife and daughter-in-law. This reflects the true status of women in a traditional society. Their attitude is not found changing at a satisfactory pace in tune to their new role in politics. They always follow the dictate of their family and male counterparts.

Table IV.20
Ranking the Roles

(Percentage distribution)

	1	*2*	*3*	*4*	*5*	*Total*
Political role	25.00	20.00	12.50	8.75	33.75	100.00
As house manager	31.25	26.25	31.25	5.00	6.25	100.00
As mother	28.00	22.00	23.75	16.25	10.00	100.00
As wife	21.75	32.75	40.75	4.75	-	100.00
As daughter-in-law	12.50	12.00.	18.00	31.25	26.25	100.00

Surprisingly, even after a decade of enactment of historical 74th Amendment to the Constitution, Indian women irrespective of their caste and creed remain fully involved in family affairs. Family and family related roles are their focal concerns and they keep imposed political role at the low pedestal.

V

ADJUSTMENTS AND CONFLICTS IN POLITICAL ROLE

The Municipal Acts provide for elected as well as nominated members for urban local bodies. To get the views of diverse sections, both types of women representatives were contacted and personally interviewed. About four per cent women representatives belonged to nominated category and the remaining were the elected ones.

Entering into Role

On being asked to divulge the reasons for joining the politics every two out of five women councilors felt that they had no choice and political role was imposed upon them by their family members. Since 74th Amendment to the Indian Constitution provides for not less than one-third of seats reserved for women, the local leaders, old politicians and influential persons having hold in local politics were forced to place women candidates. In such cases women are found to be mostly disinterested and ignorant about their political role as people's representative and the entire municipal/ official works are handled by the male members. However, there are about one-third of women (35 per cent) who joined politics because they wanted to pursue a career in politics. These women representatives are found to be quite active in their political/ municipal role. There are many others who entered in this arena for gaining social status and a negligible number to utilize their education. Pleasantly, every seventh woman representative is there for rendering social services.

Table V.1
Reasons for Joining Politics

Factors	*Indepe-ndence*	*Good Status*	*Career in Politics*	*Utilise Educat-ion*	*Impos-ed by family*	*Social Service*	*Total*
Respo-nse(%)	1.25	12.50	35.00	2.50	40.00	8.75	100.00

As regards their stay in politics, majority of the women representatives are since few years only. There are many others in this field for 10 to 15 years. These women councilors are found more active and confident than colleagues who are first timers. Those who are new in this role experience more conflict because they are not yet adapted to this new role.

Table V.2
Political Experience

Experience (in years)	*1-5 yeas*	*5-10 years*	*10-15 years*	*15-20 years*	*20-25 years*	*Total*
Response(%)	72.00	23.00	2.50	1.25	1.25	100.00

As regards commanding respect in municipality it is glaring those women representatives are liked by all. The officials of municipality as well as their male counterparts in urban administration pay respect to women councilors. (Table V.3). Women representatives are respected and liked most because they are found to be sincere and sensitive towards the needs and problems of the citizens of their area. They are sobre, soft and gentle. Their behaviour with officials and peers is congenial, friendly and cooperative.

Table V.3
Respect in Municipality

	All like	*Most like*	*Some like*	*Indifferent*	*Total*
Response(%)	50.00	37.00	11.25	1.25	100.00

It is observed that women members are not authoritative and they get works done in office by personal touch (17.50 per cent) and by persuasion (31.25 per cent). They prefer working in cooperative manner without causing any dispute or conflict. However half of the councilors use their authority to get the work done (Table V.4). The women representatives using authority include mostly chairpersons or mayors. They are found to be quite authoritative and they get work done in office by virtue of their authority. Hence difference in position does play a major role in their style of functioning.

Table V.4
Getting the Work Done

Measures	*By Authority*	*By Persuasion*	*By Personal Touch*	*Blending Reward and Punishment*	*Total*
Response(%)	50.00	31.25	17.50	1.25	100.00

In respect of attitude and behaviour of municipal officials, they get help from officials in discharging municipal functions frequently. They find municipal officials quite cooperative to them. In spite of all co-operations many women representatives some times feel lacking their duties towards municipality due to family

Table V.5
Help and Neglect from Officials

Freque-ncy	*Always*	*Frequ-ently*	*Some time*	*Rarely*	*Never*	*Total*
Help	21.25	35.00	33.75	7.50	2.50	100.00
Neglect	12.50	7.50	8.75	15.00	56.25	100.00

obligations (Table V.5). Many of the woman councilors are found committed towards their duties and responsibilities even they do not get sufficient help from officials.

Decision Making

As a part of decision making powers vested in them, about half of the woman representatives initiate discussions in board meetings frequently. But observations reveal that women councilors generally hesitate in sustaining discussions and the male members are found to be more dominating in board meetings. Most of the women representatives either just keep mum or support the move of their male counterparts in meetings. They generally fail to express their views or they do not take their role seriously. Although women members claim to participate in discussions, some of them hesitate due to lack of knowledge, confidence and interest in municipal functions. (Table V.6).

Table V.6
Initiating Discussion in Board Meetings

Frequency	*Always*	*Somo time*	*Frequently*	*Never*	*Total*
Response (%)	7.50	43.75	45.00	3.75	100.00

Table V.7
Participation in Discussion

Participate		*Frequency*					*Total*
Yes	*No*	*Always*	*Sometime*	*Frequently*	*Never*	*Not hear*	
96.25	3.75	46.25	31.25	12.50	6.25	3.75	100.00

It is encouraging to note that women representatives are always encouraged to put forth their views by female colleagues (62 per cent), by male colleagues (56.25 per cent), by President/ Mayor (65 per cent) and family members (62.50 per cent). But it is observed that male members ignore views of female members because women councillors are not treated seriously as they seldom take independent decisions without consulting their male counter parts. Interestingly, women members feel more encouraging and free in expressing their views and put forth the problems where there is female Mayor/Chairperson than in the board having been presided over by a male.

Table V.8

Encouraged to put forth views

	Yes	*No*	*Some time*	*Always*	*Total*
By Female Colleagues	62.50	11.25	25.00	1.25	100.00
By Male Colleagues	56.25	10.00	31.25	2.50	100.00
By President/Mayor	65.00	7.50	25.00	2.50	100.00
By Family Members	62.50	16.25	18.75	2.50	100.00
Average	**61.56**	**11.25**	**25.00**	**2.19**	

In respect of taking decisions on municipal works it is observed that most of the decisions are taken by the women representatives in consultation with male family members (65 per cent). Many the times women representatives feel uncomfortable in taking independent decisions. They work only as rubber stamps for husband and male family members. Surprisingly active male family members, who have been in politics for many years, take decisions independently (16.25 per cent) on behalf of female representatives.

Table V.9
Decisions in Municipal Works

Taken by	*Response (%)*
Independently	16.25
With the help of male family members	65.00
Male Colleagues	2.50
With the advice of officials	-
By family members	13.75
In consultation with female peers	-
Forced by party members	2.50
Total	**100.00**

Relationship with Chairperson/Mayor

Women representatives generally try to maintain good relations with chairperson/mayor. However, at times there are adjustment problems with male chairperson/mayor. Women members do not get due importance and do not feel free to express their views and problems. But where there is woman chairperson/ mayor, women members feel quite free to initiate and participate in discussions. They are able to communicate freely and put forth their problems and suggestions.

Women councilors feel always getting cooperation and support (76.25 per cent), recognition for advice (78 per cent), appreciation (72.50 per cent), encouragement (71.25 per cent) and sometimes also comments for mistakes (13.75 per cent). The women members having experience and knowledge of municipal administration and aware about their roles and responsibilities unhesitatingly express this views even with male chairperson/ mayor. The number of such members is of course not more. Most of the women representatives just come and go unconcerned. They do not bother much and many of them leave all the problems on their family members. Majority of them enjoy their new role as a ritual and not as a challenge and opportunity.

Table V.10
Response from President/Mayor

(Percentage distribution)

	Always	*Frequ-ently*	*Some time*	*Rerely*	*Never*	*Total*
Cooperation/ Support	76.25	16.25	1.25	-	6.25	100.00
Recognition for advice	70.00	18.75	5.00	-	6.25	100.00
Appreciation	72.50	17.50	3.75	-	6.25	100.00
Comments for mistakes	-	-	3.75	13.75	82.50	100.00
Encourag-ement	71.25	17.50	6.25	-	5.00	100.00
Average	**58.00**	**14.00**	**3.25**	**(-)2.75**	**(-)5.55**	

Relationship with Female and Male Peers

Interestingly, most of the times female colleagues of women councilors are found to be cooperative and supportive (78.75 per cent) with them. They always encourage (76.27 per cent) and appreciate (75 per cent) one another and never pass teasing comments (92.50 per cent). In few cases political affiliation, however, creates differences temporarily.

On the other hand women chairpersons/mayors also express getting full support and cooperation from female members. It is because of their support that they feel confident and are able to perform their role effectively.

Table V.11
Behaviour of Female Colleagues

(Percentage distribution)

Frequency	*Always*	*Frequ-ently*	*Some time*	*Rarely*	*Never*	*Total*
Cooperation/ Support	78.75	15.00	5.00	-	1.25	100.00
Recognition	72.50	16.25	10.00	-	1.25	100.00
Appreciation	75.00	15.00	8.75	-	1.25	100.00
Teasing Comments	-	-	2.50	5.00	92.50	100.00
Encourage-ment	76.25	10.00	7.50	3.75	2.50	100.00
Average	**60.50**	**11.25**	**5.75**	**(-)2.5**	**(-)17.25**	

Table V.12
Behaviour of Male Colleagues

(Percentage distribution)

Frequency	*Always*	*Freque-ntly*	*Some time*	*Rarely*	*Never*	*Total*
Cooperation/ Support	71.25	25.00	1.25	1.25	1.25	100.00
Recognition	1.25	23.75	3.75	70.00	1.25	100.00
Appreciation	-	30.00	3.75	65.00	1.25	100.00
Teasing Comments	-	2.50	37.50	11.25	48.75	100.00
Encouragement	10.25	23.75	5.00	68.75	1.25	100.00

As regards behaviour of male colleagues, female members express to find them cooperative and supportive in words but in reality they do not give them importance the women members deserve. Male members have apprehensions about the ability of female councilors hence their relationships are not always good. Though many women members get cooperation and support but rarely get recognition (70 per cent) or appreciation (65 per cent) or encouragement (68.75 per cent). They some times receive teasing comments also from male members. Ironically, traditional male dominance still prevails and the male members have not changed their mind set.

Relationship with Officials

Similarly women representatives always get cooperation and support (75 per cent) from municipal officials. But they rarely get recognition (68.75 per cent) and obedience (52.50 per cent) from

Table V.13
Behaviour of Officials

(Percentage distribution)

Frequency	*Always*	*Frequently*	*Some time*	*Rarely*	*Never*	*Total*
Cooperation/ Support	75.00	18.75	3.75	-	2.50	100.00
Recognition	1.25	21.25	8.75	68.75	-	100.00
Obedience	50.00	23.75	15.00	2.50	8.75	100.00
Ignore Orders	2.50	23.75	27.50	21.25	25.00	100.00
Comments	6.25	1.25	1.25	2.50	88.75	100.00

officials. Women councilors find officials more sincere, obedient and cooperative with male members. Sometimes they are found ignoring orders (27.50 per cent) also as the lower level staff do not give women members due importance. The lower level officials many a time do not take the women members seriously but higher level officials give due respect and recognition to the female members.

Scope for Adjustments and Conflicts

Demands of political role are quite contradictory to the basic nature and societal role expectations of a woman. Because of these women representatives have to make a lot of adjustments and changes both in their attitude, behaviour and lifestyle. Women's family role as a wife, mother, daughter-in-law and the political role as a representative of the people are quite incompatible in nature. Hence to bring balance between both the roles and for making them more compatible, require lot of adjustments both inside and outside the home. The incompatible demands from both fronts are the major reason for role conflict among women representatives.

Surprisingly, every fifth women representatives took up this role because of compulsion from her husband or family members whereas identical number of women entered into local politics for maintaining the family traditions. Since seats are reserved for women, husband and family members interested in politics bring forward their wives, daughter-in-laws, etc. to fulfill their own political ambition. However, there are a few women representatives who opted for this role because of their own interest in politics. Such women are found to be very much active and they take independent decisions on all aspects. About one fourth of women chose the political role for personality development and scope for social service. This may however be a cover point as the politicians at all levels claim to practice politics for rendering social service. Social service in a real sense is not their ultimate aim but they claim to do so. For social service every politician wants to grab power whatever it may. This is true in case of local women politicians as well.

Table V.14
Ranking of Reasons for Entering into the Role

(Percentage distribution)

Factors	*1*	*2*	*3*	*4*	*5*
Interest in politics	18.75	12.50	13.75	10.00	6.25
Maintaining family tradition	20.00	12.50	10.00	8.75	-
Under compulsion	20.00	12.50	6.25	8.75	12.50
On moral conscience	6.25	7.50	10.00	12.50	12.50
Enjoy new role	3.75	10.00	10.00	10.00	18.75
From Free home work	2.50	8.75	8.75	12.50	12.50
Feel freedom & Independence	-	-	5.00	12.50	12.50
Scope for personality Development	13.75	16.25	20.00	12.50	2.50
Scope for social service	15.00	20.00	16.25	12.50	12.50
Fear of in-laws/ parents	-	-	-	-	10.00

In connection with continuing with the political role majority of the women representatives want to continue to get an enhanced social status. By accepting this new role their status has raised both in society as well as in the family. About half of the women members wish to continue in this new role for shaping a career in politics, while some feels it a proper platform for utilizing their time and making use of their education. Overall most of the women feel good about their new role and wish to continue. It seems that they have tasted the fruits of political role and are not willing to go back within the four walls of house despite constraints and problems. Financial benefit may be one but the women members like independence and they wish to increase their mental faculty through this challenging role. About one fifth are there to prepare a political background for their family, whereas more than one third wants to utilize their time properly by continuing with this new role. This indicates the initiation of process of empowerment among women, although in a confusing state of affairs.

Table V.15
Reasons for continuing in New Role

(Percentage distribution)

Frequency	*Always*	*Some time*	*Rarely*	*Never*	*Total*
Financial Gain	15.00	8.75	6.25	70.00	100.00
Independence	30.00	18.75	10.00	41.25	100.00
To get social status	75.00	7.50	8.75	8.75	100.00
Shaping a career	55.00	15.00	6.25	23.75	100.00
Utilise education	40.00	13.75	7.50	38.75	100.00
Utilise time	38.25	22.50	7.50	31.25	100.00
Increase mental faculty	31.25	25.00	5.00	38.75	100.00
Prepare background for family	21.25	13.75	12.50	52.50	100.00

The women members wish to continue with the political role because they enjoy their new role to a great extent (60 per cent). However, about one third are not comfortable in this role but are not dissatisfied as well.

Those who were brought in this role under compulsion find the responsibilities very demanding hence do not enjoy their role very much (36.25 per cent). As regards contesting local elections again in future majority of the women members wish to contest elections and come back. But those on whom the political role has been imposed lack independent opinion and leave the decision of contesting elections in future on their male counterparts. It reflects that women in general are not allowed to be empowered, less by circumstances, more by male chauvinism, even after a decade of initiating the new dispensation.

Table V. 16 (A)
Role Enjoyment

Extent of enjoyment	*Great Extent*	*Some Extent*	*Not at all*	*Not at all*
Response (%)	60.00	36.25	3.75	100.00

Table V.16 (B)
Contesting Elections in Future

	Response (Percent)
Yes	80.00
No	3.75
Depends upon family members	16.25
Total	**100.00**

Further probing reveals that the political role sometimes create obstacle in maintenance of family (46.25 per cent), personal care of husband (33.75 per cent). It creates hindrances in keeping them as good wife (26.25 per cent) and good mother (38.75 per cent). Every twelfth woman member however does not feel any obstacle as a result of her political role. (Table V.17) There are aberrations and some may treat it a good beginning, as it has opened a pandora's box and the demand for reserving seats for women to the tune of one-third, if not in proportion of their number in total population is gaining a ground.

Table V. 17
Political Role creates obstacles

(Percentage distribution)

Frequency	*Always*	*Frequently*	*Some time*	*Rarely*	*Never*	*Total*
Maintaining family	12.50	6.25	46.25	25.00	10.00	100.00
Personal Care to husband	7.25	12.25	44.75	22.25	13.50	100.00
Keeping as ideal house manager	7.50	17.00	34.25	27.75	14.50	100.00
Being good mother	12.50	6.25	38.75	31.25	11.25	100.00
Average	**9.94**	**10.44**	**40.94**	**26.56**	**12.12**	

Surprisingly, even after having been elected as people's representative in urban local bodies, for women there is no concession in responsibilities and duties towards their family, children and husband. They are expected to perform these duties and responsibilities in perfection while the political role creates obstacles and leads to conflicting situations. In Indian society, family is the sole responsibility of a woman and all other roles come later on and are secondary. The women belonging to middle and lower classes having higher ambition are being crushed in between their traditional and imposed roles. The male dominated society and traditional family attitude both are the culprits for such a state of affairs.

In managing the responsibility belonging to this new role half of the women respondents sometimes feel depressed. A little less than that become nervous and more than one third suffer from anxiety, and about one third feel morally guilty for not being able to fulfill the responsibilities successfully at both the ends (Table V.18). When they are unable to manage the demands of both family and municipality they experience lot of stress and strain. This is the major cause of role conflict among women representatives. Many a time they are found unconcerned and apathetic with municipal administration to the extent that their familial role is not at all disturbed. Scope of conflict arises when the women members perform their new role actively. Most of them are found not sincere about their new role hence less scope for role conflict.

Table V.18
General feelings of Women Members

(Percentage distribution)

Frequency	*Always*	*Frequ-ently*	*Some time*	*Rarely*	*Never*	*Total*
Shyness	6.25	12.50	18.75	12.50	50.00	100.00
Submissiveness	62.50	-	18.75	13.75	5.00	100.00
Neglected	3.75	6.25	27.50	18.75	43.75	100.00
Depressed	6.25	12.50	50.00	8.75	22.50	100.00
Nervousness	12.50	3.75	45.00	13.75	25.00	100.00
Anxiety	2.50	3.75	37.50	10.00	46.25	100.00
Moral guilty	12.50	6.25	32.50	17.50	31.25	100.00

It is presumed that women representatives have to devote lot of time towards municipal functions in addition to pressure on them for managing the family affairs. Those who take both the roles seriously face heavy work load (33.75 per cent), pressure from husband (41.25 per cent), pressure from children (66.25 per cent) and mental tension (35 per cent) which affect their performance in this new role as representative and also as house manager (Table V.19). Contrarily for those who enjoy the political role because of imposition, it is a ritual and hence no conflict. They seldom feel any pressure of work and tension in life. They take it easy without any botheration. The serious players face problems at both the ends if family members are not cooperative and positive. It is observed that with the passage of time they have reconciled with the situation and adjustments have been made in most of the cases, exceptions are rare.

Table V. 19
Impact of New Role

(Percentage distribution)

	Always	*Some time*	*Rarely*	*Never*	*Total*
Health deterioration	8.75	30.00	40.00	21.25	100.00
Mental Tension	35.00	30.00	25.00	10.00	100.00
Heavy Work Load	33.75	27.50	25.00	13.75	100.00
Rigid Social Norms	3.75	28.75	38.00	37.50	100.00
Sleep deprivation	7.50	16.25	37.50	38.75	100.00
Ugly situation	2.50	11.25	38.25	47.50	100.00
Pressure of husband	49.25	22.25	12.50	16.00	100.00
Pressure of family	1.25	15.00	30.00	53.75	100.00
Pressure of children	66.25	5.00	27.50	1.25	100.00
Pressure of acqua-intances	1.25	3.75	22.50	72.50	100.00

Women representatives feel that though their new role has favoured them a high status, it has some negative effects on the family. Due to involvement in the new role they are unable to pay full attention towards family needs. They feel politics has hampered their children's education (32.50 per cent), family development (35 per cent) and family harmony (33.75 per cent) (Table V.20). Due to involvement in new role there are lot of grievances and disputes within the family which affect the harmony and create stressful situations. This may be one of the reasons that many a women have stopped taking new role seriously. They don't want to vitiate their family because of politics. However, instances are available where women have shown brevity and are playing new role in a serious manner with commitment without caring for criticism from family members including sometimes from husband also. They are truthful and sincere to their new role.

Table V.20
Joining the Politics Hampers

(Percentage distribution)

	Fully	*Great Extent*	*Parti-ally*	*Little*	*Not at all*	*Total*
Children's education	32.50	21.25	25.00	15.00	6.25	100.00
Children's health 10.00	13.75	18.75	20.00	37.50	100.00	
Husband's love	8.25	42.00	33.75	12.25	3.75	100.00
In-Laws (Parents)/Care	28.00	24.75	35.75	17.50	4.00	100.00
Family Devel-opment	35.00	8.75	35.00	15.00	6.25	100.00
Family harmony	33.75	18.75	12.50	22.50	12.50	100.00
Average	**37.92**	**21.54**	**26.79**	**17.04**	**11.71**	

Leaving the negative aspects aside, women representatives overall are found quite happy with their new role. Earlier they were confined only to the four walls of their house and did not have any identity of their own but after joining the local politics they have gained social prestige (70 per cent), earned high status for family (42.50 per cent), enhanced honour and respect (95 per cent), love and affection within the family (87.50 per cent), security and protection (85 per cent). Due to new role they have tremendously acquired social awareness (83.75 per cent) and increased their mental faculty. They feel very happy in helping the society (95 per cent) and also their own family (37.50 per cent). After becoming representative at urban local bodies they have gained a lot (Table V.21).

Table V.21
Feelings in the Family with new Role

(Percentage Distribution)

	Always	*Some times*	*Rarely*	*Never*	*Total*
Honour & Respect	95.00	5.00	-	-	100.00
Love & Affection	87.50	11.25	1.25	-	100.00
Security & Protection	85.00	11.25	2.50	1.25	100.00
High status in family	42.50	10.00	13.75	33.75	100.00
Social prestige	70.00	17.50	2.50	10.00	100.00
Help to society	95.00	3.75	-	1.25	100.00
Help to family	37.50	8.75	20.00	33.75	100.00
Social awareness	83.75	10.00	-	6.25	100.00

On enquiry as to how would they find without this role, the women representatives feel that they would become again victim of tradition (16.25 per cent), lose their self confidence and development (12.50 per cent), lose freedom (11.25 per cent) and would feel insecure and under pressure (Table V.22). This seems that women in general are found enjoying this role despite having lot of conflicts and problems.

Table V. 22
Feeling without this Role

(Percentage Distribution)

	Always	*Some times*	*Rarely*	*Never*	*Total*
Victim of tradition	16.25	8.75	36.25	38.75	100.00
Lack of self development	12.50	7.50	37.50	42.50	100.00
Lack of freedom	11.25	7.50	35.00	46.25	100.00
Insecurity	6.25	7.50	32.50	53.75	100.00
Under pressure	5.00	7.50	33.75	53.75	100.00

Indian politics is becoming a dirty game and often involves violence, muscle power and money. Women representatives find

Table V.23
Costs of New Role

(Percentage distribution)

	Always	*Some times*	*Rarely*	*Never*	*Total*
Loss of feminism	21.25	22.50	18.75	37.50	100.00
Outside risks	35.00	28.75	26.25	10.00	100.00
Character Assassination	12.50	28.75	7.50	51.25	100.00
Social impeachment	6.25	38.75	6.25	48.75	100.00

themselves difficult to adjust in such an atmosphere and very often feel prone to outside risk (35 per cent) associated with game of power and politics. They realize that due to new role they are losing their feminism and often become victim of character assassination and social impeachment (Table V.23). But all these infuse confidence and capacity in the woman councilors to fight these evils.

While disclosing their major cause of dissatisfaction towards municipal administration women representatives find low work culture (42.50 per cent), low privileges (38.75 per cent), non-cooperative colleagues (32.50 per cent) and non-cooperative staff (40 per cent), problems of citizen (21.25 per cent) and personal

Table V.24
Cause of Dissatisfaction

(Percentage Distribution)

	Always	*Some times*	*Rarely*	*Never*	*Total*
Low privileges	25.75	38.75	7.50	25.00	100.00
Low work culture	23.75	42.50	12.50	21.25	100.00
Non-Cooperative staff	5.00	40.00	33.75	21.25	100.00
Non-Cooperative colleagues	3.75	32.50	37.50	26.25	100.00
Authoritarian President/ Mayor	6.25	21.25	36.25	36.25	100.00
Away from family / husband	11.25	20.00	20.00	48.75	100.00
Low prospect in Politics	12.50	32.50	18.75	36.25	100.00
Personal problems	11.25	21.25	26.25	41.25	100.00
Problems by citizen	21.25	21.25	31.25	26.25	100.00

problems (21.25 per cent) (Table V.24). However a good number never feel dissatisfied with their role and its performance. Despite these problems and conflicts majority of the women representatives are not thinking to quit the politics and they want to continue with this new role. This indicates the courage and confidence having been emerged in these women. This is a healthy sign for the country and its democracy.

As regards this role, half of the women representatives find their role satisfactory and challenging. In spite of the problems they are found to be sensitive towards the needs and problems of urban citizens. Over all their performance level is found to be higher than their male counterparts, and urban citizens are quite happy and satisfied with their performance (Table V.25). It is surprising that women who enter into new role due to circumstances also feel satisfied and are found happy in their new avatar. However, every fifth woman member is either dissatisfied or indifferent. These may include the women on whom the role has been imposed.

Table V.25
Role of Elected Representative

	Response (%)
Fully satisfactory	25.00
Satisfactory	40.75
Indifferent	6.25
Dissatisfied	12.25
Happy	6.25
Imposed	4.00
Unhappy	4.00
Burdened	1.25
Total	**100.00**

In sum there are a number of areas causing conflicts, but women members are more or less satisfied and happy in their new role. It seems that either they are not very serious about their role and their reluctance or easy going make them satisfied or they are not allowed to act freely nor willing to act independently. The women members seem to have reconciled and adapted to the new situations. Majority of woman in local politics are satisfied because they have no role to perform. They are there only to fulfill the constitutional provision. They act as rubber stamp for their male counterparts who are the real actors of municipal functions. This has made the mockery of the supreme law of the land.

VI

STATUS IN WIDER SOCIETY

Women councilors of urban local government have major responsibility not only towards their family and municipality but towards society as well. In spite of the problems of managing dual role of family and municipality, they are found to be more sensitive towards the needs of people and society. It is observed that women representatives are more active and concerned about the welfare of the people in any comparison to their male counterparts.

It is depicted (Table VI.1) that about one-fifth of women councilors are members of some social organization. Majority of them participate actively in social works despite their family obligations and other responsibilities. A good number of the women representatives take active part in development of the society. Six out of ten women respondents regularly visit slum areas for undertaking and supervising development works. Despite busy schedule at home as well as in municipality and dual role responsibility more than half of the women spend some time with common masses in their respective area. This indicates their interest in social activities. Some of the women are even president of many social and civic organizations. They are secretary and active members as well. Thus the women representatives are found actively involved in local social activities.

Table VI.1
Interest in Social Activities

(Percentage distribution)

		Yes	*No*	*Total*
1.	Member of any social organization	17.75	82.25	100.00
2.	Participation in any social work	67.50	32.50	100.00
3.	Taking up any development plan of society	62.50	37.50	100.00
4.	Visiting slums/areas for development work	65.00	35.00	100.00
5.	Spending some time with common man in your town	55.00	45.00	100.00

During study their attention was drawn towards other social problems like dowry, inter-caste marriage, inter-religion marriage, child marriage, widow marriage, divorce, family welfare programmes etc. Their responses on this count are appreciative and praise worthy. It reflects their perceptions, consciousness and concern about social problems.

It is heartening that women representatives are found quite aware and concerned about the social issues and problems. Almost all women respondents condemn dowry system. About half of them advocate inter-caste marriage but they all disapprove contractual marriage. An absolute number favour love marriage while majority support widow marriage. None favours child marriage while compulsory family planning is supported by all. They support job reservation for women. Every four out of five women want wicked husbands to be punished. Thus the perception ofwomen representatives about civil society is quite clear and encouraging. If given a chance they would contribute tremendously in creating a society of their dream.

Table VI.2
Approval of Social Issues

(Percentage distribution)

	Always	*Some times*	*Never*	*Total*
Dowry system		6.25	93.75	100.00
Inter-caste marriage	13.75	48.75	37.50	100.00
Contractual marriage (living partner)	-	-	100.00	100.00
Love marriage	15.00	72.50	12.50	100.00
Widow marriage	66.25	15.00	18.75	100.00
Child marriage	-	-	100.00	100.00
Divorce	21.25	35.00	43.75	100.00
Compulsory family planning	100.00	-	-	100.00
Job Reservation for women	93.75	3.75	2.50	100.00
Punishing wicked husbands	76.25	21.25	2.50	100.00

Table VI.3
Views on Women's Freedom

(Percentage distribution)

	1	*2*	*3*	*4*	*5*	*Total*
Limited to home management	18.75	26.25	33.75	6.25	15.00	100.00
Given full freedom	12.50	12.50	25.00	28.75	21.25	100.00
Home first, freedom later	50.00	17.50	25.00	5.00	2.50	100.00
Freedom first, home later	-	-	6.25	48.75	45.00	100.00
Balancing mix of tradition and freedom	18.75	43.75	10.00	11.25	16.35	100.00
Total	100.00	100.00	100.00	100.00	100.00	

After their views on various social issues, women representatives were requested to give their opinion on women's freedom. With regard to women's freedom half of the women representatives feel that family should be given priority and freedom should come later. Every two out of five women members favour a balancing mix of tradition and freedom. Some give priority to only home management while others feel there should be full freedom. Thus, women representatives prefer to lead a balanced life – a blend of happy home and a responsible and responsive people's representative.

Time for rest and recreation is necessary for every person. Under the new dispensation women representatives are burdened with many responsibilities. Their day schedule is tight and they often suffer from tension, fatigue etc. It was therefore thought imperative to know as to how they spend their leisure time. Due to dual role responsibilities women representatives hardly get time for themselves. When ever they get opportunity they like spending their leisure time playing with children and watching television. They spend some time on shopping and visiting friends and relatives also (Table VI.4).

Table VI.4
Spending Leisure Time

(Percentage distribution)

Sleeping	*Watching TV*	*Shopping*	*Visiting Relations/Friends*	*Playing with children*	*Attending House holds*	*Grossiping /talking*	*Any other /Reading*	*Total*
6.25	31 25	6.25	12.50	23.75	7.50	7.50	5.00	100.00

Thus women representatives are facing lots of problems while performing their role at home and in municipality. The tradition oriented family where the typical pattern of husband – wife relationship has been 'male dominance and female dependence' is gradually changing. With the assumption the additional role of woman representative out side the home, her task is enlarged. The new role on one hand brings the woman out of the limited spheres of home and on the other makes continuous demands on her time and energy. In doing so some of the expectations of other members of the family may be left unfulfilled, thereby creating conflicting situations. In order to make life happy and harmonious most of the women representatives try to strike a balance and make adjustments through different means in every sphere of life. It seems that a good beginning in right direction has taken place. Period of a decade (post 73rd and 74th CAA) is not sufficient to change the societal mind set towards women. The seed has been sown, germination is taking place and within a couple of decades healthy society may emerge where women would have equitable status and role.

VII

ADJUSTMENT WITH FAMILY MEMBERS

Role of women in any area cannot be discussed in isolation. They are a member of the family, joint or nuclear. The behaviour of other members of the family (other than husband) casts a bearing on the effectiveness of woman's role. In the traditional middle and upper middle class families women generally spend whole life with in the family. She does all the work but without any credit or value. Mostly male family members are involved in decision making. It has been desired women representatives get full help and support from family members in discharging municipal functions. Family members are found involved in municipal decision making as well. Most of the time family members do all the municipal works..

Table VII.1
Sparing Time

(Percentage distribution)

	Fully	*Great extent*	*Some extent*	*Total*
Home management	32.00	20.00	48.00	100.00
Care of children	40.00	24.00	36.00	100.00
Care of husband	42.00	22.00	36.00	100.00
Family functions	68.00	24.00	8.00	100.00
Social functions	68.00	32.00	-	100.00

Familial background has a great role in determining the status of woman in politics. It is noted that more than half of the families do not have political background while less than that have active political background. Those women who do not belong to family having political background face problem of adjustment between family and municipality.

As regards occupation of the family largest number of families belong to business class followed by service class. Family occupation is an important indicator of the family status and the independence

It is felt by the family members that women members always manage home, care children, parents, husband and other family members despite their busy schedule in new avatar women representatives invariably attend family and social functions (Table VII.1). There remains always a scope of conflict between her home duties and other duties but she manages this all the time.

Table VII.2
Help Required

(Percentage distribution)

	Always	*Frequently*	*Occasionally*	*Never*	*Total*
Attending board meeting	48.00	8.00	24.00	20.00	100.00
Attending officials	48.00	12.00	16.00	24.00	100.00
Attending official works	50.00	8.00	16.00	24.00	100.00
Election time	100.00	-	-	-	100.00

According to members of their family, women representatives require help in attending meetings, discharging municipal functions and other official works because they are fully dependent on family member's specially male members. Some times, male members themselves perform all the official responsibilities at their own. Male member works on their behalf.

Table VII.3
Extent and way of Extending Help

(Percentage distribution)

	Always	*Frequently*	*Occasionally*	*Never*	*Total*
In discharging day-to-day problems	20.00	4.00	48.00	24.00	100.00
In attending meeting	40.00	24.00	16.00	20.00	100.00
In getting works done by officials	16.00	8.00	48.00	28.00	100.00
By relieving from work at home	-4.00	20.00	52.00	24.00	100.00
By accompanying her to meetings with official	24.00	40.00	16.00	20.00	100.00
By accompanying her to board meetings	56.00	8.00	16.00	20.00	100.00
By encouraging her	72.00	8.00	4.00	16.00	100.00
By supporting her morally	72.00	8.00	4.00	16.00	100.00

It is evident that family members help her in discharging day-to day municipal works. They help in attending meetings, performing municipal functions, and always encourage and support her morally. But some time male family members do not cooperate with her in household works. The family members act (unauthorisedly) as people's councilors in the name of women representatives who are asked to look after home, children and family. In real sense, in most of the cases women representatives are treated as a tool in the hands of their male family members.

Table VII.4
Rating her in New Role

(Percentage distribution)

Excellent	*Highly Successful*	*Successful*	*In learning process*	*Total*
40.00	16.00	36.00	8.00	100.00

In respect of rating her in new role, the family members rate her work as excellent. She is co-operative, obedient and a good decision maker. She is commanding respect in municipality very well. She always supports her colleagues. Some family members however put her in learning process. But ground realities are quite different in majority of cases. The women under new dispensation are in the phase of learning their new role, but they are not at all allowed to develop and work independently.

With regard to developing her career in politics most of the family members are interested in developing her career in politics. Female members feel that they are able to fulfill their duties and political functions most of the time. Family members always support in politics and they like her to continue in politics. It is however observed that in many cases once the seat is reserved male members do not allow women to contest the elections. It is clear that women are brought under compulsion because of seats reserved for women. This practice is not a healthy sign. Even if the role is imposed on women, and once they are allowed to participate in decision making, they should be given full support and encouragement to continue in their new avatar of people's representatives. Some of the family members think that female members should quit politics, but their number is much less.

VIII

ADJUSTMENT WITH OFFICIALS

It was thought imperative to corroborate the views of woman councilors and thus observations of municipal officials were also fetched. Hence a few officials from each local body were interviewed. It is observed that officials give full support and cooperation to all members including woman councillors. They behave like an obedient officer but some time they also ignore orders and become critical towards woman representatives.

Table VIII.1
Women Attend Board Meetings

(Percentage distribution)

Regularly	*Some time*	*Often*	*Total*
50.00	40.00	10.00	100.00

As regards women members attending the board meetings majority of the officials feel that women attend board meeting regularly. Some find women members disinterested in municipal functions. Some express that female members do not attend board meetings regularly because of lack of time out of their household duties and they also need some male member to accompany them. Many a time male member attends meeting on behalf of a woman member despite contrary advice from the officials, and strict directives from the state government.

Table VIII.2
Participation in Discussion

(Percentage distribution)

Always	*Frequently*	*Occasionally*	*Some time*	*Total*
20.00	40.00	20.00	20.00	100.00

In respect of participation in discussion officers find many women always participating in discussions. However women members who don't participate in discussions are those who don't have any knowledge of municipal functions and their husbands do the entire work on their behalf.

Table VIII.3
Women Members get full Co-operation from Male Members

(Percentage distribution)

Yes	*No*	*Some time*	*Total*
70.00	-	30.00	100.00

In respect of extending support officials opine that women members get full support and cooperation from male members and due to lack of confidence and knowledge about municipal affairs, male members generally avoid involving female members in discussion and other matters. Even in many cases women themselves are not interested and they just extend passive supports to the decisions taken by male members. Many of the women representatives are guided by their male family members.

Municipal officials observe that women are not able to form pressure group because their number is less in comparison to

Table VII.4
Women form a Pressure Group in Municipality

(Percentage distribution)

Yes	*No*	*Some time*	*Total*
20.00	70.00	10.00	100.00

male members. Most of the women representatives have no independent opinion of their own and hence disinterested in municipal functions.

Table VIII.5
Women Accompanied by Males

(Percentage Distribution)

Always	*Frequently*	*Occasionally*	*Some time*	*Total*
40.00	20.00	20.00	20.00	100.00

Analysis shows that women members are invariably accompanied by male counterparts. In view of officials most of the female members are accompanied by their male members because they are fully dependent on their male counterparts for municipal functions. They are just for namesake and their male counterparts act like real representative.

Table VIII.6
Accompanying Males are allowed in Meeting

(Percentage distribution)

Yes	*No*	*Some time*	*Forced entry*	*Total*
10.00	70.00	10.00	10.00	100.00

In respect of male family members attending board meetings on behalf of women councillors, officials offer no comments. A few admits that family members are allowed to sit in the meetings. The officials feel that rules do not permit male family members inside the meeting room but some do enter forcefully. In many cases officials have to compromise because of political affiliation of women representatives and their family members.

Table VIII.7
Rating the Women Members

(Percentage distribution)

Satisfactory	*Cooperative*	*Learner*	*Disinterested*	*Have no full Freedom*	*Total*
20.00	10.00	20.00	30.00	20.00	100.00

Municipal officials find female members cooperative, learner, but disinterested because they have lot of responsibilities related to house and family management etc. Most of them are disinterested in municipal functions because they mostly act as rubber stamps of their husbands.

Officials observe that women participate in the discussions and always like to participate in the discussion. Some women are active and always take part in discussions in the board meetings. They get full cooperation from male members and officers. The women member coming from lower strata of society however lack confidence and knowledge. They need to be oriented towards their new roles and responsibilities. The first timers are not equipped managerially and educationally to perform municipal functions. Male members unnecessarily interfere and their domination is uncalled for. If the women councilors are oriented properly towards their new role and are allowed by male family members to act independently, officials feel, women can pick up easily as they are by nature sincere, perseverant, cooperative, adaptive, laborious and devoted. Generally, male chauvinism does not allow women to develop and work independently. Although a new beginning has taken ground, it will take decades or even centuries to bring change in social mind set of male dominance having been in place since time immemorial.

IX

EPILOGUE

Problems of working/professional woman, mainly due to her dual role, are not a new one. A house wife gets more time and energy to devote to the fulfillment of the demands of her family members. While a working/professional woman with the additional role set she has to handle, if the members of the family continue to have similar expectations from her like that of the house-wife, her chances of being getting frustrated are indeed great. Lack of sympathetic appreciation of new situation, new set of demands on her new status and unpreparedness to modify the expectations and demand structure are the major causes which lead to disharmonious functioning of the family structure. Lack of adequate articulation of roles in role-sets and of the role expectations and demands among the members of the role-set etc. are no less important causes to disturb the family harmony. Marital harmony is greatly facilitated where care is taken to forestall the above mentioned problems.

The problems of women representatives are all the more pronounced. The women representatives have multidimensional roles to perform. As a house wife, she holds the traditional status of a mother, wife, sister, daughter-in-law and as people's representative she has to perform for the fulfillment of people's aspirations and expectations. Therefore as compared to their other counterparts in society, these women representatives have to perform two sets of roles i.e. traditional or prescribed as a woman in a male dominated Indian society and an achieved or ascribed by acquiring political status. Her role is now divided into two sets of roles for family and for society. This leads to a constant and continuous phenomenon of role conflict.

The present work is a humble attempt to study the role conflict and problems of adjustment of women representatives in urban local government. The data were collected with the help of a set of questionnaires. Analysis was done on the basis of the responses received through personal interviews, discussions and personal observations.

The findings of the study reveal that women representatives face maximum adjustment problems and conflicting situations at home. Women representatives having more number of smaller/ minor children and those who do not have satisfactory child-care provisions at home while they are out for municipal functions, face more role conflict. Time constraint and grievances of children are major areas of concern creating stressful situations.

The study further highlights that those women representatives whose husbands do not help them in household chores and do not have favourable attitude towards their political role face maximum stressful situations and role conflict. It is observed that major grievance of husband is, less time given by their wives towards home, children and in-laws. Though most of the husbands support their wives in political career they still carry a traditional mindset of women's role and want them to give priority to home affairs. These problems are more faced by those women representatives who are active in their political role and have serious involvement in municipal affairs. They are constrained to devote sufficient time towards husband and family and face adjustment problems in managing both roles effectively.

Attitude of family members is very important in the performance of both roles. It is observed that in-laws of women representatives though are supportive do not cooperate extensively in both household chorus and official functions. Women representatives face conflicting situations when their role as daughter-in-law gets neglected due to other role.

Relations and friends though appreciate women's new role but in most cases are not all that cooperative and supportive. Women representatives face criticism when they are unable to fulfill any social and family obligation.

Results also point out that type of family, availability of modern kitchen aids and having or not having economic obligations towards the family are other factors which have a direct bearing on role conflict among women representatives. In a nuclear family women representatives experience low degree of role conflict. Contrarily, those living in joint families do get help from other family members and are more prone to role conflicts.

With regard to their political role it is found that most of the women representatives are new in this field and do not have prior knowledge, proper orientation and experience of this field hence they are not very much clear about their role. Since entry of women in politics at local level is a recent phenomenon, there is no set pattern of behaviour, so adaptability in new role will take some time.

It is observed that majority of women representatives were brought in this new role by their husband and male members.

Some were brought under compulsion because of their seats reserved for women. Such women representatives work only as rubber stamps for their husband and male members. These women representatives are found to be totally dependent on their husbands. They do not take independent decisions and all municipal and official functions are done by their husbands. They are found to be disinterested and hence lack initiative. Such women do not face problem of role conflict, as they seldom perform their ascribed role.

But those women representatives who are active in politics and have come in this role on their own for making a career in politics are found to be very active and independent in their role as representative. They take all decisions independently and take active part in municipal and urban affairs. Such women are found confident and are able to display good leadership qualities, but more prone to role conflict.

Women representatives who have been in politics for more than 5 to 10 years have been able to develop good rapport among the local people and are found to be performing much better than their male counterparts. The male chauvinism however fails to appreciate, hence conflicts arise.

In respect of relationship between male and female members it is observed that though male members speak positive about women representatives, in practice their attitude towards women counterparts is not encouraging all the time. They are generally given second class treatment in the municipal functioning such as planning, decision making and implementation of the development programmes. The disinterested women representatives enjoy their non-involvement, hence no conflict, but the state of affairs in case of active women is otherwise.

Observations reveal that where there is male chairperson/ mayor, women representatives feel uncomfortable and hesitate in putting forth their views. If they dare to give opinion contrary to their male counterparts, role conflicts appear unfailingly. Contrarily, where the chairperson/mayor is a woman, the women members are found to be comfortable and they actively participate in the planning, decision-making and implementation of the development programmes. In the situation less scope for role conflict, because all sail in the same boat.

It is observed that though women representatives wish to participate actively in municipal affairs and devote more time towards urban problems and issues, the household responsibilities and pressure from husbands, children and relatives deter them to work in their full capacity. The social norms and social taboos associated with the women folk in society adversely affect the participation of women in the affairs of urban local government. The demands of dual role most of the time overburdens them and inability to perform both political and familial roles effectively dissatisfies them and creates conflicting situations.

The study further highlights that a major factor behind the low performance of women representatives in urban local bodies is their low educational status and lack of proper knowledge of the municipal affairs and prior experience in dealing with multidimensional urban development issues and its complexities. Due to this reason women councilors are found dependent on their husband and other male family members. The women dependent on their male family members face little or no conflict because real performers are their husband and other male family members and not the women councilors.

Besides, role of money power, muscle power, backroom dealings, communalization and criminalization of politics also prevent women in practicing active participation in local governance. Many a times these evils create artificial conflicting situations for women performers.

In spite of these problems and conflicts women representatives are making sincere efforts towards gaining high political efficacy. They are aware and sensitive towards the needs and problems of urban people. Their level of participation is also rising. This new role has given them a new status, a new image, a new position, a new hope and this in turn shapes their personality and perceptions and helps them to discover a new person in them.

In sum, for better appreciation of the problems faced by women members, two pronged strategy needs to be followed. On one hand they should be oriented towards their new roles and responsibilities through vigorous training and development activities and on the other the societal mind set needs to be changed. The women representatives specially belonging to vulnerable class of society need to be empowered educationally, mentally, psychologically and socially.

Although, 74th Amendment to the Indian Constitution is a turning point and land mark in the history of urban local government in the country, the community should be empowered to bear the fruits of democratic decentralization. The Government of India in the Ministry of Urban Development is concerned about the political empowerment of women, especially from lower strata of the society and the state governments have to show sufficient administrative and political willingness to help achieve the desired results. The governmental interventions would not accomplish the objectives unless and until social transformation takes place. Hence, the male dominated society needs to change its mind set in tune with the change of time and circumstances. A class of women is also responsible for their own plight and social harassment. The elites in women representatives enjoy sufficient power and they never encourage the common colleagues to come forward. The new enactment is a good beginning and the time is not far off when women will be able to occupy their due status in all fields of society, politics and economy. The male chauvinism and domination are reducing, of course, on a snail's pace and the women are getting empowered and conflict areas reducing in a slow but steady and sustainable manner. The grass root administration in the country is breaking the ice and women are heading in the desired direction of empowerment and development. The sudden change in perception may lead in aggravating the conflicting extent as the community in general and women in particular are not made ready – mentally, socially, and psychologically, aesthetically to practice the political role imposed overnight as a result of democratic decentralization. Had the decentralization process preceded the societal preparedness, the situation would have been quite different. However, a ray of hope is emerging and the move is in right direction. The period of a decade or so is not sufficient to facilitate the social transformation but a good beginning has been initiated. The male dominated society is getting ready of course reluctantly to appreciate the ascribed role of women.

References and Bibliography

Seth, Meera (2002), Women and Development, Sage, Delhi.

Singh, S. and Srivastava, S.P. (eds) (2002), Gender Equality through Women's Empowerment, Bharat Book Co., Lucknow.

Kapur, P. (1940), The Changing Status of Working Women in India, Vikas, New Delhi

Kapur, R. (1969), Role Conflict among Employed Housewives, Indian Journal of Industrial Relations, 5(1)

Orden, S.R. and Bradburn, N.M. (1968), Working Wives and Marriage Happiness, American Journal of Sociology

Hemlatha, K. and Suryanarayana, R. (1983), Gender and Houshold Domain in Asia, Allied Publications, Bombay

Srivastava, Abhilasha (2001), Role Multiplicity of Lower Middle Class Working Women with Special Reference to the Primary and Higher Secondary Women Teachers of Lucknow City, Ph.D. Thesis, Lucknow University, unpublished

Forbes, G. (1996), Women in India, The New Cambirdge History of India, IV.2, Cambridge University press, Cambridge

Agarwal, S.P. (2001), Women's Education in India, Vol. 3, Concept, Delhi

Narsimhan, S. (1999), Empowering Women, Sage, Delhi

Sams, S. (ed) (1991), Women, Law and Social Change, APH, Delhi

Pandey, G.S. (2001), Political Participation of Women in India, New Royal Book Co., Lucknow

Purushothaman, S. (19968), The Empowerment of Women in India, Sage, New Delhi

Jena, S.K. (1993), Working Women and Modernization, Ashish, New Delhi

Reddy, C.R. (1986), Changing Status of Educated Working Women, Asia Pub., Delhi

Rana, Kranti (1998), Modern Working Women and the Development Debate, Delhi

Sharma, Anita (1990), Modernisation and Status of Working Women in India, Delhi

Gupta, Anjula (1994), Modernizing Working Women, Delhi

Mishra, A.D. (1994), Problems and Prospects of Working Women in Urban India, Concept, Delhi

Singhal, Tara (2003), Working Women and Family, APH, Delhi

Lashmiswaramma, M. (1991), Working Women and Infant Care, Delhi

Shah, Beena (2002), Women, Higher Education and Empowerment (Challenges & Prospects), Delhi

Tapan, Neeta (2000), Need for Women Empowerment, Delhi

Mishra, P. and Mahapatra, U (2003), Women Administrators and Professionals – A Global Perspective, Kalinga, Delhi

Bakshi, S.R. (2002), Empowerment of Women and Politics of Reservation, Mittal, Delhi

Singh, U.B. (ed), (2005) Empowerment of Women in Urban Administration,

Serials, New Delhi.

Government of India (1988), Perspective Plan on Women

Kundu, S.K. (1999), Role Conflict Among Employed Women: A Case Study of Bhubaneshwar City, Ph.D. Thesis R.M.L. Awadh University, Faizabad (unpublished).

Sinha Pushpa (1982), Role Conflict among the Working Women, Janki Prakashan for Anmol, Delhi.

Acharya Itishree Padhi (1998), Working Mothers: Role Conflict and Adjustments, Reliance Publishing House, New Delhi, pp. 43-58.

Bhatty & Bhatty (1971), "Demographic Portrait of Professional Women Employed in India" in Educated Women in Indian Society Today, Bombay: Tata Mc Graw Hill.

Chakraborty, K., (1977), Conflicting Worlds of working Mother, Calcutta Progressive Publishers, Kolkata

Dohlstrom, E. (1967), The changing roles of men and women, London, Gerald Dickworth.

Hoffman, L.W., (1963), "Parental Power Relations and the Division of Household Tasks" in Nye and Hoffman (eds) Employed mother in America, Chicago, Rand Mc Nally and Company.

Kala Rani, (1976), Role Conflict in Working Women, New Delhi, ChetanPublications.

Rapoport, R. and Rapoport, R.N., (1969), "The dual Career Family", Human Relations 22(1), 3-30.

Goode, G.T., (1960), "A Theory of Role Strain" American Sociological Review, 25: 483-496

Menon, R., (1964), "Indian Working Woman – She Stands Alone", Social Welfare, 11 (5), 3-4.

Mahajan, A., (1966), Women's two roles: A Study of Role Conflict", Indian Journal of Social Work, 25 (4), 377-80.

Powell, K.S., (1963), "Family Variables" in I.F. Nye and L.W. Hoffman's (eds) The Employed Mother in America, Chicago, Rand Mc Nally and Company.

Raja, Gopalan, (1963), Social Change: An Analysis of role conflict and deviation," Indian Journal of Social Work, 16(4), 219-223.

Wardwell, (1952, The reduction of strain in a Marginal Social Role, American Journal of Sociology, 61, 16-24.

Holahan, C.K. and Gilbert, L.A. (1979), Inter-role Conflict for Working Women: Careers Versus Jobs, Journal of Applied Psychology, 64(1), 86-90.

Sullerst, E. (1971), Women, Society and Change, London: World University Library.

D'Souza, A.A. (1968), Should Wives Work, Social Action, 18 (1), 15-24.

Singh, K.P., (1972), Career and Family – Women's two Roles (A Study in Role Conflict), Indian Journal of Social Work, XXXIII (3), 277-281.

Nevill, D. and Demico, S. (1974), Development of a Role Conflict Questionnaire for Women: Some Preliminary Findings, Journal of Consulting and Clinical Psychology, 42(5), 743-749).

Blood & Hamblin, (1958), The effect of the Wife's Employment on the Family Power Structure, Socials Forces, 36, 347-352.

Blood, R.O. Jr., (1963), The Husband – Wife Relationship, in I.F. Nye and L.W.Hoffman (eds.). The employed mother in America, Chicago: Rand McNally and Company.

Bailyn, L. (1970), Career and Family Orientation of Husband and Wives in Relation to Marital Happiness, Human Relation, 23(2), 97-113.

Nichol, K. (1975), Economically Independent.... Emotionally Crushed, "Social Welfare', XXII (6-7), 37-40.

Arora, K.K., Bhattacharya et. al. (1963), Women and Career, A Group Project Report, Submitted to the Tata Institute of Social Sciences, Bombay.

Kapur, P. (1974), Changing Status of Working Women in India, Delhi: Vikas Publishing House Pvt. Ltd.

Dhingra, O.P. (1972), Women in Employment (unpublished Report), Shri Ram Centre for Industrial Relations and Human Resources, New Delhi, 197-236

Tripathi, H. (1967), Changing Attitude of Woman in Post Independent India, Journal of Gujarat Research Society, XIXX (2/114) 92-97.

Styanand, K. (1973), The Status of Working Women in India, 'Eves Weekly', 5, 15.

Desai, A.S. (1963), Women and Part Time Employment, Social Welfare, 10(7)40-44.

Suchdev, J. (1974), Working Mothers: An Interview, Social Welfare, 21(2) 10-27.

Weller, R.M. (1968), The Employment of Wives Dominance and Fertility, Journal of Marriage & Family, 30, 437-442.

Vasantha Kumar, K. (1964), Her Emotional Problems, Social Welfare, Q95) 12-13.

Hall, D.T., Garden, F.E. (1974), Self-image Stereotype of Family: Their Relationship to Women's Role Conflict and Coping, Journal of Applied Psychology, 59(2), 243-243.

Burchard, W.E. (1954), Role Conflict of Military, Chaplins, American Sociological Review, 19, 528-535.

Kahn, R.L. 91964), Organisational Stress: Studies in Role Conflict and Ambiquity, New York: Wiley.

Phadke, M. and Kulkarni, A.V. (1977), Field – Dependence – Independence and Employed – not employed as Factor in the Adjustment of House Wife, Indian Journal of Psychology, 52(1), 85-89.

Index

I

J

K

L

M